Fair Labor Lawyer

SOUTHERN BIOGRAPHY
Andrew Burstein, Series Editor

Margolin in the 1950s.
U.S. Labor Department photo. Courtesy of Malcolm Trifon.

FAIR LABOR LAWYER

The Remarkable Life of
New Deal Attorney and Supreme Court Advocate
BESSIE MARGOLIN

Marlene Trestman

Louisiana State University Press   Baton Rouge

Published by Louisiana State University Press
Copyright © 2016 by Marlene Trestman
All rights reserved
Manufactured in the United States of America
First printing

Designer: Barbara Neely Bourgoyne
Typeface: Ingeborg
Printer and binder: Maple Press (digital)

Library of Congress Cataloging-in-Publication Data

Trestman, Marlene, 1956– author.
 Fair labor lawyer : the remarkable life of New Deal attorney and Supreme Court
advocate Bessie Margolin / Marlene Trestman.
     pages cm. — (Southern biography)
 Includes bibliographical references and index.
 ISBN 978-0-8071-6208-8 (cloth : alk. paper) — ISBN 978-0-8071-6209-5 (pdf) —
ISBN 978-0-8071-6210-1 (epub) — ISBN 978-0-8071-6211-8 (mobi) 1. Margolin, Bessie.
2. Lawyers—United States—Biography. 3. Labor lawyers—United States—Biography.
4. Women lawyers—United States—Biography. 5. New Deal, 1933–1939—Biography.
6. United States. Department of Labor—Officials and employees—Biography. I. Title.
 KF373.M292T74 2016
 340.092—dc23
 [B]

                                                                    2015035232

The paper in this book meets the guidelines for permanence
and durability of the Committee on Production Guidelines for
Book Longevity of the Council on Library Resources. ∞

In loving memory of my foster mother,
Lillian Gurry Rodos,
February 14, 1918–January 9, 2013

CONTENTS

ILLUSTRATIONS

PREFACE

In a life that spanned every decade of the twentieth century, Bessie Margolin contributed to some of the most significant legal events in modern American history: she defended the constitutionality of the New Deal's Tennessee Valley Authority; drafted rules establishing the American military tribunals for Nazi war crimes in Nuremberg; and, on behalf of the United States Department of Labor, shepherded the child labor, minimum wage, and overtime protections of the Fair Labor Standards Act of 1938 through the nation's highest courts. In crowning achievements on the eve of her retirement, she also argued and won the first appeals under the Equal Pay and Age Discrimination in Employment Acts. *Fair Labor Lawyer* captures the forces that propelled Margolin's journey and reveals the inner life of this trailblazing woman, who has been largely ignored in accounts of these historical events.

Yet, in her day, Margolin attracted a fair share of attention. As a striking woman of cultivated charm, she turned heads. Her courtroom accomplishments received press coverage, and her photograph regularly appeared in newspapers and magazines. To the editors of *Glamour* and *Time,* she was a pioneering professional woman, the quintessential lady lawyer. After her 1972 retirement from the Labor Department, however, Margolin seemed to disappear from the public record. A student of women's legal history might relate a sentence or two about her in passing, but that was pretty much the extent of coverage of her four-decade career up to now.

Margolin was raised in New Orleans, in the Jewish Orphans' Home, which entitled her to a first-class education at the Isidore Newman Manual Training School. Together these two institutions—both founded upon a bedrock of Hebrew benevolence and social justice—taught Margolin that good citizenship, hard work, and respect for authority were a means of achieving economic and social status. With these values Margolin used her intellect and ambition, along with her femininity and southern charm, to win acceptance and respect from classmates, colleagues, bosses, and judges—almost all of whom were men—enabling her to work shoulder to shoulder with some of the most brilliant legal minds of her time.

She launched her legal career in 1930, when only 2 percent (3,385) of America's attorneys were female and far fewer were Jewish and from the South. Margolin worked hard to be treated as one of the boys, never shying away from a late-night brief-writing session or poker game. But she did not settle for acceptance alone. Margolin's passion for her work and meticulous preparation drove her to an astounding record in appellate advocacy, both in number of cases and rate of success. In the Supreme Court alone, she argued twenty-four times, one of only three women in the twentieth century to achieve this distinction, and prevailed in all but three instances. Even today, almost fifty years later, the highest number of Supreme Court arguments presented by a woman has reached only thirty-three. Margolin remains one of only a few dozen women and men to attain such standing in the elite world of Supreme Court advocates—a feat all the more impressive because she accomplished it at a time when that world was almost exclusively male.

Margolin's acclaim in legal circles came largely from her enforcement of minimum wage and overtime laws for America's workers, using each legal victory to develop what U.S. Supreme Court chief justice Earl Warren described as the "flesh and sinews . . . around the bare bones" of the Fair Labor Standards Act. Although she spent most of her professional life advancing her own career as she enforced the nation's labor standards, Margolin ultimately became an outspoken advocate for women's rights with the 1963 passage of the Equal Pay Act and was a founding member of the National Organization for Women. Even then, Margolin distanced herself from what she considered radical approaches to feminism. She used femininity to her advantage, serving as her own best evidence to debunk the myth that career women were destined to become "de-sexed" or "unfeminine." True, she married a career instead of a man, but it was not because she lacked opportunity or motive for traditional romance. She loved and admired men. They had been her role models, supporters, and mentors. Margolin enjoyed men professionally and socially, including intimately. And there was little Betty Friedan or Helen Gurley Brown wrote in the 1960s in *The Feminine Mystique* and *Sex and the Single Girl* that Margolin had not figured out long before; as early as 1929, she had taken to heart the feminist credo of Virginia Woolf's *A Room of One's Own,* which extolled for women the importance of having their own space, literally and figuratively. Margolin would not marry a man who interfered with her career or her independence.

A generous mentor, Margolin assisted the careers of countless lawyers and staff, both men and women. She attracted good people. The reputation she built for the appellate work conducted by the labor solicitor's office was second only to that of the U.S. solicitor general. To women attorneys she offered advice on proper courtroom attire and hairstyle while insisting they aim to be accepted and treated as one of the men. Known to her staff as a relentless perfectionist and intellectual elitist, Margolin often expected they keep the same late hours as she did; she also left many lawyers indebted to her for teaching them how to argue appeals and write briefs.

Throughout her life Margolin remained closely connected to the two New Orleans institutions that reared her—the Jewish Orphans' Home, later known as the Jewish Children's Regional Service (JCRS), and the Isidore Newman School—eagerly responding to a miscellany of requests. In 1974, two years into her retirement, she was asked to meet a Newman graduate who was heading to college in Baltimore. Margolin assented, touched that the young woman, a Jewish orphan, had experienced a childhood somewhat like her own; Newman had admitted the student to honor the same historical obligation that gave Margolin her life-changing education. For more than a decade, throughout the student's time at college, law school, and into her own career as a government lawyer, Margolin graciously invited her to dinner and the theater and for weekend visits, offering helpful advice, letters of recommendation, and captivating recollections. I was that student.

Although I first spoke publicly about Margolin's remarkable life and career in 1993, as part of Newman School's ninetieth anniversary celebration, it was only after her death in 1996 that I began to think about writing her life story, a dalliance that turned purposeful in 2005. Almost everyone I called upon to help me rescue Margolin from undeserved obscurity welcomed the opportunity to repay a personal debt of gratitude or fill a void in legal, gender, Jewish, southern, or some other facet of history. Their help was all the more essential because Margolin preserved only a hodgepodge of her work records, filling a pair of disorganized file cabinets with correspondence, legal briefs, speeches, and news clippings. If she had not prepared her professional life for a prospective biographer, she did far less to chronicle her personal affairs: no oral history, journal, or scrapbook. She left behind a few bundles of photos and private letters, many unidentified:

in some cases addresses had been ripped from envelopes and postcards, while the most intimate letters she wrote and received had been penned with initials or a pet name, perhaps to confound prying eyes.

Notwithstanding the limitations and challenges of Margolin's papers, her nephew Malcolm Trifon and his former wife, Mary Catherine Trifon, lovingly preserved them and generously granted me their long-term use, without which this biography would have been sorely lacking, if not impossible. To fill in the gaps and offer important personal and legal context, her relatives and colleagues graciously granted interviews, particularly Malcolm Trifon, Toby Trifon, Robert and Charlotte Margolin, and other members of Margolin's family, professor and former labor solicitor Carin A. Clauss, Donald S. Shire, Robert E. Nagle, Eva Bowers Fitzgerald, and Judge Laurence H. Silberman, former labor solicitor and undersecretary. I especially appreciated the courtesy and candor extended by relatives of Robert B. Butler Jr., James Lawrence Fly, and Robert W. Ginnane, Margolin's three great loves. Along the way the Hadassah-Brandeis Institute, the National Endowment for the Humanities, and the Supreme Court Historical Society fueled the endeavor with financial support and prestigious institutional recognition, for which I am grateful.

Archivists aided me when I sought material from their depositories, skillfully finding Margolin's needles in other people's haystacks. Notable among these are Amanda Strauss and Diana Carey at the Schlesinger Library; Robert Ellis and Rodney Ross at the National Archives; Susan Tucker, Ellen Brierre, Leon Miller, and Ann Case at Tulane University; Jona Whipple at Chicago-Kent College of Law; Barry C. Cowan at Louisiana State University; Kristen La Follette at Columbia University's Oral History Office; Marcia Zubrow at the University of Buffalo Law Library; staff of the Louisiana Division of the New Orleans Public Library; and Linda Stinson, the former historian at the U.S. Department of Labor. JCRS executive director Ned Goldberg welcomed me into his office to review treasured records of the old Jewish Orphans' Home and connected me to its dedicated alumni and their families. At the Isidore Newman School, "Greenie" Genie McCloskey opened the archives, while David Prescott, my ninth grade civics teacher who introduced our class to the wonders of Washington, D.C., scoured the library's files to assist my research.

Legal historians, biographers, and other scholars and authors promptly responded to my calls and emails, generously providing documents, advice, and encouragement, particularly Clare Cushman, Jonathan Bush, Daniel Ernst, John Q. Barrett, Norman I. Silber, Sheldon Goldman, Dianne Marie Amann, Jean H. Baker, Alice Kessler-Harris, Laura Kalman, Kirsten Downey, Steve Luxenberg, Catherine C. Kahn, and Robert A. Caro. Serendipity connected me with Harvard's Caroline E. Light, allowing us to share archival research while she completed her wonderful book on southern Jewish benevolence. The members of the Feminist Legal Biography Workshop, including Constance Backhouse, Barbara Babcock, Jane DeHart, Mae Quinn, Tomiko Brown-Nagin, Penina Lahav, and Sally Kenney, welcomed me into their highly specialized fold and offered priceless feedback and expertise. Biographers International Organization (BIO) and its leader, James McGrath Morris, provided a wealth of practical advice and camaraderie. Early versions of the manuscript were bravely read in whole or in part by Clare Cushman, Ann Thorpe Thompson, Margaret Hutchins Campbell, Andrea Giampetro-Meyer, Jonathan Bush, Caroline Light, Barbara Babcock, Dianne Marie Amann, and Malcolm Trifon, whose thoughtful comments I deeply appreciated.

I thank Louisiana State University Press, especially series editor Andrew Burstein, Rand Dotson, and MaryKatherine Callaway, for recognizing the importance of Bessie Margolin's story and giving me the chance to tell it. Heather Lundine, a skillful and kind developmental editor, helped this first-time author transform research into a book. Elizabeth Gratch provided expert copyediting, graciously and painlessly.

It is impossible to quantify the love and inspiration I received from my husband, Henry D. Kahn, who suffers my foolishness gladly and encouraged me to pursue this project full-time, and from our wonderful children, Helene M. Kahn and Eli B. Kahn, who never doubted me in this venture—or were smart enough not to tell me.

Finally, I acknowledge the JCRS and the Isidore Newman School, in their historic and current iterations, and their visionary benefactors and administrators for providing life-changing social services and educational opportunities to thousands of children, including Bessie Margolin and me.

Fair Labor Lawyer

1

CHILDHOOD, 1909–1925

Earliest Years and the Journey South

"Becy Margolyn" was the way the midwife recorded the name of the baby girl born to Rebecca Goldschmidt Margolin and her husband, Harry, on February 24, 1909. She was the second child for the Russian-Jewish immigrant couple, whose native Yiddish confounded their attempts at English spelling.[1] Only four years earlier, at age twenty-five, Harry had journeyed from Kiev to Brooklyn, New York, where he worked odd carpentry jobs to earn enough money to allow Rebecca and their two-year-old daughter, Dora, to join him. The Margolins ventured to America for a new life, free from the religious persecution they faced in Russia.[2] But New York's tough and crowded conditions also challenged the young family. Like thousands of other immigrant Jews who were being resettled from large northeastern industrial cities to smaller, more welcoming communities in the South and Midwest, the Margolins found their way to Memphis, Tennessee.[3] There they found a thriving Jewish community, including the "Pinch," a small neighborhood that was home to other Yiddish-speaking newcomers like them.[4]

In April 1911 Rebecca gave birth to a son, Jacob. She died a year later, reportedly from Hodgkin's disease coupled with anemia.[5] Reflecting the Margolins' traditional religious roots, she was buried in Memphis's Old Jewish Cemetery, which was affiliated with Baron Hirsch Synagogue, an Orthodox congregation. Rebecca's death left Harry a single parent with no formal education struggling to provide for his three young children.

Harry's plight caught the attention of Rabbi Max Samfield, a revered spiritual leader in Memphis's Reform Jewish community, who represented the city's chapter of B'nai B'rith's District Grand Lodge No. 7 on the Board of the Jewish Orphans' Home in New Orleans. In exchange for financial support, the Home admitted children from the district's member states: Alabama, Arkansas, Louisiana, Mississippi, Oklahoma, Tennessee, and

Texas.[6] Samfield recommended, as he had for many needy Memphis Jews, that the Home admit the Margolin children, or at least the two girls for the time being.[7] As part of the process, Samfield certified that the girls were Jewish, with no living relative to adequately care for them. In exchange for its promise to care for his children, Harry gave the Home full and complete control over them, surrendering his right to any wages his children might earn.[8] Whether Harry Margolin believed he was making a sacrifice to secure his children's admission is unknown. After the Home approved the girls' application, they moved to New Orleans, leaving behind their father and baby brother.

The Jewish Orphans' Home

In 1913, much like today, streetcars clanged and swayed along New Orleans's gracious St. Charles Avenue under a canopy of live oak and palm trees. The Jewish Orphans' Home, then standing where the tracks cross Jefferson Avenue, was a grand brick building that prominently occupied the entire block. Rising three stories and crowned with three ornamental towers, the Renaissance-style structure was proclaimed a magnificent monument to progressive Hebrew benevolence when it opened in 1887.[9] Notably, the Home was not in New Orleans's Dryades Street neighborhood, which, although not as well delineated as Memphis's Pinch, was the religious, social, and commercial center of the city's Eastern European Jewish immigrants. Instead, the Home comfortably shared the Uptown neighborhood with the mansions of New Orleans's most affluent and influential citizens, Jews and non-Jews.[10]

The Home was the second orphanage built by the Association for the Relief of Jewish Widows and Orphans, a group of Jewish leaders who organized in 1855. Obeying the biblical commandment—repeated in the Torah no fewer than thirty-six times—to protect orphans and other vulnerable community members, the association sought to aid the parentless children left in the wake of the city's yellow fever epidemics.[11] As the association decreed, the Home was to foster, maintain, and instruct Jewish orphans and half-orphans of both sexes and thus encompassed children who had lost both parents or whose sole parent was incapable of providing necessary support.[12] When the number of needy children exceeded the capacity of the original orphanage, the city's Jewish leaders, buoyed by their economic prosperity, rallied again to build the new, larger structure on St. Charles Avenue.[13]

The Home was both a stunning contrast to the humble origins of its young residents and an inspiring symbol of what each could—and indeed many of them did—achieve. Noted architect Thomas Sully's design, competitively selected, and the elegant furnishings of its public rooms demonstrated the passion and finances New Orleans's Jewish community had dedicated to transform the Home's children into productive and patriotic American Jews.[14] To its young residents the Home was an imposing but not overpowering institution in which they found—amid regimentation and discipline—comfort, security, and opportunity not possible within their own families.[15]

When Bessie and Dora entered the Home on June 5, 1913, this ethos was cultivated by its superintendent, Leon Volmer.[16] The thirty-four-year-old Arkansas native lived there with his wife and young daughter. Volmer had previously served as rabbi of a Reform congregation in Charleston, West Virginia, where he earned a reputation as a lovable and compassionate man.[17] Since assuming charge of the Home in 1911, Volmer had advocated for progressive methods of institutional child care, such as self-governance and after-care.[18] He believed his job was to provide far more than mere subsistence for his charges. "If the Orphanage has any good reason for existing," wrote Volmer when Bessie was seven, it "must be to take the unfortunate child and provide a home for him, the atmosphere, the activities and the moral and spiritual life of which will make of the child a Social Force in the Social Construction of Society."[19]

The Home was well suited for Volmer's ambitious plans. Compared to Jewish orphanages in big cities like New York and Cleveland, which housed nearly eight hundred and five hundred children, respectively, the Home had far fewer wards. During Bessie's first year she lived with seventy-one girls and one hundred boys—the largest enrollment in the Home's history.[20] Much like New Orleans's relatively small Eastern European population, the orphanage never exceeded the welcome or wealth of its small but prosperous Jewish community or the genteel courtesy of the city's Christian majority.[21] Moreover, the children's lengthy stays in the Home gave Volmer plenty of time in which to mold his young charges. Absent a parent or relative willing and capable of assuming care, a child's discharge from the Home generally required self-sufficiency, as determined by age and maturity. Although some children stayed for a few years or less, an equal number spent their entire childhoods there; Bessie would live in the Home for twelve years.[22]

Quarantine and Generosity

Bessie and Dora went through the same process all new admittees encountered at the Jewish Orphans' Home. After they were registered, they were sent to the infirmary for a mandatory two-week quarantine, in which they found themselves far from the home they had left in Memphis but not yet a part of the Home's regular routine.[23] During the brief but strange interlude, they could see other children pass under the infirmary's windows and hear them walking along the corridor or singing prayers in the synagogue down the hall where Superintendent Volmer led Shabbat and holiday services.[24] After two weeks of being examined, observed, and inoculated, the sisters emerged from quarantine with clean bills of health.

Four-year-old Bessie went to the nursery, a small room next to the infirmary. Amid cribs, a team of rocking horses, and a few other toys, Bessie was assigned her own small bed and locker. Under the watchful eye of nursery helpers, Bessie and her young companions were expected to share the responsibilities of Home life; they were taught to dress themselves, make their beds, and put away their clothes.[25] As in New Orleans's well-to-do families, the caregivers and household staff were primarily black women. The children developed strong emotional bonds with their trusted caregivers, who were known to the children only by their first names.[26] By age six Bessie joined Dora in the girls' dormitory building, where they shared a large, sparsely furnished room with two dozen girls.[27] By then baby brother Jack had joined them in the Home, taking Bessie's place in the nursery.[28]

From her earliest days in the orphanage Bessie experienced the generosity of an entire community. The names of donors were carved on tall white marble tablets that lined the walls of the polished entranceway. For their less fortunate peers, New Orleans's wealthy Jewish children reportedly donated the Home's picturesque fountain, a favored backdrop for countless photographs.[29] Gifts regularly flowed in from across the region, including dresses, laces, and embroidery for the girls, straw hats and suspenders for the boys. Katz & Besthoff drug store sent talcum powder, and the United Fruit Company delivered bunches of bananas. Special treats appeared for birthdays, such as ice cream and cake, while a steady stream of tickets offered excursions and entertainment outside the Home, including movies, concerts, and sporting events. The press and the Home publicly acknowledged these acts of loving kindness, which in turn kept the children who lived there in the hearts and minds of the community.[30]

The Home groomed its wards to be all-American boys and girls who honored the local Jewish community and reflected the values and culture of their prosperous benefactors. To accomplish this goal, in addition to providing clothing, nourishment, and medical care, the Home adhered to three overlapping facets of child development: a secular education; training in obedience, industry, and civic engagement; and a Reform Jewish religious education. For Bessie and her siblings these developmental priorities produced a powerful foundation for independence and upward mobility.[31]

Learning by Doing

When the 1913 school year opened, Bessie and the other children lined up behind Superintendent Volmer and filed out of the Home for the two-block walk to the Isidore Newman Manual Training School. Although recalled by one alumnus as rigid and militaristic, the daily march to school produced pride in another as Volmer stopped traffic for the children to cross St. Charles Avenue.[32] Established by the Home's benefactors a decade earlier, "Manual," as Bessie knew the school during her student days, was born from the notion, new to New Orleans, that practical skills, such as home economics and woodworking, should be taught in addition to traditional academic knowledge.[33] Beyond its rigorous curriculum, Manual was important and unique for the children living at the Jewish Orphans' Home in that it fostered life outside the institution. Not only was the school physically separated from the Home; it was also integrated with children from the community. Further, Manual educated a broader cross-section of New Orleans's children, as the Home's board resolved that the school admit students without discrimination because of creed, but only after providing for its own wards.[34]

Although Manual was founded to educate the Home children, by the time Bessie began her education, students from private families, including the grandson of benefactor Isidore Newman, outnumbered them. All Home children attended Manual through the lower grades, but not all Home children continued there through high school. Children who were less academically inclined were encouraged or allowed to pursue vocational training at other local schools. As the city's only private, coeducational, and nonsectarian school, Manual also attracted many paying students. As a result of these factors, as early as 1913, its graduates were gaining admission to Tulane University, Newcomb College, Louisiana State University, the University of

Michigan, Cornell University, the University of Virginia, and Smith College. Manual, the school for Jewish orphans, had become one of the South's finest college preparatory schools.[35]

The school's essence was conveyed in its motto, "Discimus Agere Agendo" (We learn to do by doing). Teaching its students to work as well as to think permeated the curriculum.[36] When Bessie was in third grade, for example, she did not simply read stories about the ancient Greeks; her teacher, Viola C. Rareshide, a Newcomb College graduate with a master's degree from Tulane University, had the boys construct armor and weapons while the girls fashioned gowns and sandals, which they wore in a performance. Among the soloists Bessie shared the spotlight with her classmate and lifelong friend, Katherine Polack. Kate came from a prosperous Jewish family, and her father served on the Home's board. After Kate introduced the program, Bessie recited a poem to classical piano accompaniment, and then they both joined the class in a "dance of the nymphs."[37]

Every day Bessie left the Home and attended a school where she learned and played on equal terms with children of New Orleans's most affluent families, both Jews and Gentiles. The Home and non-Home children were forced to mix, a process aided by the Home's earlier elimination of uniforms. Bessie saw the world of possibilities enjoyed by her classmates and their middle- and upper-class parents—vacation homes, maids, and for some children a chauffeur.[38] Academically talented, Bessie found she could hold her own with boys and girls from the finest families in New Orleans. When invited to Kate Polack's lovely St. Charles Avenue house for visits and parties, Bessie learned social and cultural lessons that could not be taught in a classroom.[39] In turn Kate and other non-Home children who visited the orphanage for cultural events or to socialize with friends often were fascinated by life in the Home, some even envious of a place offering round-the-clock playmates with whom to play hide-and-seek or make hot chocolate on a radiator.[40]

"The Golden City"

Intended to instill civic and social responsibility, "the Golden City," as Superintendent Volmer proudly explained, was a system of self-government he believed was as important to the children's development as their secular and religious education. A training innovation devised by Volmer's prede-

6

cessor and emulated by other Jewish orphanages, the Home instituted the Golden City in 1910.[41] Throughout Bessie's time there Volmer continued to "unqualifiedly pronounce it to be the best method for the development of the 'whole child.'"[42] By design the Golden City emphasized the value of independence, the dignity of fair wages earned through hard work, and the notion of government as a participatory and protective institution.[43] The Golden City's lessons informed Bessie's life.

As a Golden City "Builder," the name given to citizens in good standing, Bessie was subject to a basic legal system in which the children served as judges and lawyers for prosecution and defense and held trials for violations of the Golden City's high standards of honor and morals.[44] Their judgments were subject to Volmer's approval, in his role as the Golden City's mayor. Further, the children were divided into "Families," each led by an elected Big Brother and Big Sister, who meted out privileges such as weekend outings, use of the Home's social room, and the amount of money paid for chores.[45] During Bessie's early years she could earn a few cents each week for sweeping and bed making, a portion of which she could spend on sweets and toys; she was required to deposit the rest in a savings account to learn thrift and economy.[46] The Golden City, according to Volmer, mitigated "the evil effects of institutional rearing" and made each child "feel that he is a human being and not merely a cog in a well-oiled machine."[47]

Despite the Golden City's virtues, its reliance on older children to discipline their juniors led to abuse.[48] The "Seven Soap Scrubbers" were a group of Big Brothers who devised their own discipline for younger boys who broke minor rules. The younger boys never knew when the Scrubbers might drag them to the showers, rough them up, and rub a bar of soap all over their teeth.[49] Moreover, the system elevated institutional order over the needs of individual children. Volmer strictly enforced harsh discipline and rigid routines, such as bells to signal activities and lining up for inspection.[50] Breaking rules, such as being late for school or failing to obtain permission for simple activities, could lead to extra chores or lost privileges such as Saturday night silent movies and weekend outings.[51]

In spite of these difficult experiences, Bessie's peers also recalled happy times and kind peer leaders. As adults, many Home alumni prospered academically, professionally, and socially. Some came to recognize that all children have good and bad times, and some even acknowledged that Volmer's rigid discipline had some enduring character-building effects.[52]

Bessie never mentioned the Golden City's darker aspects and enjoyed an active social life there. She participated in the Home's club activities, which Volmer promoted to teach self-reliance and self-expression.[53] Bessie joined the Girls' Leaders Club, which organized itself around industrious purposes but also had some fun, such as when it threw a "Baby Party" to celebrate the high school graduation of two Home girls. In one of the earliest examples of her writing, fourteen-year-old Bessie described the lively party in which the club's dignified ladies for one night assumed silly behavior, securing her first byline in the Home's newsletter, the *Golden City Messenger*.[54]

Reform Judaism

For Volmer and the Home's board, religious education in accordance with the ideals of Reform Judaism was another crucial facet of the children's transformation into productive Jewish American citizens. As practiced by the Home's leaders and benefactors, largely German Jewish immigrants, Reform Judaism represented a modernized Jewish life in which ritual observance was no longer inviolate but instead served to reinforce prophetic ideals of justice, freedom, and peace. It abandoned traditional Orthodox Jewish practices that alienated Jews from non-Jews such as dietary laws of kashrut and codes of dress. In addition, moving the main Shabbat service to Friday night freed Reform Jews to pursue their occupations on Saturdays in conformance with the non-Jewish community. These changes in practice accompanied a new theology; the focus of prayer shifted from the coming of the Messiah and rebuilding the biblical Temple in Israel to the Jews' historic task of bringing social justice to the world.[55]

The Home's alliance with Reform Judaism was a clear break from Orthodox Jewish observances, traditions, and Zionist politics that prevailed among recent Eastern European Jewish immigrants, including many of the Home children's families. This inculcation of Reform Jewish observance significantly enhanced the children's chances to assimilate and acculturate as American Jews; adhering to Reform Judaism had in the same way enabled the Home's benefactors and leaders to achieve financial prosperity and gain acceptance in New Orleans.[56]

Bessie, like other Home children, learned Hebrew, attended Sunday school, and observed religious holidays in accordance with Reform Judaism. At age thirteen she celebrated her confirmation in the Home's synagogue, just as Kate Polack and other Jewish classmates at Manual were doing at New Orleans's Reform congregations.[57] To involve the larger Jewish community in the children's religious life, the Home's Rosh Hashanah and Yom Kippur High Holy Day services were open to and attended by the community.[58] Similarly, the children's lavishly decorated sukkah—the temporary booth that marks the harvest festival of Sukkot—in the Home's courtyard and the Home's Passover seder attracted alumni and board members and were promoted in local newspapers and Home publications.[59]

For the children who lived there, the Home's religious life produced a range of reactions. Some later said they were very conscious that they were Jewish children and that it was a good and happy feeling.[60] Others fondly recalled services in the Home synagogue on Friday nights and the High Holy Days.[61] One spoke about Yom Kippur, the Day of Atonement, when the children were required to practice forgiveness by shaking hands to end squabbles with peers.[62] Others enjoyed the food, gifts, and costumes that accompanied other holidays.[63] Although she was a nonobservant Jew as an adult, Bessie always considered herself Jewish.[64] Moreover, she was identified as a Jew by others, and not always to her advantage. Bessie's Jewish education and experiences in the Home gave her a solid foundation for lifelong friendships with other Jews as well as a personal reason to oppose anti-Semitism, which would inform her work for the Nazi war crimes trials in 1946, and to travel to Israel in 1962 (while forgoing a trip to Baghdad the same year).[65] Moreover, Reform Judaism's emphasis on social justice, regularly invoked in the Home's speeches and practices, would shape her professional life.

Beyond the differences in their religious observance, it is not surprising that Bessie and her siblings faced an ever-widening gap with their father socioeconomically, educationally, as well as emotionally. The Home limited visits by parents or relatives, at least on paper, to weekends.[66] Although not exclusively the basis for limiting such contact, the leadership harbored a not-too-subtle bias against its wards' families. In his 1916 report to the board, Volmer described children who entered the Home from the "lowest stratum of society with hereditary traits, mental and moral weaknesses." The same year B'nai B'rith's regional president praised institutional care for children whose widowed mothers lacked force of character to exact respect or obedience or who, feeling the pinch of poverty, would find the few pennies the child brings home from working in factories or from street occupations more alluring than the rewards of faithful studies at school.[67]

In 1925, the same year Bessie left for college, the Home's president explained that one mother was incapable of properly raising children because she was "a typical Russian immigrant, filthy, hardly capable of expressing herself in the most common English words."[68]

These prejudices and practices inevitably influenced Bessie's relationship with her father. As she said in later years, Harry moved to New Orleans from Memphis when she was about twelve years old and visited her and her siblings in the Home from time to time. She spoke of her father as sweet but frail due to asthma, which apparently prevented him from acting on his dream to open a carpentry shop.[69] At other times Bessie and Dora disparaged their father for peddling clothes in New Orleans's red-light district. They attempted to live with him after their discharge from the Home but quickly left, after he proved to be incompatible.[70] At a minimum Bessie experienced a very different life than her father's.[71] Although Harry continued to live in New Orleans until his death in 1940, his role in his children's lives was attenuated at best.

Anniversaries and Orators

By far the Home's grandest and most unique festivity was the anniversary of its founding, celebrated each year in early January.[72] The children eagerly anticipated the special activities and plentiful food, while the adults used the day to honor the Home's proud history and sustain community support.[73] Open for public inspection on this day each year, the Home was extra bright and cheerful and the children wore their best clothes.[74] Bessie celebrated twelve Home anniversaries, all filled with pageantry, banquets, and influential guest orators.

Although their messages varied, the anniversary speakers conveyed the Home's beliefs to the children and community. Distinguished Home alumni inspired the children to strive for success. Louis Yarrut, for example, just ten years after leaving the Home, returned as a partner in his own law firm, providing fourteen-year-old Bessie her first encounter with a lawyer who had been raised in the orphanage. Yarrut told the children to be proud of their time in the Home and to show their gratitude by sustaining the charity, humanity, and Americanism it had instilled in them.[75] Esteemed spiritual leaders, too, addressed the anniversary crowds, calling for reform and social justice. During Bessie's early years Rabbi Emil W. Leipziger called for a modern philanthropy, one that demanded a "social vision" that would enable them to see that orphanage, widowhood, social and industrial diseases, child labor, imprisonment, and inadequate housing are all allied problems. He implored the capable crowd to address these root causes that led to each child's admission.[76] He pointed to a young girl in the audience, acknowledging the moral grace and the worldly knowledge the Home had instilled in her. Yet he challenged the Home's benefactors to do more by posing a question, an uncanny prophecy about the laws that Bessie would one day enforce in the nation's courts: "But does the sight of her quicken you to the duty to fight for decent standards of wages and working conditions in the industrial or commercial world in which she will ultimately find herself?"[77] The pursuit of success and the moral imperative to fight for social justice were repeated and modeled throughout Bessie's childhood.

The Finer Things in Life

Beginning at age twelve, Bessie was afforded another important opportunity that would have a profound impact on her. The Home recruited prominent Jewish women in the community, volunteer "Matrons," to guide its adolescents safely through uncertainty and temptation.[78] The program also introduced Home children to the world of New Orleans's financial and social elite. Home alumni appreciated their Matrons for many things, including the chance to visit in their homes and learn about the finer things in life. This was especially true of Bessie's relationship with her Matron, Hanna Bloom Stern, who had a long history of service to the Home and to the community. Stern's husband was Home trustee Maurice B. Stern, a German-born Reform Jew who had made his fortune as president of the cotton brokerage firm Lehman, Stern & Company.[79] During the five years Hanna Stern served as Bessie's Matron, her son Edgar married Edith Rosenwald, the daughter of Sears, Roebuck & Company magnate Julius Rosenwald, further cementing Hanna's place among New Orleans's Jewish high society.[80]

As Bessie's Matron, Stern not only exposed Bessie to her family and their lifestyle, including their palatial St. Charles Avenue mansion, known for its fine furnishings and alluring garden.[81] Stern also used her position to help Bessie's transition from the Home to Newcomb College, recommending her for housing and other services. As reflected in Stern's letters, Bessie had endeared herself to Stern, who cheerfully fulfilled her duty as Matron to "mother" Bessie and raise her standards in every way possible. Stern described Bessie as a splendid girl who was not only appreciative but also industrious, ambitious, respectful, and capable.[82]

Knowledge Is Power

Bessie enjoyed many interests, activities, and academic successes at Manual, earning frequent accolades in the *Golden City Messenger*. Bessie's Home peers named her "Brightest Girl" and their "shining light," noting her habit for earning As in every academic subject.[83] Bessie read many of the classics, no fewer than four per year, beginning her freshman year with Washington Irving's *Sketch Book* and Charles Dickens's *Tale of Two Cities* and ending her senior year with William Shakespeare's *Midsummer Night's Dream* and James Russell Lowell's *Vision of Sir Launfal.*[84] Although her classical readings provided neither female author nor protagonist as a role model, they gave Bessie a strong foundation of grammar and vocabulary.[85]

In high school Bessie first discovered her lifelong love of writing, which also provided opportunities for leadership. As a junior, she was coeditor of the *Pioneer,* the school's prose and poetry magazine, under the direction of its first female editor-in-chief. As editor, Bessie learned to review other students' work and to write lengthier pieces of fiction, revealing her industry and creativity and her fascination with boys and romance. What she had not learned from the classics, Bessie apparently learned from the popular romantic literature of the time; in keeping with the genre, Bessie's female protagonists were inevitably positive and appealing characters who, after trials and setbacks, ended up engaged or married to their true loves.[86]

Drawing from her own life, Bessie created two female characters who were young, attractive, and intelligent orphans. In both stories Bessie used trickery to unite these young women with their lovers. In "Gypsy Matchmakers" Bessie wrote about Madge Dell, a self-supporting teacher adored by two students who, while dressed as gypsies on their way to a costume party, use a fortune-telling scheme to unite Dell with her shy suitor, Mr. Guilford. In the second story, "In Somebody Else's Shoes," George convinces his friend Bob to impersonate him and fulfill his obligation to visit his aunt. While there, Bob (as George) falls in love with Beulah Basel, a beautiful orphan.[87]

Bessie described her female protagonists much as she might have described herself. Madge's face, wrote Bessie, "though not beautiful, was expressive and wore an intelligent look. Her eyes, however, were beautiful. Large, expressive, hazel eyes, shaded with long, curling brown lashes, caused some people to call her a beauty." Beulah dazzled Bob with her "beautiful, well-shaped face," "little cherry lips," and "slight figure." "Gypsy Matchmakers" also revealed young Bessie's imagination for dramatic yet discreet romance. Mr. Guilford, wrote Bessie, "turned to Madge and took her slim, soft hands in his large, strong ones. Then after a long, loving look into her beautiful eyes, which were shining with happiness, he drew her fondly toward him and whispered softly something, which we need not know, into her ear."[88]

In addition to her love of reading and writing, Manual also gave Bessie the opportunity to develop what became another trademark of her professional career—her skill for oral advocacy. Years later, explaining her decision to go to law school, she wrote, "I suspect that I always had something of a penchant for debating, which I recollect having enjoyed in high school."[89] Evidencing her budding forensic abilities as well as her future political leanings, in a 1924 debate Bessie argued that the Democratic Party should win over the Republican Party in the presidential election. Three faculty judges agreed and named Bessie as the best speaker.[90]

Bessie graduated from Manual in June 1925 as a sixteen-year-old leader who was comfortable competing, succeeding, and winning respect in a coed setting. In addition to editing the *Pioneer,* Bessie sang in the glee club, presided over the debate club and the girls' student council, received a chemistry essay prize, and won the coveted scholarship to attend Newcomb College. From her thirty-one classmates, only four of whom lived in the Home, Bessie was chosen to deliver the commencement address, an honor that previously had been given only twice to a Home resident and only once to a girl.

Her academic successes did not impede her social life. Bessie endeared herself to classmates and Home residents alike, comfortably moving from one social world to the other. After graduation Bessie joined Kate Polack's family—instead of her own—for a celebratory dinner.[91] A fellow Home resident, writing in the *Messenger,* paid Bessie a hearty compliment: "Bessie is worse than a cross word puzzle, because she is also a flapper, besides being an athlete and a scholar."[92] True to her studious side, her senior yearbook photograph was aptly captioned: "Knowledge Is Power." But the tributes paid by her classmates elsewhere in the yearbook reflected a broader, and likable, persona: "Willing to do anything that she is called upon to do,

Bessie is always cheerful and sunny—everybody's friend. Manual is losing one of her most loyal students when Bessie leaves, for she entered into everything wholeheartedly—nothing half way. Good luck, Bessie, you're bound to succeed wherever you go."[93] Bessie's mischievous nature, which went unmentioned in the school and Home publications, was not lost on her closest friends. Years later high school classmate Evelyn Flonacher delighted in reminding Bessie about their old Manual days, playing hooky from French class.[94]

Lifelong Connection to Home and School

Throughout her life Bessie remained connected to her childhood home and school. She returned to the Home and Manual, which had become known as Newman, on several occasions. She was Newman's Founder's Day speaker in 1929 and again in 1968, and for more than two decades beginning in the mid-1950s arranged for its ninth graders to meet with a Supreme Court justice while on their annual civics trip to Washington, D.C., often joining them for lunch. During her last year of law school, in January 1930, Bessie spoke at the Home's Diamond Jubilee Anniversary, sharing the stage with Rabbi Leipziger. Reminiscent of Louis Yarrut's speech years earlier, Bessie expressed her deep appreciation to the Home.[95] In January 1955 the Home, which became a nonresidential service agency when the orphanage closed in 1946, celebrated its one hundredth anniversary.[96] As one of its most accomplished alumni, Bessie agreed when the Home asked her to be the subject of a feature article in the *New Orleans Times-Picayune,* "From Orphanage to Supreme Court."[97] For Superintendent Volmer, his successors, and all her benevolent benefactors, Bessie was a shining example of the Home's sacred task to strengthen her soul and develop her character, allowing her to become a force for social justice—or in Volmer's oft-repeated words, "a Social Force in the Social Construction of Society."

If educational, cultural, and economic opportunities are the yardstick, Bessie and her siblings were unquestionably fortunate to have been admitted to the Home. This is not to suggest that life in the orphanage was idyllic for all children or that even Bessie had only positive experiences. Some emerged from the Home resenting its strict discipline, regimentation, and the lack of individual attention. Moreover, the Home underwent dramatic physical changes and programmatic reform shortly after Volmer's departure in 1926.

Although the changes reflected shifts in child development, they were also a critical evaluation of Volmer's tenure, specifically his implementation of the Golden City and the children's insular experiences. Questions continued to be raised about the Home's insistence on institutional care instead of providing financial support to single parents or arranging foster placements. Within months after Bessie left there for college, child welfare experts generally cautioned Volmer and the board, "It seems a travesty on human kindness for a child who has been deprived of one parent by death to be deprived of the other solely for economic reasons and to be removed hundreds of miles from his original environment in order to receive aid."[98] Whether travesty or great fortune, or both, Bessie's and her siblings' lives were forever changed by their admission to the Home, which afforded the South's neediest Jewish children all the benefits of an elite religious boarding school.

Like Bessie, her siblings Dora and Jack remained strongly tied to the institution for years. After moving out of the Home in 1923 at age eighteen, Dora returned there to work as its nurse for several years. In 1936 she celebrated her marriage in one of the parlors on the main floor. Having entered as a baby, Jack lived in the Home for fourteen years and later returned to live and work there as a boys' supervisor while he attended Tulane University. Despite her enduring connection to it, in later years Bessie spoke about the Home infrequently and with little detail. When she talked about her childhood, however, she expressed only strong, positive sentiments. "It may be hard to climb from some charitable homes, but this one is an exception," Bessie told a reporter. "They pushed me and gave me my opportunities and I owe them a lot."[99] She was also grateful that the Home had kept her siblings together and had "promoted a family feeling for the three of us."[100] She summed up her childhood, telling her family, "I always felt loved."[101]

2

COLLEGE AND LAW SCHOOL
1925–1933

Newcomb College

At age sixteen Bessie Margolin moved out of the Jewish Orphans' Home and entered Newcomb College. Although she was free of the Golden City and its rules, for the next five years the Home and its superintendent continued to be her guardian. The Home provided her, as a nonresident ward, financial and social support to ease her transition to independence and boarded her in a private house within easy walking distance to the campus shared by Newcomb College and Tulane University.[1] Her scholarship was substantial, $125 for each of her four years, but it did not cover the entire tuition, room, and board. Although the Home funded the difference, Margolin contributed to her upkeep and earned spending money by working in the college library.[2]

Margolin had moved from one important New Orleans institution to another. As the nation's first degree-granting college for women within an all-male university, Newcomb sought to provide young women of Louisiana and adjoining states the quality liberal education that Tulane University offered its young men, and that women's colleges offered elsewhere in the country.[3] It aimed to combine the advantages of a women's college and a coeducational institution without suffering from the disadvantages of either.[4] But at Newcomb, Margolin attended academic classes, for the first time in her life, with only women. Despite Newcomb's progressive roots and the opportunities afforded by its relationship with Tulane, the coordinate arrangement during Margolin's time, which lacked feminist leadership and did not value learning by women as in the women's colleges, largely measured its students' success by the education of the men they could attract as husbands.[5]

Chances are that Margolin gave little thought to gender equality in education when she started at Newcomb. By the time she was twelve, women had already won the vote, secured certain property rights, and acquired legal access to divorce and custody of their children.[6] Arriving at Newcomb in the middle of the Roaring Twenties, Margolin's contemporaries were preoccupied with matters more immediate to their lives than emancipation, which had been the concern of the previous generation's suffragists.[7] Rebelling against Victorian mores, especially its sex taboos, young people of Margolin's day embraced a radically different style of fashion, dance, and morality. Epitomized by "flappers," young women known for their scant clothing and the energetic way they moved in it, the 1920s generation was tagged as hungry for fun and freedom. It was the generation of short skirts, cigarettes, automobiles, wild dancing, athletics, and speakeasies.[8]

In reality most young women in the 1920s, including Bessie and her Newcomb classmates, did little more than adopt fashionable hairstyles and wardrobes and drive in cars. Even their bobbed hair had its nonliberating drawbacks, often requiring time-consuming coaxing with pomades and celebrated oils.[9] The fear that students would use cars as "bedrooms on wheels" also infringed on their newfound freedom. During Bessie's sophomore year Newcomb's student president returned from a conference to report the consensus among women's colleges' representatives: automobile riding should be chaperoned.[10] The college apparently took no action on this recommendation, yet it reflects the tension between greater freedom and lingering conservative attitudes about "ladylike" behavior college girls faced, especially in the South.

At Newcomb, Bessie immersed herself in a familiar yet expanding social circle. She stayed close with Manual classmates, including Kate Polack and Evelyn Flonacher, but explored new activities and made new friends. Margolin pledged a Jewish sorority, Alpha Epsilon Phi (AEPhi), and won the position of secretary-treasurer.[11] She joined the French Circle and Debating Club, served on the finance committee for the *Jambalaya*, the university yearbook, and played forward on the intramural basketball team.[12] The *Times-Picayune*'s society pages offer a glimpse of her activities and also reveal the extent to which New Orleans respected its Jewish community while maintaining separate social circles. Adjacent to stories about the wives and daughters of New Orleans's socially elite Protestants and Episcopalians, including young debutantes who were introduced at elaborate Mardi Gras balls that were off-limits for Jews, Bessie Margolin's name appeared as a guest at events held primarily by and for Jews. The society columnist noted

17

Margolin's attendance at a sorority sisters' dance in the French Quarter, dinner parties and teas organized by New Orleans's Jewish women's organizations, and a luncheon for AEPhi pledges at New Orleans's West End Country Club, which Jewish businessmen had founded after being excluded from the city's old-line clubs.[13]

After her first semester, suggesting a desire to live among other students on campus while respecting the Home's limited after-care budget, Margolin sought housing in Newcomb's Club Dormitory, a cooperative residence hall reserved for academically strong students with limited finances.[14] Because applicants competed for the few spaces, Margolin enlisted her influential Matron, Hanna Stern, who was pleased to provide an excellent report that cited Margolin's willingness to do household work and her determination to support herself.[15] With Stern's favorable report, Newcomb promptly approved Margolin's application, provided she maintain satisfactory grades and share cheerfully in the operation of the house.[16]

Before moving into the Club Dormitory, Margolin spent the summer of 1926 in Baton Rouge selling encyclopedias.[17] Despite the convincing case she made for the value of knowledge, there is little evidence that Margolin sold many books. Years later she described the experience, walking door to door lugging the weighty tomes in the Louisiana summer's heat and humidity, as "the most miserable job" she ever had.[18] She never again came so close to becoming a peddler like her father.

Despite the distractions, academics remained Bessie's primary focus, and she continued to excel in them, earning grades of 90 and better in all of her courses.[19] After Margolin's sophomore year, Newcomb's counselor for women, Anna Many, a 1909 Newcomb alumna and math professor, lauded the excellent scholastic work and intellect that placed Margolin among the top ten in her class. Having frequently encountered Margolin over the past two years, Many observed that eighteen-year-old Margolin was not sensitive and was very self-confident. Many added that Margolin dressed rather elaborately for a person of her means but understood that many of her clothes had been given to her. This comment suggests that Margolin's attire not only appeared to be too expensive for a former ward of the Home, and perhaps out of place on a college campus, but also was the subject of discussion. Many also remarked, without elaboration, that Margolin did not make friends easily. This ambiguous comment is difficult to interpret given Margolin's active social life and sorority activities, although it echoes a reticence Margolin exhibited in later years, attributed by some observers to modesty and shyness and by others to intellectual elitism.[20]

More than a decade would pass before Margolin herself offered context to interpret Many's comments about her college wardrobe and not making friends easily. When interviewed by a reporter about her college days, Margolin said she had made her own clothes, a claim bolstered by the strong grades she earned in her sewing class at Manual.[21] Although her ongoing close friendships with her well-heeled friends Kate Polack and Evelyn Flonacher helped Margolin fit in, she was nonetheless one of few girls from the Home ever to attend Newcomb and was the only one in her class. "I don't remember any self consciousness," Margolin claimed in the 1939 interview; she was by then beginning to wear the smart, tailored fashions that would distinguish her professional persona. "Maybe there was and I've forgotten it, but if any embarrassment existed, it wasn't strong enough to remember." Yet Margolin recognized that she had managed to cross a socioeconomic boundary, harking back to the counselor's observations. "Many of the wealthy girls at Newcomb were my friends then, and are still my friends," she added defensively. "Why, I correspond with a dozen of my old school chums."[22] The upwardly mobile career woman was unwilling to acknowledge that her childhood in the orphanage presented any handicap or inferiority—in her attire, social life, or otherwise—that she could not overcome.

Tulane Law School

With her academic success, Margolin could have sailed through Newcomb to graduation. But instead, during her sophomore year, Margolin set her sights on law school. Reluctant to ask the Home to finance her education for an additional three years, Margolin discovered one of the great advantages of Newcomb's coordinate program: Tulane allowed a limited number of students to combine a liberal arts curriculum with the study of law, obtaining both degrees in a total of six years.[23] Tulane not only admitted Margolin to its law school but also transferred her from Newcomb to Tulane's otherwise all-male College of Arts and Sciences to complete her liberal arts degree.

Although Margolin later cited only her penchant for debating, her bold decision to attend law school seems driven by a sense of entitlement to pursue opportunities enjoyed by men. Tulane Law School had admitted its first woman in 1898, but there had been very few. When Margolin entered in the fall of 1927, she was the sole woman not only in her first-year class but in the entire law school.[24] She had few, if any, role models. No other girl from the Jewish Orphans' Home had ever gone to law school, and Tulane Law School's most recent female graduate had completed her legal studies before Margolin began.[25]

Tulane was not unique in having a limited number of female law students. By 1920 women had gained admission to 102 of the nation's 142 law schools, owing largely to suffrage and the declining enrollment of men due to World War I.[26] With few exceptions, however, such as Portia Law School in Boston, the first and only all-woman's law school, being a female law student in the 1920s was still rare. The 12 American law schools with the most women, taken together, enrolled only 84.[27] By 1930 the nation's 2,203 women law students represented only 3 percent of total enrollment and remained at that level until World War II.[28] When Margolin reached her third and final year of law school, she would still be 1 of only 5 female Tulane law students.[29] In other words, women attending law school during Margolin's time were very conspicuous in their classes and had to get used to being noticed, for better and for worse.

Years later Margolin admitted that she felt isolated and self-conscious her first year as the only woman in the law school. Like other pioneering women in male-dominated law school classes, Margolin faced the discomforts and fears she stirred in her male peers. They might believe that she was in law school simply to find a husband or that she was taking the place of a man who needed the education to support a family. If she did well, she might be accused of threatening class ranking or suspected of receiving her grades out of favoritism.[30] Margolin navigated such attitudes and won the support of her law classmates and professors, many of whom became friends and professional colleagues. Years later a law classmate recalled the initial discomfort of having Margolin in the otherwise all-male student body. A professor assigned a civil procedure case involving an accident in a men's room. Embarrassed to use the word *toilet* in Margolin's presence, no one wanted to recite on the case. When one poor fellow finally blurted out, "Washroom," the whole class laughed and sighed with relief.[31]

Margolin's 1927 arrival at the law school coincided with big changes there. Rufus Harris, the law school's new dean, arrived with several other talented full-time faculty members, all Yale and Harvard law graduates, and made extensive improvements in the curriculum.[32] Before Harris arrived, Tulane Law School's goal was to prepare students to practice law in Louisiana. Harris expanded the vision and raised the bar, with the law school now striving to rival the country's best legal training, which gave Margolin the background and perspective to consider a career outside of Louisiana.[33]

Harris also resurrected Tulane's defunct law review, an opportunity Margolin seized to develop and showcase her strong research and writing skills and to assume a leadership role.[34] By her second year Margolin's rank as an honors student distinguished her for selection as note editor and by her last year civil law editor, a particularly prestigious position because of the publication's emphasis on Louisiana's Civil Code, a unique legal system derived from Spanish, French, and Roman sources.

Besides editing pieces written by others, Margolin used her fluency in French to conduct extensive research in French legal sources in order to author three comments, as student essays on law topics are known.[35] In each Margolin analyzed technical and emerging commercial law issues involving negotiable instruments (whether a usufruct of promissory notes enjoyed full ownership rights to the principal or merely the interest), creditors' rights (whether the civil law remedy of "vendor's privilege" entitled a creditor to seize personal property upon the purchaser's default), and real property (when certain types of personal property became "immovables by desti- nation," or legally inseparable from real property, under Louisiana law). Impressive for their insight on commercial topics particularly relevant to struggling businesses during the Great Depression, Margolin's legal analyses were also recognized by courts and practitioners. Her comment on vendor's privilege was cited in subsequent law review articles and court decisions; in 1935 a federal appellate judge paid a rare compliment in a published opinion to a law student's work by referring parties interested in learning more about immovables by destination to "Miss Margolin's most excellent article."[36]

In addition to her connections with the faculty, during law school Margolin developed important, lifelong contacts with private practitioners and fellow students. Monte Lemann, who chaired the *Tulane Law Review*'s advisory board, was president of the Louisiana Bar Association and one of the prom- inent legal figures President Hoover appointed in 1929 to a commission to study the effects of Prohibition on law enforcement.[37] Lemann, a 1907 Harvard law graduate and classmate of future Supreme Court justice

Felix Frankfurter, kept in touch with Margolin on professional matters throughout her legal career and admired her considerably.[38] A fellow law student who remained important throughout Margolin's career was John Minor Wisdom. A Newman alumnus from a privileged family, Wisdom was one year ahead of Margolin in law school and worked with her on the law review, of which he was editor-in-chief. In 1957 President Eisenhower appointed Wisdom to the United States Court of Appeals for the Fifth Circuit, where Margolin and her Labor Department staff often appeared for argument. Known for his landmark decisions instrumental in desegregating the American South, Wisdom affectionately and respectfully referred to his law school friend as "Miss Bessie," expressing his regrets to her lawyers when she was not there to argue a case, and honored her by traveling to Washington, D.C., to attend her 1972 retirement dinner.[39]

Although Tulane's combined law and liberal arts program anticipated completion in six years, Bessie condensed her studies into only five years, with superlative grades, by taking liberal arts courses during the summer.[40] Her demanding academic schedule, however, did not interfere with extracurricular activities. She continued to participate in her Newcomb sorority and ran for vice president of the law school. Although she lost the election, she was joined by John Wisdom, who lost his bid for president.[41] She also made time for community activities. Despite having lost her own mother as a child, Margolin organized a mother and daughter luncheon for the National Council of Jewish Women.[42] She also returned to the orphanage, where she, in her words, assisted in social work with children.[43] One of those children, who had been unable to start first grade on schedule because of an illness, fondly recalled years later that Bessie had taught her to read and write.[44] During her last two years at Tulane, Margolin delivered remarks at the Home's seventy-fifth anniversary celebration and spoke at Newman's 1929 Founder's Day program, where she recalled her time at the school.[45]

Bessie's admission to law school also reunited her with Dora and Jack. When Newcomb's registrar notified Bessie that her transfer to Tulane disqualified her from the reduced-cost Club Dormitory, the siblings rented a house together.[46] With a nursing degree from Touro Infirmary, Dora was working as the Home's nurse. Jack, after graduating from Newman, was attending Tulane's College of Commerce and Business Administration.[47] By Bessie's last year of law school, Jack had moved on campus, and she and Dora rented an apartment with their father. The census that year listed Dora as head of the household, suggesting that she was using her nursing income to pay the rent; Harry's occupation was recorded as "Salesman—Clothes."[48]

While Margolin concentrated on her future career path, her closest girlfriends, including Kate Polack and Evelyn Flonacher, were assuming traditional roles as housewives and mothers, amid a dizzying swirl of pre-nuptial festivities that marked unions of prominent New Orleans families.[49] Margolin, too, desired romance and even for a while seriously considered marriage. She received her first marriage proposal during law school from classmate Robert B. Butler Jr., her moot court partner and a good friend of Harry Trifon, a Tulane medical school student who later married Dora. Bessie always remained wistful about Butler and told members of her family that she had been "really in love with him."[50] A dashing, dark-haired young man with a thin mustache, Bob was an honor student and a competitive chess player. But he and Margolin had vastly divergent religious, political, and social backgrounds. Butler's father, Judge Robert Butler, an Episcopalian and old-time Louisiana legislator from Terrebonne Parish, had been appointed to the bench in 1924, after losing his bid for lieutenant governor.[51]

In December 1929, during their last year in law school, Bob presented his "sweetheart" Margolin with a copy of *Elbert Hubbard's Scrap Book,* a collection of quotations from great authors and philosophers, ranging from Socrates to Twain and countless others in between. In neat black script Bob added lines from three poems: Emily Dickinson's "There is no frigate like a book to take us lands away" and two dramatic verses by Edwin Markham, one of which praised "the soul that knows the mighty grief" as the only one that "can know the mighty rapture." The following year, after Margolin had moved to New Haven, Connecticut, Bob presented her with a second book, *Last Poems:* a small, red volume of passionate and thinly veiled sexual love poetry written by a woman under the male pseudonym Laurence Hope.[52]

It is no wonder Margolin fell for Butler; his thoughtful gifts reflected an appreciation for her intellect and passion. Margolin, too, loved poetry and found time in her first years after law school to type and assemble into a notebook favorite poems mostly by women, such as Emily Dickinson, Dorothy Parker, and Edna St. Vincent Millay, but a few male poets' verses stand out. Between poems extolling solitude (Helen Margaret's "Lonely Things") and the pursuit of a life's dream (Elizabeth Larocque's "Introspection"), Margolin inserted Ludwig Lewisohn's "Together." "You and I by this lamp with these / Few books shut out the world," began Lewisohn's widely disseminated portrait of an idyllic marriage, which he called "the one sure sabbath of the heart."[53] Margolin also favored writing that expressed her overwhelming desire for independence and for personal and intellectual fulfillment. On every blank page and squeezed into the margins of the book of quotations Butler had given her, Margolin copied extensive passages of Virginia Woolf's *A Room of One's Own,* which had been published only two months earlier. In her groundbreaking feminist essay Woolf described the "most strange phenomenon" that most books about women were written by men and found it, as Margolin copied, "flattering, vaguely, to feel oneself the object of such attention, provided that it was not entirely bestowed by the crippled and the infirm." Margolin inscribed the book with the author's powerful words as if they were her own: "No force in the world can take from me my five hundred pounds. Food, house and clothing are mine forever. Therefore not merely do effort and labor cease, but also hatred and bitterness. I need not hate any man; he cannot hurt me. I need not flatter any man; he has nothing to give me. So imperceptibly I found myself adopting a new attitude towards the other half of the human race." Elsewhere Margolin copied, in apparent agreement, "The history of man's opposition to women's emancipation is more interesting perhaps than the story of that emancipation itself." Nearly four decades later Margolin would intone the same sentiment during her legal battles to enforce the Equal Pay Act of 1963 and to give meaning to the prohibition against sex discrimination in employment in Title VII of the Civil Rights Act of 1964.

Years later, explaining to her nephews the cause of her breakup, Margolin said only that she could not accept the traditional life Butler had intended for her. He apparently expected her to return with him to his small home-town of Houma, Louisiana, more than an hour's drive south of New Orleans, where he would practice law and she would be Mrs. Robert Butler Jr. When Margolin broke off her engagement to Bob in late 1933, ending their four-year relationship to begin her career with the Tennessee Valley Authority (TVA), the news was no surprise to those who knew her best. Her mentor Professor Ernest Lorenzen, who recommended her for the TVA job, wrote of the breakup in a letter to Bessie: "And you have broken off with Bob! Well, I am not surprised. You are too ambitious for him and as long as you can-not overcome your longing to be somebody professionally it was probably the best thing to cut him loose." He continued with what would be a pro-phetic statement about Bessie's life: "You seem to belong to those that would not be happy if you were confined to a home and children."[54] After law school, Butler returned to Houma, where he practiced law, married, and had three children and seven grandchildren.[55] Twenty-five years later Butler and Margolin met at their law school reunion, where they revealed glimpses of their affection; they sat next to each other during dinner and, while posing with the class for a photo, locked eyes on each other instead of the photographer.[56] Throughout those years, Margolin's independence prevailed. And Butler was not the last man Margolin would choose as a lover but not as a husband.

In June 1930, at age twenty-one, Bessie graduated second in her law school class of twenty-three students. In 1933, when Tulane established a chapter of the Order of the Coif, a prestigious national honor society open only to top law graduates, she was the first woman admitted.[57] To Margolin, looking back in 1967, Tulane meant "something very special to me as a woman." She considered herself uniquely fortunate that her hometown university, as one of the few in the nation that welcomed women into its graduate and professional schools, gave her "the fullest opportunity and encouragement to fulfill myself as a human being intellectually, culturally, socially, and as a citizen with rights and responsibilities equal to those of men."[58]

Yale Law School

Glowing recommendations from Tulane Law School, her brilliant academic record, and her fluency in French won Margolin a coveted position at Yale Law School working as a research assistant to Professor Ernest G. Lorenzen, a noted authority in conflict of laws and comparative law. In May 1930 Tulane's Dean Harris announced Margolin's appointment, noting she was probably the first law school coed in the South to receive such an honor, and credited her excellence in research and writing.[59] But the deserved honor almost did not come to pass.

Six months earlier, after Yale Law School dean Charles E. Clark visited New Orleans, Tulane professor Milton Colvin praised Margolin's high-quality editing on one of his books and suggested she might be useful to members of Yale's law faculty.[60] Clark agreed to keep her in mind as a research assistant but also inquired whether Colvin considered her worthy of a fellowship in graduate legal studies, which would afford the Yale faculty the opportunity to become acquainted with her.[61] Colvin would have strongly recommended her for a fellowship, he explained, but had not done so because Tulane already had recommended her classmate Wood Brown, law review editor-in-chief. If, however, Yale would award fellowships to two Tulane candidates, wrote Colvin, the faculty could avoid choosing between two deserving students.[62] Clark reported that Yale expected to award Brown a fellowship, and as there might be funds left for Margolin, she should immediately apply.[63]

Within two days Margolin wrote Dean Clark that she was eager to do legal research, whether on issues of common law or preferably comparative law, such as she had analyzed for Tulane's law review. Asked how much money she required, Margolin presented her terms cautiously, balancing her need for self-sufficiency against the harsh economic climate of the Great Depression. "I should like an allowance of enough for room and board and for absolute necessities, as I shall have no independent means of income and desire to be independent next year, if possible."[64]

But neither Margolin's preferred field of research nor remuneration concerned Yale. Instead, this was a time when the college's informal admissions policies restricted the number of Jewish students and faculty but stopped short of a formal numeric quota, an issue Margolin had not faced at Tulane.[65] Yale registrar Arlene Hadley wrote Dean Harris and without further explanation asked whether Margolin was Jewish.[66] Harris responded affirmatively. As a Yale graduate who apparently feared his bare response threatened Margolin's chances, Harris went on to praise her with a flourish of benign anti-Semitism: "I wish to state, however, that she has none of the characteristics that mark some of the people of that race as offensive." Likely unaware that Margolin's parents had emigrated from Russia and that she was born in New York, Harris wrote, "She is distinctly of a type of the Jewish race that you find so frequently in this part of the country, that is French, Spanish or Portuguese, and is therefore very much unlike the New York type."[67] Harris was sure that Dean Clark would appreciate the distinction, noting that some of New Orleans's leading and most attractive people were, like Margolin, Jewish. Moreover, added Harris, it was unlikely that the average person would ever, without being told, recognize her as being of "Jewish extraction." Harris concluded his letter, "I think I know [Clark] and Yale Law School well enough to know what kind are not enthusiastically desired, to say the least." Hadley thanked Harris for his letter: "We are very grateful for it and I am sure that discrimination will not be shown in her case, but we like such information on all applicants."[68]

Margolin was fortunate that Yale did not completely exclude Jews and that she was not a marginal candidate who could expect to be denied admission on account of religion. Instead, Dean Clark found Margolin to be a "very high grade person and one that we could use to good advantage here."[69] But now that he knew she was Jewish, Clark expressed to Harris for the first time his reluctance about raising Margolin's hope of finding a teaching position in an American law school. Given that Clark had known from the beginning "Miss Margolin's" gender, and that there already were Jewish law professors at Yale, Clark's sudden concern for Margolin's future as a law professor suggests that he believed being both a Jew and a woman was a fatal combination. With fewer than five women law instructors in the country in 1930, being a woman was in itself a nearly insurmountable obstacle to teaching law, as Margolin would continue to learn over her career.[70] Clark recommended she should not pursue an advanced degree that would equip her to teach, but instead she should work as a research assistant. On the other hand, Clark warned, if Margolin were "exceedingly ambitious and likely to be disappointed at what fate might have in store for her, it would be wiser not to start anything with her at all."[71] Harris assured Clark that Margolin was a very levelheaded girl who would set aside any thought of attempting to become a teacher. Margolin, promised Harris, agreed to abide by whatever decision Clark made to help her become a research assistant, whether it included a degree or not.[72]

Although Tulane's faculty eagerly helped Margolin obtain a job at Yale, they nevertheless may have doubted the long-term return for their efforts. Quoted in a 1937 article about Tulane's women law students, Paul Brosman, who had been assistant dean during Margolin's time and then succeeded Harris as dean, considered his women students his best scholars but noted the obstacles they faced after graduation, with very few of them becoming practicing lawyers. Brosman blamed "physical equipment, unreasoning prejudice, and a 'memory' type of mind which shows up better in college than in actual legal combat." Brosman noted that of the forty-one women who studied law at Tulane since 1912, only twenty-four had completed their course. Only seventeen of them had ever practiced law, and at least three of those women had abandoned it later for marriage. Brosman cited Margolin as one of Tulane's few female law students who continued to practice law.[73]

Despite the prejudices and restrictions, Margolin won the appointment at Yale. Before heading to New Haven, Margolin spent the summer of 1930 working for Tulane law professor Frederick Beutel, an expert on negotiable instruments, and studying for the Louisiana Bar examination.[74] A three-day ordeal, the exam was administered in July to seventy-four law graduates from Tulane, Loyola, and Louisiana State University. Just two days later the Board of Law Examiners announced the anxiously awaited results: fifty-two of them had passed, including Margolin, Bob Butler, and other Tulane law classmates. At the admission ceremony in Louisiana's Supreme Court, Margolin wore a stylish white cloche surrounded by the large group of hatless men, all of whom raised their right hands to take the lawyer's oath.[75]

When Margolin moved to New Haven to begin work as Lorenzen's research assistant, earning $1,500 per year (about $20,500 today), the Jewish Orphans' Home declared her self-supporting and formally discharged her from its care.[76] With no housing for women on Yale's campus, she took a room at the YWCA, close to the law school. Margolin thoroughly enjoyed her new job and impressed Lorenzen, who extended her appointment for a second year and increased her pay to $1,800. "Of course some day I intend to do more practical work," she told a New Orleans reporter for a story about her latest achievement, "but right now research appeals to me." She described her curiosity, the thrill of searching for an answer, and her satisfaction from finding it. Despite Clark's admonition and Harris's assurances, Margolin had not abandoned her plans for graduate studies, telling the reporter that she wanted to earn a doctorate at Yale.[77] The accompanying photograph caught Margolin in a dramatic profile, her gaze trained firmly downward, revealing long dark eyelashes, delicate features, and her sleek finger-waved hairstyle. Margolin had become a sophisticated and feminine woman who impressed the reporter as modest and unspoiled yet who "epitomized . . . the realization of ambition."[78]

With her intellect, hard work, and charm, Margolin had once again endeared herself to influential people willing to wield their influence in her favor. Her boss, Ernest Gustav Lorenzen, was one of those people. The German-born professor had joined Yale's faculty in 1917; there he was known affectionately as "Gus" and remembered for his kind and loving heart.[79] His treatises in the fields of conflict of laws (which resolves disputes over which jurisdiction's law governs a particular case) and comparative law were praised for their innovation and lasting contribution to legal scholarship.[80] As his assistant, Margolin won Lorenzen's respect and affection. During her second year at Yale, Lorenzen sought to secure her future with more than another year as a research assistant. Along with another faculty member, the young and wildly popular William O. Douglas, Lorenzen supported Margolin for one of Yale's Sterling Fellowships, of which only a limited number were available for doctoral studies in law. Although the fellowships were created in 1926 and Yale Law School officially began admitting women in 1918, no woman had ever received a Sterling Fellowship for research in any field, making Margolin's sponsors' efforts especially noteworthy.[81] In March 1932, realizing her ambition to pursue a doctorate in law, Margolin won a Sterling Fellowship for the following academic year for exceptional academic and general social qualifications. The stipend's two thousand dollars and the relative comfort of life at Yale gave Margolin financial security—a luxury enjoyed by few Americans during the Great Depression.

While being a Jewish woman rendered Margolin virtually unemployable in the outside legal world as a law professor or corporate lawyer, neither her academic nor her social life at Yale seemed to suffer. Photographs reveal Margolin enjoying the company of a small group of young, fashionably dressed companions, perched on a convertible on one occasion and relaxing on the grass on another. Whether Margolin knew that Yale had questioned her religion before she arrived is unknown. Once there, however, she entered an environment marked by a profound yet genteel anti-Semitism that included social exclusion.[82] Margolin maximized her chances for acceptance by offering little, if any, evidence of her religion. She was living in the Young Women's Christian Association, she did not attend synagogue or observe other Jewish traditions, and as evidenced by her romance with Bob Butler, she had not limited her relationships to Jews. Although there is no indication that Margolin attended synagogue while she was at Tulane, her ongoing involvement there with her sorority and the National Council for Jewish Women kept her publicly associated with other Jews. At Yale she had no such open ties to a Jewish community and instead developed long-term personal and professional relationships within the law school, including with two talented fellow students, both southerners: Henry H. "Joe" Fowler, from Roanoke, Virginia, also a Sterling fellow who later became secretary of the Treasury in the Johnson administration, and Abe Fortas, from Memphis, Tennessee, another nonobservant Jew despite his Orthodox upbringing, who was editor-in-chief of the *Yale Law Journal*.

In addition to these peers and Professor Lorenzen, at Yale Margolin met many people who aided and deeply influenced her career, such as

Dean Clark and law professors William O. Douglas, Jerome Frank, Harry Shulman, and Wesley Sturges. All of these men adhered to Yale's dominant school of jurisprudence, legal realism. Notwithstanding ongoing debate to define it and assess its importance, in general this theory of law and legal education rejected "classicism," or "conceptualism," which had been first introduced at Harvard some sixty years earlier; conceptualism preached that the law could be reduced to fundamental concepts and rules derived from studying appellate cases and that it was unaffected by judges' private prejudices or societal needs.[83] In contrast, Yale's legal realism was a functional approach that eschewed law solely as a body of abstract principles; it required empirical study, along with related disciplines. Recognizing that judges' biases and a case's particular circumstances were as important to decision making as legal concepts, legal realists focused on the intelligent formulation of policy. Margolin's professors employed this functional approach in their field of law. For Lorenzen the concept of domicile, for example, did not exist in a vacuum; it drew meaning only in the context of the case in which it was being considered, such as taxation, marriage, or inheritance.[84] For Douglas bankruptcy and corporate reorganization, hot legal topics during the Depression, required investigating the surrounding social, economic, and legal phenomena to enable the entrepreneur to avoid risky business practices and ensure greater security for the consumer and for the worker.[85]

Margolin was at Yale in the heyday of the legal realism movement. She was surrounded by professors who preached about the role of idiosyncrasy in the formation of law, the importance of focusing on the particular context of a factual situation, and the value of using social sciences to illuminate legal issues. Her Ivy League education in legal realism not only taught her imaginative and modern approaches to problem solving but legitimated the use of law as a vehicle for social change.[86] These were powerful tools for a woman who had spent her childhood listening to social visionaries in the Jewish Orphans' Home and who would later champion the New Deal's social programs.

Before she began her fellowship year, Margolin got a summer job at New Haven's Legal Aid Bureau, making news as its first woman investigator. "Woman Lawyer Joins Legal Aid," was the *New Haven Register*'s caption over her photo. Seated at a desk crowded with books, dark-eyed Margolin wore a serious expression and a sleeveless dress that exposed her slender arms. Previously, the bureau had hired only male law students but took on Margolin to assist during the summer months while most of the Yale students were away on vacation.[87] The position allowed Margolin to earn money while gaining her first practical experience in a law office that served clients who could not afford private counsel. It would be one of the last jobs Margolin held that was not highly sought after by her male peers.

Precisely when and how Margolin decided to use her Sterling Fellowship to study bankruptcy and corporate reorganization is unknown, but there is little doubt that Douglas's enthusiasm and practical approach to addressing the nation's economic failure influenced her choice. As Lorenzen's assistant, Margolin edited his conflict of laws treatise and revised comparative law readings for his graduate course. According to Margolin, her work for Lorenzen covered a very broad scope in a general way—contracts, persons and family law, criminal law, and some commercial law.[88] But by the time Margolin began her fellowship year in September 1932, she had redirected her focus to complement Douglas's work, culminating in two scholarly writings.[89] She first produced a fifteen-page comment that was published in Yale's law journal, "The Corporate Reorganization Provision in Senate Bill 3866: A Proposed Draft of a New Bankruptcy Act." She endorsed Congress's attempt to prevent dissenting minority creditors from upstaging majority-approved reorganization plans, which she argued would spare corporate debtors, and in turn their employees and the economy, from the ravages of needless liquidation.[90] To earn her doctorate, Margolin also completed her thesis, "Corporate Reorganization in France—A Comparative Study of French and American Practices," which combined her knowledge of comparative law, her fluency in French, and her new interest in bankruptcy and reorganization.

By the spring of 1932 Lorenzen dedicated himself to securing permanent employment for his star pupil beyond her one-year fellowship. Ignoring the conditions Clark imposed (and Harris reiterated) when she had first applied for the research position two years earlier, Margolin set her sights squarely on teaching law, a bold but seemingly more realistic goal than securing a law firm job in the depressed economy, especially for a Jewish woman.[91] Lorenzen urged Dean Harris to recognize that Tulane was the logical place to showcase Margolin's preeminence in civil and comparative law and to take advantage of her extraordinary mental powers. Margolin's ranking among Yale's best students had secured her Sterling Fellowship, wrote Lorenzen, the first and, for the foreseeable future, probably last awarded to a woman.

Lorenzen concluded his missive with a final plea for Dean Harris to find some way of getting her on Tulane's law faculty.[92]

Margolin wrote her own letter to Harris, soliciting his advice about whether she should pursue a career teaching law and asking whether he could hire her at Tulane. Notwithstanding her impressive abilities, Harris responded that Margolin faced obstacles in her path to teaching law. Except in the field of law librarianship, which he presumed did not interest her, Harris knew of few women who taught law and none who had attained prominence, which meant that there were no precedents to invoke in Margolin's favor to overcome the prejudice against women shown by many law teachers and deans. Harris was torn. He did not want to discourage Margolin because he had no doubt about her ability and wished to stop the irrational, "anti-feminist prejudice" in the law teaching ranks, but he did not want to sacrifice her for the cause. In his last and relatively abrupt paragraph, Harris finally delivered the disappointing news: there was simply no opening at Tulane, and financial conditions prevented adding any new positions.[93]

Although Harris had no job to offer, Margolin still had a year to figure out her next steps after Yale. Lorenzen proved relentless in his efforts to assist her, all the while cementing their close and caring relationship. Margolin confided in Lorenzen about personal matters, admitting to him—at least for a short while during her romance with Bob Butler—that she was no exception to the rule that girls are never quite happy until they have tried out matrimony.[94] Lorenzen not only offered fatherly advice about the relative timing and priorities she should assign to her career versus matrimony; he repeatedly urged her to recognize the need for spiritual fulfillment, specifically the kind discussed in the Christian Science lectures he attended.[95]

While Lorenzen was in Massachusetts in April 1932 seeking Christian Science healing for an undisclosed illness, Margolin wrote him at least twice expressing her concern for his well-being and chiding him for pretending he was healthy. She also shared personal and painful experiences, for which Lorenzen offered comfort. As no further details were needed between them, he wrote to Margolin only that "this year was a bad year for you" and then reassured her that she would find happiness in the coming year among "all the boys in the graduate department." It was also Lorenzen with whom Margolin shared the news in December 1933 that she had finally broken off her engagement with Bob Butler; this same trusted advisor knew Margolin well enough to not be surprised by her decision.[96] As close as these shared confidences suggest they were, there is nothing in the language of his few letters to indicate that the fifty-six-year old Lorenzen, widowed several years earlier with a son Margolin's age, enjoyed more than a fatherly, mentoring relationship with Margolin, an ambitious young woman whose tenuous relationship with her own father offered little as a role model.[97]

Throughout her fellowship year Lorenzen remained concerned about Margolin's career plans. In December 1932 he approached Dean Harris again, hoping that a position for Margolin had opened at Tulane. Sparing no praise, Lorenzen wrote that Margolin gave Tulane the rare opportunity to secure a brilliant mind trained in the civil and common law who was eager to return home to New Orleans. Lorenzen recommended Margolin unqualifiedly, certain she would make a most effective teacher, despite prevailing prejudice against women in general. She not only held her own with the best students, Lorenzen added, but her hiring would be recognized as a sound progressive and liberal move.[98] Before leaving for Europe that summer, Lorenzen still worried about Margolin's lack of a permanent job and wrote to Harris for the third time, hoping Harris would find it possible to hire her.[99] Responding for Harris, who was traveling, Professor Brosman, expressing his disappointment, reiterated what the dean had already said: there were no funds to hire Margolin at Tulane.[100] Impatient to find work, Margolin had taken steps of her own. She accepted a temporary research position in Washington, D.C., at the Inter-American Commission of Women, which would begin June 1, 1933.

Before then, as Yale's award of the Doctor of Juridical Science (JSD) degree depended upon approval of a thesis that made a substantial contribution to legal scholarship, Margolin focused her energies on that task. She also took law classes in credit transactions, conflict of laws, and psychology in law administration, for which she earned grades of "Good" and "Excellent." In a seminar on legislative and judicial problems, however, she failed to impress the two professors who taught it. William S. Gaud Jr., who had received his Yale law degree just two years earlier, did not mince words on her transcript, describing her work as "bad." He acknowledged without elaboration that she was bothered by "personal problems of some importance," but even so, given weeks of warning, her work product was "most inadequate," and she was the "weakest of the lot" in class discussions. Professor Walton H. Hamilton, a co-instructor, offered a milder evaluation. "Nihil obstat. I shall allow no judgment of mine to stand in the way of a degree for Miss M." Even in this regard, Lorenzen defended Margolin. She had been devoting all her time to her thesis, Lorenzen explained, and when she was ready to start her assignment for Gaud and Hamilton, she learned "most terrible news from home," which debilitated her for more than a week.[101] Neither professor explained the personal problems or terrible news, and no record exists of death or serious illness at the time among family or close friends in New Orleans. Her long-distance relationship with Bob Butler, which would end less than a year later, was a likely source of personal distress, albeit for which there exists no account. Whatever the cause, the seminar would remain one of very few times that Margolin allowed personal problems to interfere with her work. Dora's death in 1960 produced the only other recorded disruption in Margolin's work for purely personal reasons, and even then she resumed her duties promptly enough to require only a short extension to file a Supreme Court brief.[102]

Margolin's thesis on French and American reorganization practices won high praise from the three professors who supervised her work and who later recommended its publication.[103] Douglas said her meticulous work had "an air of realism about it."[104] Professor Roger Foster cited Margolin's profound comprehension of reorganization practices and problems, while Lorenzen rated Margolin among Yale's best graduate law students during his sixteen years there.[105] Margolin demonstrated her comfort in legal writing by employing humor, albeit subtle and legally technical in nature; while analyzing a French court's decision, she made a point—likely to resonate favorably with legal realists—that the law is most often unascertainable by lawyers and law professors.[106] In her readable work Margolin thus revealed a budding use of humor in legal arguments, taking a measured risk of offending a decision maker such as in this case her thesis advisors and in later years a judge or even a Supreme Court justice.

Despite its initial reluctance, Yale awarded Margolin her doctorate in law, and she won over most of the faculty during her time there. She left New Haven before the graduation ceremonies and so was not there to celebrate with her male classmates.[107] Instead, Margolin was already in Washington, D.C., starting a new job—working for a woman and, for a brief time, for women's rights.

3

SUMMER WITH A SUFFRAGIST
1933

Margolin arrived in Washington, D.C., on June 1, 1933. An air of great vitality and movement was sweeping the sleepy city.[1] In the eighty-nine days since President Franklin D. Roosevelt took office, his bold plans to rouse the country from the despondency and financial depression of the past four years were coming to life in the form of new federal agencies with far-reaching missions. Although Margolin had not come to Washington for the New Deal, she was there as it took root and as the government's ranks swelled with fresh talent eager to launch the nation's grand social and economic experiments. The bureaucracy's large demand for lawyers was met by an equally abundant supply, mostly men. Margolin would join them three months later, but until then she went to work at the Inter-American Commission of Women, to research Latin American laws that discriminated against women. It would be Margolin's first exposure, albeit brief, to the ongoing battles for women's equality being waged at the moment, both in the United States and internationally. And she could have no better introduction to those battles than with the commission's founding chair, Doris Stevens. Or so it would have seemed.

A celebrated suffragist, Stevens years earlier had agitated for women's enfranchisement with other stalwart members of the National Women's Party (NWP), who were branded by one congressman as nagging "iron-jawed angels" and "bewildered, deluded creatures" after they picketed President Wilson's White House in 1917.[2] Stevens's and her fellow suffragists' relentless protests had earned them more than nicknames; they were arrested and sentenced to sixty days at the Occoquan Workhouse in Lorton, Virginia. There, before receiving a presidential pardon, Stevens served three days with other protesters in deliberately foul and unhealthy conditions. They risked their reputations and health, even their lives, during their intensive eight-year campaign to win the vote.[3] Having secured that fundamental right, Stevens turned her energy and attention to the glaring inequities that remained for women in the United States and around the world. In 1928 the governing board of the Pan American Union created the Inter-American Commission of Women and named Stevens as its first chair; in that role she led a diplomatic effort to pass domestic equal rights legislation for women through international treaty.[4]

In early 1933, much as the suffragists earlier had examined sex-based differences in political rights state by state to urge a national suffrage amendment, Stevens decided to launch a survey of the legal codes of the commission's member countries to catalog laws that handicapped women as property owners, spouses, mothers, and citizens or infringed on their right to transmit citizenship to children born abroad. She planned to take the completed report to the December 1933 Seventh Pan-American Conference in Montevideo, Uruguay, where she would introduce an equal rights treaty.[5] First, she needed bilingual legal scholars to do the work.

In February 1933, in the midst of her thesis research and her search for a job following graduation, Margolin learned from Yale law professor Jerome Frank that Stevens, his personal friend, was looking to hire a researcher.[6] Following Frank's lead, Margolin quickly wrote Stevens, describing her qualifications for the position. Margolin confidently assured Stevens that even though her prior work had been chiefly in French law, conducting legal research in Spanish should prove no obstacle for her given the similarities between the Latin American and French legal systems and terminology. Moreover, Margolin explained, her legal training at Tulane acquainted her with Louisiana's civil law and its French and Spanish sources. Margolin politely asked Stevens for more information about the work and for the privilege of a personal interview.[7] Before Stevens responded to her first letter, Margolin wrote again, this time saying that she planned to be in New York, where Stevens lived (Margolin did not explain how such a timely coincidence had occurred), and reiterated her eagerness to meet.[8] As Margolin hoped, Stevens met her within the next two weeks and, judging from the correspondence that followed, asked Margolin to start work immediately.

There is every reason that Stevens would have taken to Margolin, a rare woman in the legal profession with stellar academic credentials and references from Yale Law School. She was impressed with Margolin's strong recommendations and enthusiasm.[9] Stevens had attended but did not graduate from law school, and it was a lawyer, the prominent Dudley Field Malone, who had finally captured Stevens's heart, apparently overcoming—at least temporarily—her avoidance of the restrictions of traditional marriage. Malone had been Stevens's legal counsel when she and other NWP members were arrested, and she served as Malone's chief researcher when he joined Clarence Darrow to defend John T. Scopes in 1925 for teaching evolution in violation of Tennessee law. At one point during that historic trial Stevens told the press: "I came all the way from New York to find that the defendant was a man, the prosecutor a man, the judge a man, the jury all men, the attorneys on both sides men. . . . One would think there weren't any women in this world or that they didn't do any thinking."[10] Margolin, having held her own at Tulane and Yale Law Schools, was changing the complexion of the law.

Although American women still had no legal right to serve on a jury in most states and under federal law, there is no evidence that Margolin was principally drawn to the job with Stevens because she wanted to join the fight for women's rights. At the same time, despite Stevens's reputation as a phenomenal organizer and lobbyist with striking good looks and legendary charm, she demonstrated radical sensibilities that were foreign to her new researcher.[11] As Margolin's lone brush with the police resulted from a speeding violation a decade later, there is little to suggest that she could see herself picketing the White House and subjecting herself to imprisonment, as Stevens had done. Moreover, not only did Stevens live in a bohemian colony of artists and activists; she had made headlines years earlier for refusing to take her ex-husband's name while they were married. Margolin believed that keeping one's maiden name after marriage was too "modernistic" for her.[12]

Nevertheless, working for Stevens, Margolin could use her keen legal research skills, expertise in civil law, and fluency in foreign languages. Besides, the lack of any other job offer made working for Stevens especially attractive to the practical Margolin. After meeting Stevens in New York, she returned to New Haven eager to convince Professor Lorenzen and Dean Clark to allow her to start researching for Stevens during the school term, possibly using the assignment to fulfill part of her graduate requirements. She soon realized, however, that it was too late in the term to start something that could materialize by June into qualifying graduate work. Margolin promptly reported back to Stevens, with regret, that she could not start the project until June, after she received her degree.[13] They agreed that Margolin was to conduct her research over the summer in Washington, D.C., mostly at the Library of Congress, earning $125 a month—$25 a month less than what she had been earning at Yale. In the meantime Stevens urged Margolin to find some time to perfect her fluency in Spanish.[14]

By April, Stevens wrote Margolin asking her to report for work on June 1 at the commission headquarters in the Pan American Union Building. Stevens suggested that Margolin might start her work on the laws of Haiti, which had challenged other researchers, but her actual assignment would depend on what countries had been finished by the time she arrived.[15] In response Margolin expressed her excitement about the job, reporting that she was working double time to finish her work at Yale. Even her daily Spanish reading was improving, and she had begun to read some of the Latin American constitutions.[16]

Margolin submitted her thesis and within two days packed her things, left New Haven, and reported to the commission's office in Washington. She quickly rented a room in a house in the District's Chevy Chase neighborhood. Over the next two weeks, when given the chance to hire a secretary, Margolin offered the job to Maxine Boord, who had just completed her first year at Yale Law School and was one of few women pursuing an undergraduate law degree at Yale while Margolin was there.[17] Margolin's hasty telegram offered Boord a summer job earning eighteen dollars per week and room and board at thirty-five dollars per month. By day's end Boord had wired Margolin that she was thrilled to accept the job and would arrive within two days.[18] In the earliest days of her own career Margolin had begun a lifetime pattern of aiding many capable women and men in their careers.

After graduating from Yale's law school in 1935, Boord went on to a distinguished law career in Kansas and later Michigan, authoring a series of sociolegal works on family and divorce laws, including a 1956 book that exposed chaotic conditions in the nation's domestic courts, from decrepit buildings and lack of court reporters to hostile attitudes toward divorce.[19] Reflecting the early impact of her summer job with the commission, Boord took a course in family law when she returned to Yale in the fall, and one of her first legal publications was a 1939 article entitled "Laws Affecting Women in Kansas."[20] That Boord's career path focused squarely on women and domestic issues strongly suggests that her experience at the commission was a positive one or at least was aligned with her earliest legal interests.

Not so with Margolin. Soon after Margolin arrived in Washington, she was disappointed to discover that the commission was a tiny operation with a shoestring budget. The Inter-American Commission of Women, she quipped in a late-June 1933 letter to Professor Douglas, was a "charmingly pompous title for an organization composed of about three women." Stevens "carries on the work from hand to mouth," she wrote, and had hired Margolin on a temporary basis because the commission did not have sufficient funds to keep her longer.[21]

As it turns out, Margolin was glad Stevens lacked additional funds to employ her on a permanent basis; her complaints about the work ran much deeper than the organization's meager management. "I fear I'm not cut out to be this kind of feminist," she confided in Douglas. "I can't scare up the least bit of enthusiasm over the legal equality between men and women in Latin America." And despite Margolin's passion for detailed legal research, she found the work she was doing for Stevens "intolerably dull." She wrote Douglas that she hoped she could tolerate the job until she could find something more interesting because she could not afford to be unemployed even briefly. "But," she lamented, "I am convinced that I could not have landed anything more at variance with my interests."[22]

Wanting to paint Douglas a fair picture of the importance of Stevens's activities, Margolin continued her letter, noting perhaps hers was the dullest and most tedious assignment: "It must be, my God!!!" Margolin was eyeing her future elsewhere; she found her work at the commission "doubly unbearable in the midst of the Washingtonian atmosphere, with such thrilling prospects as the Tennessee Valley one looming on the horizon."[23]

In spite of the antipathy she expressed for her work, Margolin's experiences would ultimately inform her career. She met and worked that summer with Burnita Shelton Matthews, who, after being rejected in 1920 by the D.C. Bar Association on account of her gender, had opened her own law firm and made a name for herself in the Washington legal scene; in 1929 she obtained for the National Women's Party a record-setting award of $300,000 when its headquarters were condemned for the new Supreme Court building. Within a year after Margolin's job at the commission, Matthews was elected president of the National Association of Women Lawyers.[24] In 1949 President Truman appointed her to the federal district court of the District of Columbia, where she became the nation's first female federal trial judge and only the second woman after Florence Allen's 1934 appointment to the Sixth Circuit Court of Appeals to hold a lifetime federal judgeship. Some thirty years after they worked together at the commission, Margolin would cite Matthews's judgeship, then still an extreme rarity for a woman, in support of her own candidacy for the federal bench.

Moreover, Margolin's research that summer contributed to the fight for women's rights. By the end of 1933, armed with the legal summaries that identified Margolin, Matthews, and other members of the IACW's Comité de Investigación, Stevens presented the commission's demand for women's equality to the Pan-American Conference in Montevideo.[25] The commission put forward an equal rights treaty and an equal nationality treaty. Although Stevens and other commission members were not official delegates and were convinced to "quietly table" the equal rights treaty, they managed to persuade the United States to join other delegations in approving the equal nationality treaty.[26]

Whatever seeds of feminism Margolin inadvertently and reluctantly took from her summer working for women's rights, they would lay deep and dormant until Margolin turned her talents and energy to enforcing the Equal Pay Act three decades later. And when she decided to immerse herself in the subject in the early 1960s, she conducted a survey of the status of women in foreign countries, the same approach she had learned from Stevens. As Margolin's feminism blossomed, it would not resemble the radical militancy of her early mentors; Margolin would take care to avoid such labels, preferring a reasonable, and mainstream, approach. Until then, before she pursued equality for all women or understood what that meant to her, Margolin had a more personal goal. She sought to advance her own career practicing law as an equal, even if it meant being the only woman in the group. In Washington, D.C., during the dawn of the New Deal, the federal government was a good place to start.

4

DEFENDING THE NEW DEAL'S
TENNESSEE VALLEY AUTHORITY
1933–1939

A Thrilling Prospect on the Horizon

When she started her legal career, Bessie Margolin was one of only 3,385 women lawyers in the nation.[1] Although that number had nearly doubled since 1920 due to suffrage and the increasing number of law schools that admitted women, Margolin and her female counterparts still comprised barely 2 percent of the legal profession.[2] Their numbers were growing, but their career paths were anything but smooth or certain. Margolin quickly learned that government service offered far better opportunities to women lawyers than private practice, whether on one's own, with a private corporation, or most elusively, in a law firm. "In government service a woman attorney is more likely to be treated on a par with men attorneys of equal training and ability," observed Margolin in 1938. But even in government service, she cautioned, opportunities were "not as available to a woman of average legal training as to a man of the same equipment."[3] She was keenly aware that women lawyers who held federal jobs largely worked in lower-paying clerical or administrative positions that required no legal training.[4]

Fortunately for Margolin, her Ivy League credentials and strong references distinguished her from women of average "equipment." Moreover, living in Washington, D.C., that summer made it easy for Margolin to respond to hiring opportunities created by the New Deal's bold plans. As she had written to Professor Douglas shortly after starting her summer job at the Inter-American Commission of Women, she saw thrilling prospects looming on the horizon in Washington and had already singled out the Tennessee Valley Authority (TVA) as the place where she would like to work.[5]

Unlike other New Deal legislation, the Tennessee Valley Authority Act was not introduced to address a crisis brought on solely by the 1929 stock market crash or the Great Depression that followed. True, the Tennessee Valley had been hit hard by the Depression, but hardship there was nothing new. Many of the four million residents of the Tennessee Valley's watershed, spanning forty thousand square miles across Tennessee, Kentucky, Virginia, North Carolina, Georgia, Alabama, and Mississippi, were impoverished, illiterate, and lived in remote, undeveloped areas where only two out of every hundred farms had electricity.

Nor was the TVA Act the first time Congress had focused on this region; it had repeatedly tried to resolve a dispute there that dated back to World War I: how to best develop the hydroelectric capacity at Muscle Shoals, Alabama, a thirty-seven-mile stretch of powerful rapids on the Tennessee River. The National Defense Act of 1916 had authorized funding for hydroelectric generation and nitrate production to supply the U.S. Army with wartime explosives while promising peacetime fertilizer for the vast surrounding acreage severely eroded by the river's annual flooding. Although the Wilson Dam was eventually completed, the war ended before the nitrate plants were operable. The National Defense Act prohibited privatization, leaving the Muscle Shoals project as idle surplus.[6]

Resolving the problem required Congress to decide whether the government would keep and operate the property or would sell or lease it to the private sector. While agricultural interests wanted inexpensive fertilizer that could be produced at government-run nitrate plants, private utility companies, which wanted to add the hydroelectric facilities to their networks, viewed public power as unfair competition and socialistic. Public power advocates, in contrast, sought inexpensive electricity free from corrupt influences of big corporations. Despite reportedly consuming more congressional time than any other issue of the 1920s, the fate of Muscle Shoals remained unresolved.[7]

It was not until April 1933 that President Roosevelt deployed the necessary political force to convince Congress to stop wasting public resources at Muscle Shoals. He implored Congress to create a flexible federal corporation to engage in national planning for the complete river watershed that would give "life to all forms of human concerns" for the general social and economic welfare of the nation.[8] Congress passed the TVA Act, which Roosevelt signed on May 18, 1933, broadly empowering the new agency to make the Tennessee River navigable and control its frequent and devastating flooding, replant forests, improve the soil, and promote better farming methods while developing the region's agriculture and industry. Perhaps most important for Margolin's future career, the act also granted TVA the right to construct dams and power plants and to produce, distribute, and sell the power generated.[9]

An independent public corporation led by a three-man board of directors, TVA represented a great experiment in the social, industrial, and agricultural coordination of a vast region that would raise its inhabitants to higher standards of living. And the lifeblood of TVA's plan was electric power. According to Harvard-trained lawyer David Lilienthal, TVA's director in charge of its power program, the agency's most important considerations, notwithstanding any adverse economic effect on private utilities, were to make power available at the lowest rate consistent with sound financial policy and to achieve social objectives that low-cost power made possible. For the same reasons, journalist Walter Lippmann declared TVA by far the most interesting of the New Deal undertakings, destined to exercise the largest and longest influence.[10]

TVA's geographic focus, too, resonated with Margolin, who had spent two early years in Tennessee and grew up in the Jewish Orphans' Home with children from throughout the region. Moreover, TVA's mission of improving lives by conserving natural resources aligned with the Home's values of social justice; like much of the New Deal, TVA was created to improve American lives, including those of the most vulnerable members of society. Margolin, still seeking a permanent job, also recognized that the new organization would need considerable legal research and opinion work, which she knew was viewed as most suitable for women attorneys.[11] Little did she realize that, if hired, she would join an elite legal team that would successfully defend the New Deal agency against an avalanche of constitutional challenges.

Unlike the men from Yale, Harvard, and other prestigious law schools who were recruited for the New Deal, Margolin received no such invitation.[12] Instead, she took matters into her own hands. By the end of June 1933 she applied for a legal position at TVA, attaching recommendations from Yale's Dean Clark and Professor Douglas that she had secured only days earlier.[13] Margolin satisfied TVA's request for a photograph with a small snapshot taken outside the Chevy Chase house where she was boarding. On TVA's questionnaire Margolin described herself as a five foot three, 112-pound, twenty-four-year-old woman who would not accept a salary of less than two thousand dollars per year. As for her use of intoxicants, with the repeal of

Prohibition still three months away, she emphatically replied, "Not at all." She listed her father, Harry, and siblings, Dora and Jack, as her family but supplied the street address of the orphanage as her permanent residence.[14]

Margolin's application arrived at TVA's Washington, D.C., office, which had just opened in space commandeered at the Interior Department. She worried that her application might get overlooked or misplaced, a valid concern.[15] TVA's personnel office was a mess, overwhelmed by submissions from more than eight thousand applicants vying for a wide range of professional and blue-collar jobs, while hundreds of people lined up for interviews daily.[16] Despite the chaos, Margolin's application caught the attention of Floyd Reeves, TVA's first personnel director, who just two days later recommended that Director Lilienthal, also serving as TVA's general counsel, hire Margolin for his legal department.[17]

At the same time, Reeves contacted Margolin's references, and they quickly responded, echoing praises from Douglas and Clark. "She is an unusual woman," wrote Dean Harris from Tulane, citing her professional ability, charming personality, and a progressive social outlook he thought aligned well with TVA's mission.[18] Professor Wesley Sturges, who had recently left Yale to join the New Deal's Agricultural Adjustment Agency, described Margolin as sincere, industrious, and keen and cautious in her thinking. Pressed for her weakest attribute, Sturges noted some lack of aggressiveness but predicted she would develop self-assurance with increased financial independence.[19] "If you have a place for a woman lawyer," wrote Richard Joyce Smith, a former Yale law professor who had recently joined a Wall Street firm, "I would say that Miss Margolin would be one of the best that you could find."[20]

Margolin's most compelling endorsement came from Professor Lorenzen, her devoted mentor. Given her remarkable academic record, he expressed his confidence that she would accomplish something really worthwhile. But Lorenzen also emphasized what he believed the men running TVA needed to hear to hire a woman lawyer—that Margolin was intent on a legal career "as a primary objective from which she would not be deflected by consideration of marriage."[21] Lorenzen was making a significant commitment on Margolin's behalf; six months later she would advise him that she had broken off her romantic relationship with Bob Butler.

In August 1933, days after being hired as TVA's general solicitor, William A. Sutherland, a partner in the Atlanta law firm of Sutherland, Tuttle & Brennan, called in Margolin for an interview. After inquiring about her education and her current job with Doris Stevens, he learned another bit of information that he likely did not elicit from male applicants: "She does not take shorthand."[22] Even with her impeccable credentials and references, Sutherland remained unconvinced and asked Washington powerbroker Thomas "Tommy the Cork" Corcoran to compare Margolin to other candidates.[23] Despite Corcoran's frequent sexist boast that he never recommended a woman for a position above the rank of secretary, years later Sutherland recalled that Margolin had received Corcoran's approval.[24] On September 8, 1933, after considerable scrutiny, TVA hired Margolin as a research attorney in its Washington office for two thousand dollars per year.[25]

For Margolin the TVA job was cause for celebration and great relief. In 1933 two thousand dollars a year went far, especially for a single person in Washington, D.C.[26] Margolin moved out of her boardinghouse and rented an apartment closer to her new office. Before she could start work, however, she was required to certify that she would uphold the Constitution and that she believed in the feasibility and wisdom of TVA's mission. For the next five and a half years she zealously defended those tenets.[27]

First Year in TVA's Washington Office

Although Margolin spent her first year in the agency's Washington office, its official headquarters were in Knoxville, Tennessee, with additional offices at Chattanooga, Nashville, and Muscle Shoals. Her time in TVA's small Washington office proved to be a disorganized introduction to the practice of lawyering. Sutherland continued his private practice in Atlanta and was a largely absentee boss, offering little daily guidance.[28] Other than her summer at New Haven's Legal Aid Bureau, Margolin had no prior experience in a law office, much less advising clients or appearing in court. But with myriad questions from newly hired administrators, she immersed herself in the TVA Act, its legislative history, the laws of the constituent states, and the mechanics of TVA's work.

Within her first week Margolin was working hard but happily. As she reported in a letter to Professor Douglas, "I am delighted with the work and the associations, and of course, am getting a big kick out of being in the thick of things and helping to 'run the country' with the rest of the Harvard and Yale students and professors."[29] Just three weeks later Sutherland and the fledgling legal department filed TVA's first condemnation lawsuits to acquire property along East Tennessee's Clinch River, where it planned to build the huge thirty-four-million-dollar Norris Dam. Often working with Howard Corcoran, Tommy's brother, Margolin was soon offering opinions and advice on questions TVA was facing for the first time, including its use of appropriations, the impact of state laws on incorporation and property taxes, and the scope of authority of the Electric Home and Farm Authority, a government-run retail sales finance company that TVA used to promote the sale of electric appliances.[30] Resolving these issues, often unglamorous and thorny, taught Margolin how to get the machinery of a new federal agency up and running.

Her hard work did not go unnoticed. Despite Sutherland's remote supervision, Margolin impressed him. In January 1934, just four months after she started, Sutherland recommended that TVA raise her salary by 50 percent, to three thousand dollars per year.[31] Marguerite Owen, TVA's respected Washington representative, reported that TVA staff and outside consultants had praised Margolin's research, valuing her precision and clarity in reasoning and expression. Convinced that Margolin could handle a regular series of assignments if the legal department had a full-time chief to oversee lawyers with clearly designated responsibilities, Owen endorsed her proposed salary increase.[32]

James Lawrence Fly Takes Over the Legal Department

By May 1934 Sutherland had resigned as TVA's general solicitor and returned to his prominent Atlanta law firm.[33] In selecting Sutherland's replacement, Lilienthal was looking for a general solicitor who could organize the legal department and at the same time remain committed to carrying out TVA's broad mandate despite mounting adversity.[34] Many facets of TVA's novel activities demanded legal skill and ingenuity, but it was TVA's power program that already was consuming the better part of its lawyers' attention, as it would continue to do throughout Margolin's time there.

To increase the supply and decrease the cost of electricity produced at Wilson Dam, then TVA's only source of power, TVA sought to purchase existing private transmission lines and distribution facilities rather than duplicating them. The process started out amicably, or so it seemed; Wendell Willkie, president of Commonwealth & Southern Corporation, one of the nation's largest utility holding companies, which provided electrical power to customers in eleven states, signed an agreement on January 4, 1934, to transfer parts of its utility holdings to TVA. But the agreement turned out to be a facade that quickly dissolved, revealing the hostility of local private electric companies' executives and stockholders, who hurled charges of socialism and communism, followed by a barrage of litigation challenging the constitutionality of TVA's power sales.[35]

In June 1934 two dozen ice and coal companies filed the first power lawsuit against TVA, alleging that the power program, including its electric appliance sales, was causing them economic ruin.[36] Lilienthal immediately assigned Margolin to research the companies' legal standing. Although the companies abandoned their case when a later suit, *Ashwander v. TVA*, proved a better litigation vehicle, the first case made Lilienthal recognize the urgency of hiring Sutherland's replacement.[37] He soon received recommendations for several candidates, but he gave serious consideration to only one: James Lawrence Fly.[38] By having successfully prosecuted antitrust cases for President Hoover's Justice Department, Fly enjoyed a reputation in Washington as a talented litigator with little tolerance for monopolies.[39] By August 6, 1934, the TVA Board hired Fly as general solicitor.[40] Fly had entered Margolin's life and would soon change it profoundly—both professionally and personally.

Larry Fly was a tall and rangy Texan with thin red hair indicative of his Scotch-Irish heritage. Thirty-six years old, he was charming, hardworking, and extraordinarily able and effective.[41] Fly had grown up on a farm in a small town outside of Dallas, the youngest of nine children. He was a fiercely proud graduate of the U.S. Naval Academy, where he had been a champion debater. After ending his naval service with a medical discharge, he studied law at Harvard, before going to work at the Justice Department. While stationed with the navy in San Diego, he had married Mildred Marvin Jones after a relatively short engagement, and she had worked to support him during law school. They had two small children when they moved to Knoxville in 1934. Yet instead of a wedding band, Fly wore his gold and ruby Naval Academy ring.[42]

Fly's impact on TVA's small legal department, then consisting of Margolin, Howard Corcoran, five other lawyers, and clerical staff, was immediate. His second day on the job, Fly outlined for Lilienthal his plans for reorganizing the department. Besides improving the inadequate law library and centralizing the ragged filing system, Fly wanted to hire ten more lawyers at once, with a goal of doubling the team in the near future. He expected his division to be part of TVA's broad vital march so it could aid the board in charting courses. Fly also wanted to promote friendly and efficient cooperation among his staff.[43] By all accounts he succeeded, soon gaining the trust and respect of his staff, to whom he became known as "Chief." As described by one of Margolin's colleagues, Fly was the general in charge whose contributions as legal strategist and supervisor "can't be overestimated."[44]

Fly's impact on Margolin was also immediate. He assessed her pay and position, as the agency had delayed her proposed raise pending Sutherland's replacement.[45] Tommy Corcoran, who was aiding Fly's transition at TVA, received a brief report on the legal staff, which described Margolin as a Washington "prima donna." She was a good kid who excelled at research, the report also noted, although she was "sadly underpaid and a bit sore on things." The author predicted she would fare well under Fly's supervision.[46] Well beyond the three thousand dollars Sutherland proposed, Fly quickly recommended that Margolin's salary be increased to thirty-six hundred dollars.[47] With the board's approval, Margolin got the raise and was promoted to associate attorney, in recognition of the valuable work she had been doing and paving the way for Fly to assign her legal matters of ever-increasing responsibility. The raise also put her salary on par with other associate attorneys, all male lawyers with comparable experience.[48]

Fly assembled a team of brilliant lawyers with whom Margolin worked, deeply shaping her experiences at TVA. Among his first recruits was Joe Fowler, Margolin's Yale classmate, who quickly became the legal department's expert on crucial navigation issues.[49] Margolin would also soon begin close lifetime friendships with three other TVA lawyers on Fly's team. Herbert S. Marks, a Felix Frankfurter protégé who had graduated first in his Harvard Law School class, had clerked for the federal judge who presided over Fly's successful antitrust prosecution of the Sugar Institute and briefly worked at the Interior Department, before Fly tapped him to join the team in 1934.[50] Joe Swidler, who had worked in Lilienthal's law firm after graduating with honors from the University of Chicago Law School, was already at TVA negotiating utility contracts as the agency's expert power attorney when Fly arrived.[51] Margolin's close circle of TVA colleagues also included Melvin Siegel, Marks's Harvard classmate, who served as Justice Benjamin Cardozo's law clerk before joining TVA.[52]

With the promise of interesting work and a strong leader, Fly created a legal powerhouse. He included Margolin in his extraordinary group of young lawyers, who had outstanding academic records and law school achievements.[53] Fly offered them jobs in the nascent and rather mystical field of constitutional litigation that would challenge their imaginations and interest and in which they could rapidly accumulate valuable experience.[54] Fly was not concerned that Margolin and her colleagues had spent little if any time in a courtroom; he was much more interested in securing lawyers who could analyze tough legal questions.[55] For litigation expertise Fly recruited William C. Fitts, a Yale law graduate and seasoned trial attorney from Birmingham, Alabama, to be his chief assistant general solicitor. Like Fowler, Fitts credited Fly as a fair and excellent administrator who set up and ran the TVA legal department as one of the government's finest.[56] Fly delegated authority to his lawyers, stepping back and giving them room to develop in their own way.[57]

Transfer to the Tennessee Valley

To implement his reorganization plan, Fly soon closed TVA's Washington, D.C., legal office and transferred Margolin and other staff who had been working there to Knoxville, Tennessee.[58] The distance between Washington and Knoxville was about five hundred miles. But compared to New Orleans, New Haven, and Washington, more than miles separated the Tennessee Valley from any place Margolin had known. On rainy days blood-red water gushed through deep clay gullies into a river that defied navigation. The neglected forest was dwindling. Malaria was epidemic. Recalling the area when he first arrived, Joe Swidler said, "There was everything bad about it."[59]

Visitors to Knoxville commented just as frequently about the soot, which fell like black rain from coal-burning chimneys and industrial furnaces, making everything dirty.[60] Whatever landed on the roofs of the buildings blew into open windows.[61] In summer TVA employees chose to let the dirt into their un-air-conditioned offices, seeking relief from Knoxville's heat and impressive humidity.[62]

Like her colleagues, Margolin adjusted to Knoxville, approaching the difficulties matter-of-factly. She worked in the New Sprankle Building, TVA's downtown headquarters, along with more than one hundred highly trained architects, engineers, economists, planners, and doctors as well as Director

Lilienthal, his two fellow board members, and their staff.[63] Seeing her new, sparsely furnished office, Margolin requested her former secretary to ship from Washington not only her law books but also the bookcase. Five years later, when Margolin returned to Washington to start her next job, it was not Knoxville's soot, heat, humidity, or lack of furniture that she recalled. Instead, Margolin longed for her cozy little office in Knoxville.[64]

It was, after all, very fortunate that Margolin moved to Knoxville and later to Chattanooga. There was no better way for her to appreciate the importance of TVA's work than to see firsthand how quickly the clay soil of farm hillsides eroded and how deep the fissures and gullies grew; hers was an object lesson in the desperate need for effective power, flood control, and soil conservation programs.[65] At the same time, both during and after work Margolin came to know the experts TVA hired to fix the region's problems. She developed lasting friendships with TVA employees outside the legal team, such as architects Alfred and Jane Clauss, whose baby girl, Carin, grew up to become Margolin's protégée and the first woman solicitor of labor.[66] Walt Seymour, a TVA statistician and key figure in its Power Planning Department, and his wife chose Margolin as their daughter's godmother, a role she warmly carried out for many years.[67]

The Ashwander Case Begins

Although Lilienthal had asked Margolin to examine the first legal claims against TVA's power program, it was Fly who immersed her in the two great constitutional challenges that were destined for the Supreme Court, *Ashwander v. TVA* (*Ashwander*) and *Tennessee Electric Power Company v. TVA* (*TEP*).[68] Both cases attacked TVA's power program, which the electric utility industry viewed as a high-stakes threat because of the government's low-cost competition. Even if the companies could not ultimately defeat the threat, they hoped that protracted litigation would weaken TVA's bargaining position if and when they were forced to negotiate the sale of their facilities.[69]

TVA's power program ultimately withstood nearly forty constitutional challenges, all filed before Margolin left TVA for the Labor Department in 1939. But it was *Ashwander* and later *TEP* that made national headlines and overshadowed all other legal work during Margolin's time there. By early 1936 she saw the Supreme Court in *Ashwander* affirm TVA's right to sell electric power produced by the Wilson Dam on the grounds that the government had the right to dispose of its property, even in the form of electricity, in any manner it chose. And by early 1939 Margolin saw the Supreme Court in *TEP* affirm the ruling that federal powers over commerce and national security, as well as its right to dispose of property, made all aspects of TVA constitutional. The New Deal's great experiment, TVA, provided Margolin, even as a junior attorney, with unrivaled legal training.

The *Ashwander* case began on September 13, 1934, when George Ashwander and other improbably vigilant stockholders of the Alabama Power Company (APC) filed suit to enjoin the company from performing Wendell Willkie's January 4, 1934, contract with TVA. Forney Johnston, a New Deal–hating lawyer from Birmingham who had filed the earlier lawsuit for the ice and coal companies, reappeared on behalf of Ashwander and his fellow shareholders. Johnston, a skillful litigator with seemingly limitless funding from the utility industry, filed a far-reaching complaint. He alleged that TVA's power program represented an intrusion in the electric power business for which the government lacked constitutional authority under the war power or property clauses and violated the Tenth Amendment's reservation of states' rights.[70]

The filing of the suit, and in particular the request to enjoin APC and TVA from performing the contract, sent TVA's legal staff into high-speed activity that Fly carefully orchestrated. The team filed papers asking the court to dismiss the complaint prior to trial for several reasons, including the shareholders' failure to state a legally sufficient cause of action. After a hearing Judge William I. Grubb, a crusty seventy-four-year-old jurist who had one month earlier become the first federal judge to declare the New Deal's National Recovery Administration unconstitutional, ruled against TVA and ordered the matter proceed to trial, signaling his disfavor of TVA's position on the merits.[71] Although he agreed with TVA's basic proposition that the government may dispose of any surplus created by exercising lawful powers, such as national defense or improving navigation, Judge Grubb preliminarily concluded that TVA's plan for a broad social program belied its claim that its sole interest in electricity was to salvage a surplus. Citing public statements by TVA officials, he found that their actual goal exceeded navigation or defense and was instead, as he described in his decision, "to create an ideal community, as a social experiment, and give it aid by supplying cheap electric power, produced by it, for that purpose."[72]

As the TVA team prepared for trial, recognizing little chance of success with Judge Grubb, Fly adopted an overarching strategy to obtain findings of fact that they would need to prevail on appeal. Although he preferred to win in the trial court, Fly repeatedly told his staff not to worry too much about what the trial judge decided on the law because the reviewing court, the Fifth Circuit Court of Appeals, was not bound by the trial court's legal conclusions.[73] Fly's long-range view proved crucial to TVA's ultimate victory, and it also gave Margolin a template that she later used to enforce the Fair Labor Standards Act.

From the beginning Fly also recognized the importance of limiting the scope of the trial to the Wilson Dam, the only TVA dam expressly built for national security under the National Defense Act of 1916. But even this limited scope required the team to prove that the dam improved navigation on the Tennessee River and controlled flooding and that electric power sales yielded revenues to offset the cost of the project, in addition to making government property—the power—available to Americans rather than wasting it. Proving these facts required many expert witnesses and an extraordinary amount of technical evidence, which Fly gave his team wide latitude to develop.[74]

Knoxvillians noticed the midnight lights that consistently burned in the windows of the New Sprankle Building's sixth floor, where TVA's lawyers worked.[75] Even though *Ashwander* was the top priority for Fly and his trial team, it was only one of the growing number of legal challenges to TVA's power program and only one of myriad legal matters requiring skillful and speedy response. In addition to her work on *Ashwander* and other power litigation, Fly continued to assign Margolin a wide range of duties with greater responsibility, giving her more hands-on litigation experience in his first few months than she had received in the prior year. Before 1934 ended, she opposed a motion for a temporary restraining order in Nashville's federal district court, participated in the Alabama Public Service Commission's review of TVA's contract with the Alabama Power Company, and helped write a brief in a major condemnation case. In January 1935, after traveling by train to Atlanta, where she met with a consultant regarding a new dam, she flew to Birmingham in time to join the team for the last week of preparation before the *Ashwander* trial began.[76] She stayed there for the month-long trial and to hear Judge Grubb's ruling.

Fly and Fitts tried *Ashwander,* with Margolin and other team members scrambling behind the scenes to prepare legal memoranda, organize evidence, and ready witnesses. After court adjourned each day, the team met to prepare for the next day.[77] When Johnston concluded the stockholders' case, Fly marshaled evidence to establish that TVA's power program was incidental to its primary objectives of navigation, flood control, and national defense.[78] Even with the "Trial of the Century"—the criminal prosecution of Bruno Hauptmann for the Lindbergh baby kidnapping—vying for the nation's attention, *Ashwander* made headlines, with the press detailing Judge Grubb's evidentiary rulings as if the trial were a sporting event.[79]

On February 22, 1935, after both sides had introduced all their evidence, Johnston and Fly made closing arguments. Fly hammered away at a central point: the only question before the court was whether TVA had the right to purchase a little transmission line to carry wasting electric power to the market that wants it.[80] As soon as Fly concluded, Judge Grubb announced he had already reached a decision. He summarily rejected TVA's initial argument that the stockholders lacked standing to sue and then addressed the merits, following the logic and approach of his earlier ruling on TVA's motion to dismiss. Attached to a constitutional power such as navigation, national defense, or flood control, reasoned Judge Grubb, the government could sell a surplus of resulting energy. Having now considered all the evidence, however, he again ruled that TVA had intended to produce energy not as a surplus but to get into the utility business and thus had exceeded its legal authority.[81] In effect Judge Grubb ruled that APC could buy power from the government and sell it to the people of Alabama but that it was unconstitutional for the people of Alabama to buy the power directly from the government.[82] The ruling's only redeeming aspect for TVA was that Judge Grubb expressly confined it to the validity of the January 4 contract regarding the Wilson Dam, finding it unnecessary to address the constitutionality of the TVA Act.[83]

Although Judge Grubb's decision was no surprise, it was still a major defeat for the Roosevelt administration, several of whose New Deal programs, such as the Railroad Retirement Act and the slum clearance powers of the National Industrial Recovery Act, already had been declared unconstitutional by lower federal courts and were headed for Supreme Court review.[84] It was also terribly frustrating and disappointing to the TVA legal team. Margolin and her colleagues watched as Fly, who kept his eye on the big picture, announced that TVA would immediately appeal.[85]

To do so, Fly decided to call in assistance. With the board's approval, he hired John Lord O'Brian as special counsel for the appeal. Mild-mannered and distinguished, the sixty-year-old Republican O'Brian was an accomplished, Harvard-educated lawyer and former U.S. attorney for the Western District of New York, who had trained Fly at the Justice Department's Antitrust Division. With extensive public service and Supreme Court experience, O'Brian was considered a leader of the American bar.[86]

Although Senator Hugo Black and other congressmen wanted TVA to appeal the trial court's ruling directly to the Supreme Court, Fly insisted on taking one step at a time, appealing first to the Fifth Circuit. Predicting the Supreme Court would declare unconstitutional at least some of the New Deal programs then headed its way, Fly did not want TVA to be first up to bat.[87] By April 1, 1935, TVA filed its notice of appeal from Judge Grubb's decision to the Fifth Circuit, and Fly assembled his lawyers to prepare the brief. Margolin's work on the first appellate brief of her legal career was a heady experience. To aid TVA's lawyers, in addition to O'Brian and solicitor general Stanley F. Reed, Fly enlisted an impressive group of consultants, considered the New Deal's finest, including Paul Freund of the Justice Department, who had worked on Harvard's law review with Marks and Siegel, and Abe Fortas, who had left Yale to join William O. Douglas at the Securities and Exchange Commission.[88] With the group's work product in hand, Margolin drove with Fly and Fowler to the printer in St. Louis, where they made last-minute changes before filing the *Ashwander* brief on June 1, 1935.[89]

Two weeks later Margolin sat in the packed Atlanta courtroom to hear the argument. O'Brian, who split TVA's allotted time with Fly, recounted an unbroken line of decisions regarding government property to argue that the United States owns the power at dams it builds, which entitles it to dispose of the power as it sees fit. When it was Johnston's turn, he showered invectives on TVA, including its audacity to create a collectivist system in bad faith.[90] Reflecting the urgency of the case, the Fifth Circuit ruled in TVA's favor within one month. Fly immediately advised Lilienthal by telegram, "Unanimous decision represents sweeping victory on major issues."[91]

Margolin saved the extra edition of the *Knoxville News Sentinel* from that day, which announced in bold letters: "TVA Wins in U.S. Court."[92] News accounts across the country touted the New Deal's first appellate victory, with editorials reflecting the sharply divided political landscape. The *Christian Science Monitor* reported that by winning at the Fifth Circuit,

Fly had chalked up the only major score of the season for the Roosevelt administration on a constitutional issue.[93] The *Wall Street Journal* likened the Fifth Circuit's approval of TVA to a reprieve to a condemned man, coming "at a time when the Roosevelt policies seemed so legally discredited that an unprecedented condition existed and a vital and overshadowing issue loomed."[94] Margolin followed the press accounts carefully, a practice she continued throughout her career. Angered by a bare two-line reference to TVA's victory in the *New Republic,* she wrote the editor, revealing neither her gender nor her employer. After lauding the oral arguments of TVA's "two able attorneys" and the circuit court's decision as "singularly lucid, logical and convincing," Margolin revealed her passion for her cause and her willingness to speak her mind: "One would think that a magazine of the reputed liberality of the New Republic would grasp the opportunity to convey a clear account of the case for TVA to an interested public confused by the widely-published canned legal opinions expensively made-to-order by hirelings of the Power Trust."[95]

An Introduction to the United States Supreme Court

As expected, Forney Johnston petitioned the Supreme Court to review the Fifth Circuit's ruling. TVA, now joined by the Justice Department, did not oppose review, eager to have the Supreme Court remove all doubt about TVA's right to carry out its power program as Congress required.[96] After the Supreme Court granted review, the TVA team devoted the next two months to prepare for the December 1935 oral argument. TVA renewed O'Brian's contract as special counsel, and Fly kept in place essentially the same legal team that had worked so well together for the trial and the Fifth Circuit appeal, now decamped to Washington to prepare a new brief and argument.[97] After seeing galleys of Johnston's brief, Fly was determined to present TVA's case clearly and convincingly to refute the "accusations and spectres" Johnston conjured up.[98] Back in Knoxville, excitement mounted as loyal TVA employees planned to charter a bus to Washington to attend the argument at the grand new Supreme Court building, which had just opened in October 1935.[99]

On the day of the argument, after Solicitor General Reed presented the required motion, Chief Justice Charles Evans Hughes admitted Bessie Margolin of New Orleans, Louisiana, to the Supreme Court Bar, entitling her to sit in one of the spaces reserved for bar members. Not only was Margolin one of the few female attorneys in the country authorized to practice at the High Court, but she was also one of even far fewer who had actually done so by either filing a brief or arguing there.[100] Margolin's name appeared on TVA's brief under the names of Attorney General Homer Cummings, Solicitor General Reed, O'Brian, Fly, Freund, and Fowler, making her the first and only woman whose name appeared on the Supreme Court brief of any of the New Deal cases.[101] That day Margolin watched and heard O'Brian and Reed present the arguments she had helped create. It would be ten more years before Margolin herself would argue at the Supreme Court, joining the nation's most elite circle of lawyers, male and female.[102]

As appellants, the stockholders' lawyers argued first and had the last word in rebuttal. It was perhaps a good sign for the government that Chief Justice Hughes interrupted Johnston's dramatic recitation of TVA's evils and asked him to explain what the suit was about, who brought it, and why.[103] Later in the argument Johnston's cocounsel, James M. Beck, who had been President Harding's solicitor general and by 1935 was a vigorous New Deal critic, articulated TVA's true menace. The circuit court's ruling, he argued, paved the way for the federal government to use the electricity it generated to make shoes or steel or any other commodity it wished, no matter how greatly it invaded the states' right to control industrial activity.[104]

In contrast to his formidable opponents, O'Brian spoke in measured terms, demonstrating his experience from dozens of Supreme Court appearances. He was conversational with the justices; he answered their questions and anticipated what was troubling them. When Justice George Sutherland asked whether the Wilson Dam was built to improve navigation, O'Brian answered confidently, "Undoubtedly, your Honor," and swiftly cited the page in the appendix that contained supporting statutory language.[105] Justice James C. McReynolds, a conservative curmudgeon, on the other hand, did not hide his disapproval. He fired questions at O'Brian, trying more than once to bait him into conceding that the federal government's claimed right to sell the power it created at the Wilson Dam allowed it to compete with utility companies across the country, beyond the reach of state regulation.[106] O'Brian refused to take the bait, redirecting the colloquy by emphasizing the huge amount of power that would be wasted if TVA were not permitted to transmit it, and then boldly posed a rhetorical question: "Can it be that under an interpretation of the Constitution we are deprived of the right of realizing the value of that for the people?"[107] Breaking the silence, O'Brian answered his own question, noting that once electric power was generated by the dam, "we cannot do anything with it except seize it instantly and deliver it on transmission lines or it is forever gone."[108] O'Brian, a master advocate who would be Margolin's lifelong mentor, was demonstrating to an eager disciple how to seize every advantage in oral argument.[109]

When court resumed the next day, Solicitor General Reed had fifteen minutes to resolve remaining questions and convince at least five justices to affirm the Fifth Circuit's ruling. The team had spent the previous evening helping Reed prepare, an exercise that was instructive for Margolin in later years when she, too, would find herself in front of the Supreme Court for an argument spanning two consecutive days. When Reed took the podium, he stressed that the Court need not reach the broad question of the TVA Act's constitutionality.[110] For the TVA team the most exciting moment during the *Ashwander* argument came when Justice Willis Van Devanter and several other justices gently acknowledged that the dispute was confined to a single contract to be fulfilled solely by the Wilson Dam—the one point on which their whole case depended.[111]

After the argument, days and then weeks passed without a decision. In the interim Fly promoted Margolin from associate attorney to attorney and increased her pay to four thousand dollars per year, citing her excellent work that proved particularly valuable in difficult and important research and brief-writing problems and noting that she had contributed more to the *Ashwander* briefs than any other attorney.[112]

Finally, on February 17, 1936, the Court issued its ruling; with Justice McReynolds as the lone dissenter, it affirmed the Fifth Circuit's decision and made TVA the first New Deal agency to survive Supreme Court scrutiny.[113] People across the South rejoiced. In Knoxville factory whistles blared, and the high school band played to cheering crowds in the downtown streets. The citizens of Norris, Tennessee, where TVA was building a dam, assembled to give thanks in prayer for the decision. Alabama citizens of Florence, Sheffield, and Tuscumbia reportedly celebrated, while Florence's mayor declared the decision the greatest victory ever won in the industrial and commercial life of the American people.[114] At the same time, Forney Johnston and officials of the Alabama Power Company declined to comment; a representative of a manufacturer's association warned that any expected savings from electric energy would be more than offset through increased taxes.[115]

Fly generously credited the hard work of his talented, young staff, light-heartedly claiming they all but wrote the Supreme Court's opinion.[116] Other observers also noticed the striking similarity between TVA's brief, O'Brian's oral argument, and the Supreme Court's ruling, including one article titled "O'Brian and Fly Are Real Heroes in Victory of TVA—Brief Shows Supreme Court Ruling Followed Their Arguments All the Way."[117] Margolin saved the article, along with another that praised TVA's brilliant legal team, a comment she underscored in blue ink with apparent satisfaction.[118]

It was not long before the legal team's exhilaration over its victory in *Ashwander* was tempered by reality. Although newspapers called it sweeping, the ruling validated only the Wilson Dam contract and the transmission of power from it. Fly's strategy to limit the scope of the case had worked, but it left unresolved questions about TVA's power program for dams still under construction. A great battle had been won, but the war over the TVA's constitutionality definitely was not over. At Fly's request, in early March 1936 Margolin prepared a lengthy memo analyzing unfavorable interpretations that might be accorded the limited scope of the *Ashwander* decision.[119] She concluded her analysis by offering a prescient assessment of the challenges ahead. To prevent future litigation by power companies in spite of their contracts, Margolin queried whether TVA might secure the companies' agreement to discourage shareholders' litigation. Unless they could secure some such agreement, Margolin advised Fly, she expected lengthy litigation in connection with every contract TVA made with power companies.[120]

TEP v. TVA

Even if it had wanted to demand such agreements, TVA had little chance before new lawsuits were filed. Margolin's second round of involvement in litigation that would reach the Supreme Court began just three months after the *Ashwander* decision. This time the Tennessee Electric Power Company (TEP) joined forces with other privately owned electric power companies, eighteen in total, to challenge TVA's entire power program, or at least everything not validated by the Supreme Court in *Ashwander*. The companies claimed that TVA threatened to destroy them by building dams unrelated to any federal function and that even if TVA had lawfully acquired the energy produced by the dams, TVA's method of disposition was unconstitutional. Because of its broad scope, the *TEP* suit promised to dwarf the *Ashwander* litigation.

Over several days in December 1936 Tennessee federal district judge John J. Gore held hearings on the companies' request for a preliminary injunction, an extraordinary form of temporary relief a court may grant before trial when the moving party shows that failing to preserve the status quo will cause irreparable harm and that success at trial is likely. The TVA crew worked around the clock to oppose the injunction, dictating, typing, consulting witnesses, and preparing affidavits. On the last day of the hearing, however, just minutes into argument, Judge Gore astonished both sides by announcing that he had heard enough. Convinced that the suit raised grave questions of law and fact and that the loss to TVA from the injunction would be less than the damage likely to be suffered by the power companies without it, Judge Gore granted the injunction.[121]

His order was far-reaching. Although it allowed TVA to complete certain power lines and substations then under construction, it prohibited the agency from extending its facilities, adding new customers, connecting to existing rural lines, and generally engaging in any service beyond the project's current scope.[122] Stopping short of completely paralyzing TVA, the injunction rendered a devastating blow for the region's people, who had come to depend on TVA for income and electricity. According to Margolin, when Fly heard the ruling, he shocked everyone present when he suddenly cried out to Judge Gore what she and the entire TVA legal team were thinking: "You can't do that! You're going to throw millions of people out of work. Don't you realize what you're doing?"[123]

TVA immediately appealed the injunction to the Sixth Circuit. Margolin went to Cincinnati to help prepare for the argument. One month later the Sixth Circuit reversed Judge Gore's injunction order but rejected TVA's attempts to dismiss the entire case on jurisdictional and procedural grounds.[124] Unsatisfied with a partial victory that sent TVA back to a hostile Judge Gore, Fly decided to seek the Supreme Court's review of the Sixth Circuit's ruling. After working with the team to quickly draft the petition, Margolin oversaw the printing of the brief in Louisville and then its filing at the Supreme Court.[125]

Less than two weeks later, the Supreme Court denied TVA's petition for review, which sent the case back to Judge Gore.[126] According to Fly, it was not long before Judge Gore, while hearing another pretrial matter, condemned TVA's position on the merits while claiming to withhold his judgment until after the trial.[127] Fearing the trial was doomed to be a farce, Fly went to Washington to seek legislation that would mandate a three-judge court in constitutional cases against the government, including the one pending against TVA. Having three judges, implored Fly, was at least as important as expediting appeals in such cases, which the House Judiciary Committee was then considering.[128] Fly was so determined to prevent a single judge such as Gore from derailing TVA that he resorted to unorthodox methods of persuasion, including barging in while the House Judiciary Committee chairman was taking a steam bath.[129] His efforts paid off. By the end of August, Congress passed the Judicial Reform Act, providing for three-judge courts in constitutional cases against the government and mandating direct appeals to the Supreme Court. Consequently, *TEP v. TVA,* the first case to be tried under the new law, was tried by a three-judge panel consisting of circuit judge Florence Ellenwood Allen, as chief judge, and district judges John J. Gore and John D. Martin.

Fly wanted his team in Chattanooga, where *TEP* was to be tried. In August 1937 Margolin, now a senior attorney making forty-six hundred dollars per year, was one of fourteen TVA employees Fly transferred from Knoxville to Chattanooga.[130] For months she worked almost exclusively on the *TEP* case, drafting pleadings and briefs and helping develop direct and cross-examination of witnesses and legal arguments.[131] One week before trial the TVA team moved into makeshift offices in Chattanooga's Read House Hotel, where Fly had reserved twenty-two rooms. Padding around in slippers, Fly directed his staff as they prepared for battle.[132] Regardless who won this round, the inevitable appeal in *TEP* would go directly to the Supreme Court, a certainty they did not have in *Ashwander.*

The trial began on November 15, 1937. In the crowded Chattanooga courtroom Margolin sat directly behind John Lord O'Brian and the rest of the TVA legal team, witnessing what *Life* magazine called "one of the most far-reaching cases in U.S. constitutional history" that would determine "the fate of President Roosevelt's whole dream of reshaping American life with electricity."[133] Across the courtroom sat nearly one dozen hard-hitting lawyers, with some forty in the background, representing southern utility firms whose assets totaled a billion dollars.[134] The companies' lead counsel was Newton Baker, the former mayor of Cleveland, Ohio, and secretary of war during World War I, who reversed his initial support for Roosevelt's New Deal when TVA was created.

After Baker delivered a sweeping opening statement lambasting TVA on largely political grounds, Fly sought to redirect the panel's attention to a fundamental legal issue, whether Congress had acted within its constitutional power by authorizing TVA to build dams for navigation, flood control, and national defense, which in turn created the by-product of power. And under the principles set forth in *Ashwander,* as Fly told the court, that power was the property of the United States government.[135] In the six-week trial that followed, the TVA legal team used the lessons they had learned from *Ashwander* to keep their theory prominent amid their opponents' skillful arguments and massive evidence. To do this, they prepared an army of witnesses, ranging from engineers to workers who erected the power lines, to testify on subjects such as hydraulic engineering and stream flow. Fly kept Margolin deeply engaged in the work, analyzing testimony, preparing questions for direct and cross-examination, and framing the legal arguments.[136]

Margolin was not the only woman playing a key part in this landmark trial. This fact was not lost on the public, as the *New York Times* made clear in one of many headlines devoted to the trial: "A Woman Presides over the Tribunal Hearing of One of the Most Important Constitutional Cases in American History."[137] The selection of Judge Florence Allen to lead the panel prompted more than fascination among TVA's legal staff. At the beginning of the trial the team was concerned about having drawn a woman judge, an unidentified TVA lawyer admitted to a reporter, but she quickly impressed them. Not only did the lawyer appreciate Judge Allen's disarming and engaging smile but found that she went to great lengths to be fair.[138] Although the lawyer did not specify whether Margolin shared the original concerns, Allen likely impressed her too. Not only was Allen the first and only female federal appellate judge at the time (and likely the first female judge Margolin had ever seen), but at the time of the *TEP* trial President Roosevelt was seriously considering Allen to fill Justice George Sutherland's seat on the Supreme Court.[139] Six years later Margolin argued before Judge Allen on behalf of the Labor Department and on more than one occasion cited Allen's lone female federal appellate judgeship in support of her own candidacy for a seat on the federal bench.[140]

Judge Allen received her federal judicial appointment in 1934, after a dozen years of distinguished service on the Ohio Supreme Court, where she was the first woman elected to sit on the highest court of any state. At the time of the *TEP* trial she was fifty-four years old, kept her straight hair closely cropped, and favored long, loose-fitting patterned dresses that she wore with laced-up, short-heeled shoes. Despite her extraordinary legal career, Allen appeared frumpy and old-fashioned, once publicly describing herself an old maid.[141] She presented a striking contrast to twenty-eight-year-old Margolin, who then wore her hair softly curled and favored high-heeled pumps, a crisp white blouse with a form-fitting jacket and skirt, revealing shapely legs almost up to her knees.[142] Despite their differences, Judge Allen provided Margolin with a compelling model of a woman who commanded a courtroom efficiently, decisively, and with good humor. When a utilities lawyer launched a lengthy description of a witness's excluded testimony, Allen cut him off, citing the rule that required counsel to make such offers succinctly.[143] She promptly rejected as irrelevant large categories of the power companies' evidence, bearing on matters unrelated to the statute or Constitution, such as TVA's alleged conspiracy with other public agencies, rates charged by TVA and the companies, and nonofficial TVA statements in speeches and press releases.[144] Judge Allen also used humor to lighten the courtroom's tense mood, a tactic that Margolin later employed as an advocate. While questioning a witness, Fly mispronounced a city in Judge Allen's home state of Ohio. "You may mispronounce Tupelo in this court," Allen quipped with a smile, "but not Gallipolis!"[145]

In all other respects Fly's courtroom performance was impressive, occasionally interrupting his methodical presentation for an unexpected dramatic flourish. In one memorable instance plaintiffs' counsel called Wendell Willkie to testify, asking him little of substance; it was part of an apparent strategy to induce Fly to ask questions on cross-examination that would allow Willkie—a gifted orator who less than three years later would run a formidable presidential campaign as the Republican nominee—to testify broadly against TVA. When plaintiffs' counsel tendered Willkie for cross-examination, Fly took a moment to confer quietly with his team. He started to approach Willkie, documents in hand, seemingly ready to launch an aggressive interrogation, but then dramatically announced, "No questions for this witness."[146] Willkie was stunned. All he could do was sit there flabbergasted until he quietly left the stand.[147] Exiting the court later that day, Willkie revealed to reporters his admiration for Fly: "He's the most dangerous man in America—to have on the other side."[148]

While preparing for closing arguments in *TEP*, just as in *Ashwander*, TVA's lawyers engaged in intensive strategy sessions that provoked vibrant debates among its sharp and strong-willed team members, with Margolin an equal force in the tussles over every word and every line of the briefs.[149]

According to Fowler, it was only after he and Mel Siegel had finally won over Herb Marks and Margolin that the team framed the final arguments to focus on the standing issue, that is, to show that the companies lacked the legal authority to sue because of their limited franchise rights, a strategy that proved crucial at the Supreme Court.[150] In mid-January 1938, after Jackson and Fly presented the closing statements, the three-judge panel adjourned to deliberate its decision.[151]

Within a week the court was ready to rule. Spectators stood at the back of the packed courtroom, while others filled the jury box. Counsel for the utilities sat at one table, and at the other Margolin and the rest of the TVA legal team surrounded Fly.[152] They all listened for more than an hour as Judge Allen read the decision she had authored for the panel.[153] Absent fraud, malice, or coercion, announced Allen, there could be no conspiracy among public officials in administering the law. And even though the court agreed with the utility companies that TVA intended to undercut their prices, any such finding constituted "damnum absque injuria"—damage without legal injury.[154] When Judge Allen finished, the popping of flashbulbs added to the excitement in the courtroom; Margolin beamed while posing with the TVA team for a newspaper photograph.[155]

As expected, the companies appealed directly to the Supreme Court, authorized by the new statute. Having taken *Ashwander* and the earlier *TEP* ruling to the Supreme Court, Margolin and the team knew their next steps.[156] In October 1938 the TVA lawyers filed their 261-page brief asking the Supreme Court to uphold the panel's decision, with Margolin listed among its authors.[157]

At the same time, along with several other TVA lawyers, Margolin was busy presenting a major condemnation case against the Southern States Power Company to a commission in Asheville, North Carolina. For nearly three months witnesses testified and the lawyers argued, amassing five hundred exhibits and filling six thousand pages of transcripts.[158] On November 5 Margolin interrupted her work on *Southern States* to go to Washington to help prepare for the *TEP* oral argument at the Supreme Court, this time to be presented by O'Brian and Fly. Afterward Margolin returned to Asheville, where she remained until concluding the *Southern States* hearing on December 23, 1938. Two days later she returned to TVA's Knoxville office.[159]

Margolin had much to celebrate as 1938 drew to a close. She had not only completed her work on the *TEP* oral argument and the *Southern States* hearing, but she had also received a raise from forty-six hundred to five thousand dollars.[160] Before leaving Knoxville for Chattanooga, Margolin rewarded herself by buying a brand-new car—a 1939 Hudson coupe, with only twenty-two miles on the odometer—costing her nearly two months of her new salary.[161] In 1939 Margolin was among roughly one in five Americans who owned a car and even fewer of whom were women.[162] Automobile advertisements at the time featured stylish women but almost always as passengers or waving bystanders, not as drivers.[163] Margolin did not need ads to fuel her love of nice cars and would repeatedly splurge on them. Years later she would cherish the white convertible Alpine Sunbeam sports car that she shipped back from London. Although she was never known for a good sense of direction or keen driving skills, these deficiencies did not stop her, even when motoring alone on uncertain and poorly marked roads that predated the interstate highways.[164] She compensated with speed, resulting in her arrest on one occasion and a sixty-day suspension of her license on another.[165] Undaunted and accustomed to operating in a man's world, Margolin used her hard-earned money to buy the independence that owning a car provided.

Whether by car, train, or even the occasional airplane flight, Margolin traveled extensively during her time at TVA. From July 1934 through December 1938 she spent 488 days on the road, almost 30 percent of her time. The novelty of travel gave way to its gritty reality, but Margolin seemed to thrive on it. She learned to fend for herself as a single, attractive woman, often traveling overnight, sometimes with her male colleagues and other times alone, raising eyebrows either way. On overnight train trips TVA authorized Margolin to purchase a Pullman berth, which provided another form of adventure. After a porter had turned the seat into a bed, Margolin reached her upper berth with a ladder and drew curtains for privacy. Men and women shared train cars, so getting dressed inside a berth required skill and some contortion. It was not unusual for a passenger to be awakened by another who, whether sleepy or intoxicated, had climbed into the wrong berth.[166] As a result, Margolin learned tact and survival skills, not to mention how to pack, avoid wrinkles in her clothing, and stay neatly dressed—experience that proved invaluable as she crisscrossed the country for the Labor Department, meeting with regional attorneys and arguing hundreds of cases.

In May 1938 Margolin shared some thoughts about her blossoming career in her sorority's magazine. The field of law was still too greatly restricted for women with considerable prejudice against them, Margolin advised her Alpha Epsilon Phi sisters around the country. But she wondered whether young women fostered that prejudice by readily abandoning their profession for marriage. Margolin offered her view not as criticism but because she sympathized with a very real problem—one that she expected to endure "unless and until something can be worked out to permit and encourage the woman attorney to maintain interest in her profession notwithstanding marriage and children."[167] Indeed, although she did not disclose the fact in her article, Margolin had won her TVA job with a pledge, made for her by Lorenzen, that she would marry her career instead of a man. Nor did she mention that within months after Lorenzen's pledge, she had honored it by ending her engagement to Bob Butler, once and for all.

In a field dominated by men, Margolin further advised, a woman attorney "must manage to be accepted and treated as another man and must be willing to take responsibility, criticism, and hard work in the same spirit as do the men attorneys. In short, she must aim to become one of the men, without, however, becoming masculine and overly aggressive in her approach." This was tough advice for a woman lawyer to follow, especially if she wanted to do trial work. Ability notwithstanding, Margolin's forays into courtrooms, especially in southern cities and towns, were met with resentment from attorneys, judges, and even witnesses who, according to other TVA lawyers, were not yet ready to accept a woman lawyer.[168] Despite the challenges, Margolin followed her own advice. She had earned an equal place among TVA's talented, brilliant men. John Lord O'Brian, for example, recognized that Margolin's "special gift of lucidity" in writing had contributed materially to the character of TVA's briefs. He appreciated that Margolin not only had a "legal brain," as he put it, but also was "a very feminine person, and a very nice person."[169] Margolin used these qualities outside the workplace to endear herself to her colleagues personally, earning a regular seat at the TVA legal department's poker nights, where she held her own, betting and bluffing against Swidler, Fowler, Marks, Siegel, and Fly.[170]

On January 30, 1939, the Supreme Court issued its decision in *TEP*, ruling in TVA's favor. The Court affirmed the panel's decision but on different grounds, adopting TVA's argument that the utility companies lacked standing to maintain the suit.[171] When the Court ruled, Margolin was in Miami taking a short but well-earned vacation. She sent a gleeful letter to

Herb Marks expressing her eagerness to revel over the decision with him and half-jokingly complained, "It was a trifle disappointing not to get some little word on the merits—don't you think?"[172]

Even before the Supreme Court had announced its decision, Margolin began to look for other job opportunities. In her nearly six years at TVA she had undergone exquisite legal training, including the two constitutional cases that had whetted her appetite for litigating important issues from inception to resolution by the Supreme Court—and against which any other assignment at TVA now paled by comparison. James Barr, Fly's former assistant at TVA, had just joined the Labor Department's new Wage and Hour Division, established to enforce the Fair Labor Standards Act of 1938. Aware of Margolin's interest in making a job change, Barr related that the division was looking to hire a lot of people, making it a particularly good time for her to apply.[173]

Fly was also interested in leaving TVA to return to Washington, and by January 1938 he was campaigning to succeed Robert H. Jackson to head the Justice Department's Antitrust Division. In recommendations to the president, O'Brian and Lilienthal praised Fly not only as a skillful and talented lawyer but as an administrator who had kept his capable and independent-minded lawyers working together in harmony.[174] Although Fly did not get the antitrust job, his staff shared O'Brian's and Lilienthal's opinion. Despite the years of high-pressure, high-stakes litigation, Fitts could not recall any serious disagreement with Fly throughout five years as his deputy, noting that he was closer than anyone else in the legal department to Fly—except for Margolin.[175]

5

BACHELOR GIRL

Margolin had joined TVA when she was twenty-four and left shortly after she turned thirty. During that time, as her sister and closest female friends married and assumed traditional roles as wives, mothers, and homemakers, Margolin went from being considered "single" to "unmarried."[1] Honoring Professor Lorenzen's pledge that she would not be distracted from her career by consideration of marriage, Margolin proved she would not abandon the law. She also avoided the public disapproval generally shown toward married workingwomen who were accused of neglecting their families, although she could still be criticized for stealing a job from a man. Even the federal government's "marital status clause"—which provided that in any personnel reduction employees whose spouses also worked for the federal government were to be dismissed first—was implemented to retain the male half of the couple.[2] With so many factors working against a married woman having a successful career, it is not surprising that Margolin avoided marriage.

Margolin not only embraced the professional ambitions associated with men, but she also enjoyed the social and sexual freedoms traditionally associated with the male bachelor. Although it was not the norm, she was by no means the only young woman enjoying her freedom. Since the turn of the twentieth century, independent, single, urban women were often called "bachelor girls." It was a mostly complimentary term, acknowledging that single women were not simply spinsters but could, like single men, live irresponsible, pleasure-filled lives.[3] The namesake "Bachelor Girl" of a popular film released in 1935 was Marion Forsythe, a bohemian globetrotting artist who was persuaded by a tabloid publisher to pen her autobiography, especially her romances. "A bachelor girl lives alone with her memories," teased the movie's trailer, while "a spinster just lives alone."[4] Yielding to the cultural canon that marriage was the proper goal of a woman's life, even Forsythe's fiercely independent Bachelor Girl ultimately gave up her career to settle down and marry her publisher.[5] Margolin never would so yield.

Perhaps because of her attractiveness, Margolin was often characterized as a bachelor girl, rather than a spinster. She did little to discourage this portrayal. In 1939 a chatty reporter for the *New Orleans Item* who was fascinated by Margolin's story wrote a feature about the local orphan girl who made good. Given the way she posed for her picture and answered questions, Margolin did not seem to mind that the story focused as much on her appearance and marital status as her academic and professional achievement. Echoing the popular romance genre of the time, the reporter introduced Margolin as a brunette with flashing black eyes and stunning figure who looked like a million dollars—all the money she did not have. Margolin's pretty face made the reporter wonder why she still had *Miss* tacked on before her name.

Margolin's full-length photo, strategically positioned above the fold of the newspaper's front page, underscored the point. A young woman in a figure-revealing skirt and demure silk blouse perched on a windowsill, gazing outside. More cheesecake than lawyerly, the photo would have made a mockery of Margolin's career but for the reporter's accolades. This was one of many photos and articles that portrayed Margolin as a woman lawyer with both brains and beauty who chose to dedicate herself to an important career instead of a husband, at least for the time being. After pressing Margolin to explain why she had not married, the reporter recounted Margolin's response: "'I haven't had time for love.' Then she smiled. 'But I'm not immune, I'm just uncontaminated.' Dr. Margolin brushed back a lock of soft black hair. 'So far,' she added."[6]

Margolin's witty comment, which seemed ripped from a movie starring Katharine Hepburn or Bette Davis, revealed the young lawyer's passion for wordsmithery. Obviously intending to be humorous, Margolin seemed neither defensive nor self-conscious about being single. Her statement, however, was not true. By April 1939 Margolin had found plenty of time for love and was hardly "uncontaminated." Given that she had ended her relationship with law school classmate Bob Butler six years earlier, it is not surprising that Margolin glossed over it. She was, however, in the midst of a romance that would last for many years. Shortly after Larry Fly arrived at TVA, he and Margolin started an amorous liaison that continued into the next stage of their careers, hers at the Labor Department and his at the Federal Communications Commission (FCC). Their affair was a well-known secret within TVA and around town. As she could not publicly acknowledge her affair with a married man who was her former boss at a high-profile New Deal agency, it seems bold, if not reckless, that Margolin said anything more to the reporter than necessary. She could have simply replied that she had not had time for marriage. And yet she had toyed with the press about her love life.

She shared the same playful attitude with her closest friends. Evelyn Flonacher, who was now divorced and enjoying her work at a New Orleans advertising agency, compared Margolin's scintillating (but unfortunately lost) letters to a mink coat—rare but worth the wait. Margolin enjoyed corresponding about romance and sex, as suggested by Evelyn's candid response to her friend's apparent inquiries and comments: "No, I haven't been seduced lately. . . . You're right, however; this town is indeed a sink of iniquity and no place for an up and coming young female attorney with melting black orbs."[7]

We are deprived of any account Margolin may have given her girlfriends about Larry Fly. His daughter, Sally Fly Connell, documented the only known instance of Margolin discussing the romance. In 1967, one year after Fly's death, Connell spoke with Margolin while researching a proposed biography of her father. After Margolin warmly recalled Fly's professional life at TVA, Connell confronted her with the affair. "I know about you and Dad," said Connell. Margolin conceded, "Sure, it wasn't a secret." When Connell requested permission to write about their relationship in Fly's biography, Margolin, who was trying to win a federal judgeship, flatly refused, threatening to sue Connell for libel if she did. Having gotten Margolin to confirm the affair, Connell nevertheless was left struggling with how to present her father fully without addressing his personal life; Connell died in 1982, never having published her unfinished manuscript.[8]

There is no record of the precise moment when Margolin's professional relationship with Fly grew personal. There was plenty of opportunity at work, where they spent countless hours together, both in the office and traveling on business. Although few, if any, of Fly's colleagues at TVA or the FCC ever squarely discussed the relationship with him, it was general knowledge that Margolin was his mistress. Those who spoke about the relationship considered it neither promiscuous nor scandalous, largely due to the genuine affection they saw between Fly and Margolin. Despite the fact that Fly was married and had young children, his colleagues did not seem troubled by his adulterous conduct. Instead, they tended to justify Fly's infidelity by pointing to troubles with his marriage, some even blaming Mildred Fly's difficult personality.[9] Some colleagues recalled that Fly and Margolin had kept their affair pretty quiet by being very discreet.[10]

Other observers, however, described Margolin and Fly as anything but discreet, contending that the couple had made little effort to conceal their love affair, especially during their time in Knoxville.[11] Nor did the pair keep it from Fly's wife, who bitterly resented his frequent absences from their home and children and who by her own account knew that her husband lived with Margolin for much of the time they worked together at TVA, a fact that also did not escape comment by people in the small community.[12] After Margolin moved to Washington, D.C., to start her job at the Labor Department, Fly followed six months later to accept an appointment to head the Federal Communications Commission. The two soon resumed the same pattern there; Fly stayed at Margolin's apartment most evenings, occasionally returning to his Virginia home.[13] Although it was never confirmed by anyone close to Margolin or Fly, the rumor was that they would have married but that Mrs. Fly refused to grant a divorce.[14]

In a series of letters to her TVA colleague Herb Marks during her last few months at TVA and her first few months at the Labor Department, Margolin provides a glimpse of her relationship with Fly. Although she wrote few details, she did not hide or explain that she was with Fly. After the Supreme Court announced the *TEP* decision, Margolin traveled to Miami, where Fly had been relaxing since his oral argument. While there, Margolin wrote Marks, relating pleasant days spent betting at the race track, using the pronoun *we* without apparent need for further identification.[15] Over the next two months Margolin used annual leave to travel from Chattanooga to Washington, D.C., to care for Fly as he recovered from hernia surgery at the U.S. Naval Hospital. Her detailed reports to Marks on Fly's condition and her concerns for his recovery reveal she had assumed a caregiving role normally reserved for a wife or immediate family member but not an employee.[16]

Fly was equally protective about Margolin, both personally and professionally, and she valued his opinion. While Margolin negotiated with her prospective boss, Calvert Magruder, about her new job at the Labor Department, Fly voiced his concerns. He thought she deserved more money but was later satisfied with Magruder's commitment to assign Margolin meaningful work and responsibility.[17] Even John Lord O'Brian, TVA's gentlemanly special counsel for the *TEP* and *Ashwander* cases, acknowledged

Margolin's close personal relationship to Fly; after O'Brian had a promising conversation with an influential friend to help Fly win the top antitrust job at the Justice Department, he reported the confidential news to the convalescing Fly—only after he had already reported it to Margolin.[18]

Margolin and Fly's relationship appears to have been consensual, caring, and happy. Margolin also remained financially independent from Fly; when she needed a loan to take her post-*TEP* vacation to Miami, she got it from Herb Marks, whom she repaid within the month.[19] The relationship did not impair Fly's overall supervision of TVA's legal department, as his legal staff praised him as an outstanding administrator who ran one of the best law departments inside or out of government.[20] There is no evidence that Fly favored Margolin in assignments or promotions or that anyone in the legal department believed he had shown such favoritism. To the contrary, colleagues considered her work excellent, in spite of the prejudices against women lawyers in Tennessee at that time.[21] Although Fly won Margolin repeated promotions, so, too, he rewarded the extraordinary efforts of all the lawyers who worked on the two major constitutional cases and regularly sought raises for the rest of his legal staff.[22]

While Fly and Margolin's relationship escaped adverse consequence while they were at the agency, TVA management did not ignore another extramarital relationship in its legal department. Billie Thompson, a divorced mother of two children, was a stenographer who occasionally worked for Margolin. In the spring of 1938 Thompson was terminated, apparently for unsatisfactory performance. A month later she met with Fly to disclose what she believed were the real reasons for her termination and to ask for reinstatement. Thompson alleged that she had been fired in retaliation by Fly's assistant, James Barr. Barr was a married man with whom she had had a two-year affair and became pregnant. She suffered a miscarriage, which led to additional medical complications that caused her to miss work. Thompson described how she fell in love with Barr when they first joined TVA and how they managed to steal away together during workdays and in the evenings when Barr's wife was away.[23] Although she did not win reinstatement, Fly helped her secure a position with the Justice Department.[24] Barr did not dispute Thompson's revelations but instead resigned to avoid further embarrassment to the agency and to Fly. To protect Barr's reputation, TVA's personnel director agreed to inform inquirers only that he had resigned for purely personal reasons.[25] Fly, O'Brian, Melvin Siegel, and Herb Marks all helped Barr secure his position in Washington, D.C., with the Labor Department's Wage and Hour Division, where Margolin later joined him.[26]

Although Fly's staff never questioned his relationship with Margolin or his loyalty to Barr, there was one personnel matter that Fly's staff thought reflected especially poor judgment. According to Fitts and Fly's daughter, Fly had hired a lawyer as part of a plan to bring the lawyer's wife, Ruth, to Knoxville.[27] Ruth earlier had worked as Fly's secretary at the Justice Department in Washington, where their extracurricular involvement prompted attempts by Mildred Fly to get Ruth transferred out of Fly's office. According to Mildred Fly, her husband had lived with Ruth in Washington, just as he later lived with Bessie Margolin in Knoxville. Claiming to have caught her husband with each woman at different times, Mildred Fly alleged that he had continued his illicit relationship with both women after becoming FCC chairman.[28] Fly's FCC colleagues acknowledged his reputation as a man around town who may have had more than one mistress.[29]

Although no one from TVA's legal department complained about Margolin's relationship with Fly, John Franklin Pierce, TVA's office services director, raised the issue with agency management in 1939, after she had left. TVA had threatened to terminate Pierce for accepting gifts from and disclosing confidential information to a TVA contractor. Pierce denied wrongdoing and lodged a countercharge; Pierce claimed that TVA's general manager was using petty or false charges to fire him while ignoring far more serious conduct by high-ranking individuals. Pierce alleged that Fly consorted with Margolin and for that reason alone paid her a salary of five thousand dollars per year and unfairly promoted her over employees with real ability; indeed, Pierce also claimed that Margolin had antagonized the judge in one of her condemnation cases, making herself the laughingstock of the local bar.[30] Pierce described Fly's relationship with Margolin as "open, brazen, and obnoxious to the community, his office, and to his family," exemplified by an episode when Fly "was forced to separate said woman from his wife who publicly attacked her in the lobby of a TVA building in the presence of witnesses."[31] Within months after lodging his counterclaim, Pierce left TVA, having resolved what he later called an internal squabble on terms he declined to disclose, citing "legal ramifications."[32]

Although it would be nearly fifty years before the law recognized sexual harassment as unlawful sex discrimination, it is difficult to imagine that Fly and Margolin were unaware of the perils of a supervisor and subordinate romance, especially given the woeful consequences of the affair between Fly's assistant and Margolin's typist.[33] Margolin acted as if her credentials, hard work, and excellent performance at TVA protected her from claims that she had used her relationship with Fly for job advancement or as if she simply did not care what others said—surprisingly risky conduct for a woman who was working so hard to be accepted in a traditionally male world. She also must have deeply trusted Fly to believe that their relationship would not end badly for her. Her letters reveal a devotion to Fly, and while the relationship does not seem to have impacted her career, knowing that she was not the only woman with whom Fly had had an extramarital relationship (perhaps concurrently) and the reported public confrontations with his wife must have caused her personal anguish. Perhaps the attraction to an intellectual and charismatic peer, if not mentor, who deeply appreciated her intellect and ability simply overwhelmed Margolin's sense of propriety or caution.

Shortly after Margolin left TVA, a new opportunity opened for Fly, which turned out to be far more exciting and controversial than the antitrust job for which he had lobbied. President Roosevelt picked Fly to chair the Federal Communications Commission, a post he assumed in early September 1939, bringing his family to Washington, D.C. Their arrival coincided with a sudden and dramatic change in the tone of Margolin's letters to Herb Marks, who had left TVA for Portland, Oregon, to become general counsel to the Bonneville Power Administration, which Congress had created to construct a hydroelectric dam on the Columbia River. Less than seven months after she started at the Labor Department, a desperate Margolin sought to get away from Washington and asked Marks if he had a job for her at Bonneville. She had been happy about moving to her apartment in Washington's Glover Park, so her request reflects her serious concerns about staying there. In an unusually distressed tone she told him: "I will have to investigate other possibilities if you have no opening. My trip for Wages & Hours to New Orleans has been postponed indefinitely but I can't postpone moving that long."[34]

Although Margolin's letter gave no clue about the nature of her predicament, Marks must have understood, as he responded quickly by telegram. He was working on the matter and asked what she was currently earning and when she could come.[35] The next day Margolin wired back with her salary, offering to come in one month, and urged Marks to decide quickly.[36] By mid-December 1939 Margolin's problem, whatever it was, had abated. She had been working in New Orleans for weeks and expected to stay another month. Her long and timely trip had made her "problem in Washington" practically disappear. When she did return to Washington, she planned to move to a new abode, which she expected should make things work out.[37]

Although she never expressly stated it, a likely source of Margolin's trouble was Fly's wife, Mildred. In late 1939 Sally Fly Connell was ten years old when her mother took her to Margolin's Washington apartment looking for Fly. Mildred beat on the door, yelling, "My husband's in there."[38] Despite this disturbing encounter, Margolin's brief desperation to leave Washington, and her problem there, Fly and Margolin continued their relationship for at least four more years.

As Margolin's public profile and responsibilities at the Labor Department were expanding, so, too, were Fly's at the FCC. Chairman Fly, the devoted New Dealer, sought greater government involvement to diversify broadcast ownership and promote meaningful programming—a regulatory approach that startled and angered the broadcasting industry and their politically conservative defenders in Congress.[39] Fly rarely escaped the media's glaring spotlight, prompted by his public disputes with broadcasters, legislators, and FBI director J. Edgar Hoover. He would soon be called "the most dangerous man in the Government."[40] But while Wendell Willkie had used the term good-naturedly to acknowledge Fly's formidable skills in the courtroom, the moniker had become decidedly hostile.

Despite their busy schedules, Fly and Margolin managed to steal private time together, as captured by a series of letters Fly wrote to her between 1941 and 1944. All handwritten in pencil on ordinary ruled legal paper, Fly signed his letters to Margolin as "L," or the occasional "Thine," never using his name—or hers. Instead, he addressed her as "My own sweetheart," "My darling of New Orleans," "Precious one," and even "Sugar Pie," among other pet names, both in the greeting and several times within each letter, reflecting a possessive intimacy that also served to safeguard their confidences should the letters fall into the wrong hands. In some letters Fly recounted the public battles he had fought that day, such as having to fend off an attack by Congressman Martin Dies (D-Tex.), chairman of the House Special Committee to Investigate Un-American Activities, known as ardently anti-Communist and anti–New Deal.[41] In another letter he shared his success in shepherding a legislative amendment through the House and his disappointment in being left off the Censorship Advisory Board.[42]

Fly also used his letters to relay support and enthusiasm for Margolin's work, apparently an essential element of their relationship, such as when he sent her a March 1944 news clipping about the Labor Department's victory in a Supreme Court case for which Margolin had drafted the brief and helped solicitor general Charles Fahy prepare for his argument.[43] Fly acknowledged and encouraged her hard work with endearing phrases: "I know you've spent so much of your own grand and sweet self in that case and that principle—that it almost seems as if it were wholly your own. And methinks it a grand principle—regardless of how the varied special interests may react to it." In other examples Fly wished her good luck on her cases and regretted that he could not be with her to hear her argue.[44] Fly once proposed that she join him for a ten-day winter getaway, offering a shorter alternative over New Year's Eve if she absolutely had to work during Christmas.[45] Elsewhere he expressed concern for her well-being, saying in one letter, "You looked so sweet but so tired, too, that I was hurting myself."[46] Margolin and Fly also exchanged small favors and domestic activities. While Margolin was traveling in 1941, Fly stopped by her apartment to run the motor of her car and then reported, "It still starts and runs beautifully, my precious."[47]

In 1943 Fly's private relationship with Margolin suddenly became fodder for a Georgia congressman's vendetta against Fly and the FCC. In January, prompted by powerful Congressman E. Eugene Cox (D-Ga.), the House broadly authorized an investigation into whether the FCC, encompassing all personnel and activities, was acting lawfully and in the public interest. While introducing the resolution, Cox claimed that small broadcasters, newspapers having an interest in broadcasting, and military officers had complained that Chairman Fly was trying to impose a dictatorship over all media.[48] Cox called the FCC a "nest of Reds" and alleged that Fly was "rapidly becoming the most dangerous man in the Government."[49] Cox's rampage was largely aimed at Fly, who had first crossed the congressman in 1941. Serving as the Defense Communications Board's ex officio chairman, Fly had testified against legislation that would have expanded the FBI's wiretapping powers. Cox alleged that the bill Fly opposed would have permitted monitoring communication to Japan before Pearl Harbor and might have prevented the disaster, a charge contradicted by claims that the FBI had actually tapped telephone communications between Hawaii and Japan under authority specifically granted by Attorney General Tom Clark.[50] Cox also wanted to derail the FCC's investigation of a twenty-five-hundred-dollar check he had received for actively sponsoring a Georgia radio station's license application at the FCC.[51] As the check constituted evidence that Cox had peddled his influence, a federal crime, the FCC submitted its investigation file to the Justice Department for prosecution.

Despite a Justice Department attorney's April 1942 recommendation to Attorney General Biddle to present the case against Cox to a grand jury immediately, no indictment followed.[52] Instead, House Speaker Sam Rayburn appointed the powerful Cox to chair the committee to investigate the FCC and armed him with a sixty-thousand-dollar budget. Cox, in turn, hired Eugene Garey, a right-wing Wall Street lawyer, as the committee's general counsel.[53] Under Cox's direction, in addition to myriad subpoenas Garey served on the FCC, nearly crippling the agency by demanding truckloads of documents, Garey also targeted Fly's personal life. He ordered federal investigators to retrace Fly's steps over the previous decade, back to the start of his tenure as TVA general counsel. Although it was public knowledge that Margolin had frequently traveled with Fly and the rest of TVA's legal team on business, senior investigator Robert B. "Bugeye" Barker spent countless hours scrutinizing the extensive TVA travel records of both Fly and Margolin. Not surprisingly, he discovered that Margolin and Fly had made a total of sixteen trips to the same places at the same time. In a lengthy report Bugeye analyzed each trip, noting in red ink each instance the vouchers showed Margolin and Fly arriving and departing at the same time, traveling together by train or car, and staying in the same hotel, highlighting each time Margolin or Fly failed to submit a separate cab or hotel receipt. In his cover note to Garey alleging Fly and Margolin's use of government money to fund their romantic journeys, Bugeye reported, "The total amount paid out by the Treasurer of the United States on these 'Honeymoon' Vouchers is: $2,478.33."[54] No doubt Cox took pleasure in learning that he could accuse Fly of a misdeed with a price tag roughly equal to his own.

It is undeniable that Margolin and Fly made these trips at government expense. While it is also undeniable that their romance took root during this time, it is clear that the purpose of the trips, most of which were taken with Henry Fowler, Herbert Marks, and other members of TVA's legal staff, was to conduct official business. Moreover, the investigator cited nothing other than the absence of a hotel bill or cab receipt as evidence that Margolin and Fly were engaged in wrongdoing. It did not matter to Cox that these so-called honeymoon vouchers actually represented legitimate TVA expenses; the investigation went far beyond the cost of Fly's travels with Margolin.

In addition to Bugeye, Garey dispatched James Dunn, a former U.S. Secret Service agent, to Knoxville and other TVA locales in April and May 1943. Dunn's reports make clear he was sent to find damaging information about Fly. At the outset of his mission he wrote, "We will drive this bastard dizzy before we are finished with him."[55] Dunn amassed more than one hundred pages of sworn testimony from a dozen witnesses, the bulk of which recounted the comings and goings of Fly and Margolin. Although no transcripts or affidavits remain, a glimpse of the testimony is available from two sources. The committee preserved untranscribed notes written in the Pitman style of shorthand, decipherable only by the original stenographer, revealing to the untrained eye little substance but numerous easily recognizable names, such as Margolin, Fly, Margolin's Knoxville apartment building, "The Fritz," and those of TVA employees, including James Barr and James Pierce.[56] The committee also saved Dunn's handwritten letters, in which he recorded his activities in Knoxville identifying witnesses and a general sense of their testimony.

Dunn's letters reflect the extent to which people in Knoxville were aware of Margolin's relationship with Fly and their willingness to talk about it. A *Knoxville Journal* reporter described Margolin as "the girl Mr. Fly ran around with" and who received a series of rapid pay raises, none of which, the reporter alleged, she had earned because she was never engaged in the practice of law.[57] A stenographer assigned to TVA's condemnation cases reportedly heard that Mrs. Fly physically attacked Fly and Margolin on the street in Knoxville, representing either a variation of the same incident that Pierce had described four years earlier or a separate encounter.[58] Margolin's cook offered that Fly nearly always stayed in her apartment, while her landlord reported that Mrs. Fly showed up one Fourth of July to demand that Margolin be evicted for her immoral conduct.[59] From other sources Dunn reported that even after moving to Washington, D.C., Fly was living out of his house and went home only occasionally.[60]

By July 1943 Cox had all he needed to publicly disgrace Fly. According to Clifford Durr, Fly's fellow FCC commissioner and friend, Cox told Fly to "be a good boy" or he would disclose the affair to the press.[61] Although several of

Fly's FCC colleagues described Cox's threat to reveal Fly's affair with Margolin as "blackmail," it is not entirely clear what Cox was demanding from Fly as the quid pro quo. Being a "good boy" likely did not mean stopping the investigation about Cox's twenty-five-hundred-dollar payment, as the matter had earlier been turned over to the Justice Department but did not go forward because of the near impossibility of securing a conviction in Georgia, where the crime had occurred. Whether Cox was actually demanding something from Fly or simply wanted to run him out of office, the situation was distressing for Fly, who anguished over the threat that his love affair with Margolin would be revealed. In contrast to Fly's unflinching defense of the FCC and its personnel from the committee's outrageous subpoenas in the past, now his FCC colleagues witnessed a sudden and inexplicable change. Fly had never been known to back away from a fight, but when Durr suggested that the FCC should resist Cox's latest abusive demand for documents, including personal financial records, Fly said perhaps they should comply. Durr then found out about Fly's affair with Margolin and understood that Fly was caught in an embarrassing position. Fly showed up at Durr's house one night during the investigation, pacing back and forth in the front yard like a caged lion, afraid that Cox would disclose the scandal.[62] Whether Fly was concerned about the resulting embarrassment and damage to his own career and reputation or to Margolin's, or both, is uncertain. Years later Durr offered an explanation for Fly's dilemma: "Well, he had two kids in high school at the time, and we didn't have the same standards of morality—they were still a little bit Victorian at that time, much more than they are now."[63]

This was a time when adulterous affairs of public figures were willingly ignored by the press and caused little scandal so long as they remained secrets, even if poorly kept. If exposed in the full glare of a newspaper's headline, however, such affairs were deemed ruinous to careers and reputations. One notable contemporary example was Wendell Willkie's extramarital affair with writer Irita Van Doren, which escaped public mention even when Willkie held press conferences from the apartment they shared. Nevertheless, President Roosevelt reportedly held news of the affair in reserve to be used against Willkie's 1940 presidential campaign if Willkie were to disclose damaging information he had gathered about Vice President Henry Wallace.[64]

Just as House Speaker Sam Rayburn had the power to appoint Cox as chairman, he had the power to stop him from making Fly's private life public. And Congressman Lyndon Johnson, who was known in Washington as "Sam Rayburn's boy," was well positioned to enlist the senior legislator's aid. Johnson also had a personal incentive for helping the FCC; Lady Bird Johnson was awaiting FCC approval to broadcast her Texas radio station twenty-four hours a day at a new frequency. Durr's loyal assistant, W. Ervin "Red" James, who was intent on stopping Cox from revealing Fly's affair, seized the opportunity to take up the matter up with LBJ, who in turn took up the matter with Speaker Rayburn.[65] James later recounted what Johnson told him: "LBJ called me and he said, 'The Speaker called the Chairman in'— he's talking about Cox—'and told him, "Now, Gene, there ain't going to be no sex in this investigation. You understand me, Gene. There ain't going to be no sex. There's too damn many of us that are vulnerable on that score."' So they dropped it."[66]

Although it is unknown whether Congressman Johnson knew the name or anything else about the woman involved in the "sex" he and Rayburn kept out of Cox's investigation, *he* would later, as president, receive a report that Margolin had had an "illicit love affair" with Fly, thanks to an FBI name check he requested in 1964 while considering her nomination for a federal judgeship.[67] In any event Johnson and Rayburn successfully stopped Cox from asking Fly about the affair in the public hearings, sparing Fly and Margolin from certain embarrassment if not serious repercussions in their careers.

We are left to wonder how much Margolin knew about Cox's threat to reveal her romance with Fly and how she felt about having her private affairs scrutinized by so many people. Again, she left no record. She had, however, ongoing relationships with close colleagues still working at TVA, who likely told her that her records had been subpoenaed and that investigators had been asking about her. Despite the intrusions on her private life, the quality of her performance at work did not suffer. She had once been a twenty-four-year-old graduate student at Yale who received an unfavorable rating from a professor for letting personal problems distract her from an assignment. Since then she had dedicated herself to her career and learned to display only grace under pressure.

The investigation into the FCC and other facets of Fly's life, however, dragged on until the end of 1944, by which time congressional leaders convinced Cox to step down. They replaced him with Clarence Lea of California, who finally authored a report in January 1945, clearing the FCC of virtually all of twenty-four charges.[68] By then the beleaguered Larry Fly had already resigned as FCC chairman, which he described to President Roosevelt as "one of the world's most onerous jobs," and went into private practice in New York.[69]

Fly and Margolin continued their covert romance during the post-Cox stages of the investigation, as reflected by dated (or datable) letters he wrote when they were apart. In one March 1944 letter to his "Darling," who was traveling in Los Angeles, Fly explained that he had not written more "lest the letters started floating around losted." He described "three tough days before the so & so's," mocking some of the latest charges leveled against him by Republican congressman Louis E. Miller of Missouri, who had assumed Cox's role as Fly's nemesis. Fly recounted to Margolin how he rebuffed Miller's accusation that the FCC's Radio Intelligence Division had sent the navy on a wild-goose chase for enemy activity in the Aleutian Islands. Fly also wrote that he successfully refuted Miller's charge that he had charged sixteen bottles of seltzer water to the government. As it turned out, Fly explained, an industry member had paid the tab. With the charm that likely first endeared him to Margolin during their high-pressure TVA days, Fly quipped about Miller's seltzer accusation, "So that fizzed out!"[70]

But his letters also reveal a disquieting tension, with Margolin seeming to distance herself from Fly's bouts of possessiveness and suspicion. More than once, Fly described the sleeplessness and unbearable strain he suffered when he did not hear from her for two days, unable to understand why she could not spare even a few minutes to write him.[71] His desperate words reflect an unquenchable thirst for Margolin, at least when she was out of touch. At other times he seemed to demand little, as in one undated letter in which he wrote a single sentence, only "to say, as ever, how very much I love you."[72]

How did Margolin, in words or deeds, express her feelings to Fly? Did she ever make similar demands for a greater share of his time, expecting priority over the many other things and people in his life, such as his family? None of Margolin's letters to Fly remain, nor do we know if Fly would have continued to encourage her career ambitions had they married. But a relationship with a married man certainly kept her free of the career-inhibiting roles of full-time wife and mother. At some point in their relationship Fly gave Margolin his gold and ruby Naval Academy ring. Years later Margolin gave the ring to her nephew, telling him rather matter-of-factly that she had received it from a man who wanted to marry her but that the relationship had not worked out because she had not been ready to settle down.[73] Although it is uncertain when they ended their relationship, Fly wrote his last dated letters to Margolin in March 1944 and by the end of that year had resigned from the FCC and moved to New York to start a private law practice.

From his New York law firm Fly continued his high-profile and often controversial quest for individual liberties in the face of growing concerns for national security. In 1947, while serving as a labor arbitrator, Fly ordered that the National Council of Jewish Women reinstate a social worker it had discharged for allegedly using her job to promote Communist propaganda.[74] In 1949 he represented labor leader Harry Bridges, who faced deportation for falsely denying his membership in the Communist Party.[75] As an outspoken board member of the American Civil Liberties Union, Fly filed an amicus brief in the criminal prosecution of Judith Coplon, who was accused of spying for the Soviet Union. In the brief Fly took no position on Coplon's guilt or innocence, arguing only that she deserved a new trial because the court had admitted evidence obtained by the FBI's illegal wiretapping. Fly used the media—newspapers, magazines, and television—to publicly criticize what he called the "dirty business" of wiretapping, which he said posed a grave threat to American civil liberties, and to demand a congressional investigation of the FBI.[76]

In these efforts and others Fly personally antagonized FBI director J. Edgar Hoover throughout the time when Margolin, a federal employee, was subject to FBI scrutiny regarding her loyalty to the government.[77] As late as August 1951, in response to a White House request for any derogatory information it had about Fly, the FBI dedicated three of seventeen pages in its report to Fly's earlier "immoral association" with Margolin.[78] Moreover, while advocating for civil liberties, Fly often pitted himself against the U.S. attorney general, the solicitor general, and others in the Justice Department—many of the same lawyers who were then entrusting Margolin with increasing responsibility for the Labor Department's Supreme Court cases.

By the end of 1945 Margolin had argued her fifth case at the Supreme Court and had appeared in every federal circuit court in the country. She would spend the second half of 1946 in Nuremberg, Germany, helping organize American tribunals for the Nazi war crimes trials after World War II. Her rising career, his public controversies, and the inconvenience of a long-distance romance provided ample incentives to curtail their relationship.

Fly divorced his wife in December 1950; he married a twice-divorced New York socialite only eighteen days later, taking his new bride for a two-month trip around the world.[79] Fly retired in 1954, and the couple moved to Florida. Margolin's later correspondence with other colleagues suggests that she and Fly rarely, if ever, saw each other after their romance ended but harbored no ill feelings. Following a 1959 gathering of her TVA colleagues, Margolin asked Fly's longtime secretary: "Did Larry and his wife ever show up? I regretted missing them."[80] And in May 1962 O'Brian wrote to Margolin while she was traveling in Europe to report that Fly had undergone a serious operation followed by a long convalescence.[81] Fly died of cancer in January 1966.[82]

Harry Margolin in 1913 with his children, *from left,* Bessie (4), Jacob (2), and Dora (8), shortly before the girls were admitted to the Jewish Orphans' Home in New Orleans. *Courtesy of Malcolm Trifon.*

The Jambalaya

ANDERS, BAILEY, BROWN
EPLEY, FENNER, FULLILOVE, GLADNEY, GOODMAN
GORDY, HAGERTY, HENRIQUES, KLEINFELDT, LOWERY
MARGOLIN, MENUET, MITCHELL, MUDD, O'NEAL
PARKER, PARLONGUE, PRICE, RAMSEY, SANDFORD
SIZELER, STAHL, WEBER, WEINSTEIN, WISDOM

150

Tulane Law School, First Year Class, 1927–28. During her first year at Tulane, Margolin was the only woman in her class and in the entire law school. She graduated in 1930 with the second highest scholastic average. *Jambalaya,* 1928. *Courtesy of University Archives, Special Collections, Howard-Tilton Memorial Library, Tulane University, New Orleans, La.*

Margolin and Robert Butler in their last year at Tulane Law School. Their law-school romance ended in 1933; Margolin was too ambitious to become a full-time wife and home-maker and honored a pledge to her employer that she would not be distracted from her legal career by marriage. *Jambalaya*, 1930. *Courtesy of University Archives, Special Collections, Howard-Tilton Memorial Library, Tulane University, New Orleans, La.*

"N.O. Girl Aid to Yale Savant." Glowing recommendations from Tulane Law School won Margolin a coveted position as a research assistant at Yale Law School, where she became the first woman awarded Yale's Sterling Fellowship for graduate studies. By the time she earned her doctorate in law in May 1933, she had thoroughly impressed her faculty advisor, William O. Douglas, who was appointed to the Supreme Court six years later and supported Margolin throughout her career. *New Orleans Item-Tribune, August 21, 1931.*

"Staff of TVA Counsel Happy over Decision." In the second of two great constitutional challenges to TVA's power program, the agency's legal team, headed by James Lawrence Fly, *seated at far left,* gathered for this photo after prevailing before a three-judge federal court. Seated right of Fly are William C. Fitts, Henry ("Joe") Fowler, Melvin Siegel, and Margolin. Standing are Herbert Marks, Joseph Swidler, and Richard Mosher. *Chattanooga Times,* January 22, 1938. *Courtesy of Chattanooga Times Free Press.*

"Opponents in Battle over Press Freedom." By 1943 Margolin was championing the wage and hour rights of American workers under the Fair Labor Standards Act in federal courts across the country. In *Walling v. Sun Publishing* she was the Labor Department's chief trial counsel and also argued the appeal at the Sixth Circuit, where she prevailed against Elisha Hanson, counsel for the newspaper industry, shown here with Margolin. *Cincinnati Enquirer,* December 1, 1943.

Margolin's army identification
card for the Nazi War Crimes
Trials in Nuremberg, Germany.
On loan from the Labor Department, Margolin drafted the rules
establishing the American military
tribunals that presided over the
"Subsequent Proceedings."
Courtesy of Malcolm Trifon.

Margolin (*circled*) listens from the gallery as Justice Jackson delivers his summation
to the International Military Tribunal on July 26, 1946, in Nuremberg. Later that day
Margolin wrote Jackson, before whom she had already argued several times at the
Supreme Court, lauding his denunciation of Hermann Goering and other top Nazi war
crimes defendants as "powerful, stirring, and thrilling—not to mention unanswerable."
Papers of Robert H. Jackson, Library of Congress.

Margolin on Supreme Court steps, with U.S. Capitol in the background, 1954.
By 1954 Margolin had argued eleven times at the Supreme Court, on her way to a
career total of twenty-four arguments, of which she prevailed in twenty-one.
U.S. Labor Department photo. Courtesy of Malcolm Trifon.

Margolin with labor solicitor Stuart Rothman, 1954. Rothman was the sixth
(and longest-serving) of Margolin's eleven labor solicitors; her thirty-three years at the
Labor Department also spanned the administrations of six U.S. presidents (from FDR
to Nixon) and nine secretaries of labor (from Frances Perkins to James Hodgson).
U.S. Labor Department photo. Courtesy of Malcolm Trifon.

Federal Woman's Award winners with President Kennedy, May 1963. *From left:*
Katie Louchheim, assistant secretary of state; Margolin, associate solicitor, Department of
Labor; Dr. Eleanor Makel, supervisory medical officer, Department of Health, Education
and Welfare; Verna C. Mohagen, director of personnel, Soil Conservation, Department of
Agriculture; President Kennedy; Blanche Noyes, air marking specialist, FAA; Eleanor C.
Pressly, head, Vehicles Section, NASA; and Katherine Mather, chief, Petrography, U.S. Army
Engineer Waterways Experiment Station, Department of the Army. *Cecil Stoughton,
White House Photographs, John F. Kennedy Presidential Library and Museum, Boston.*

Robert W. Ginnane, 1960s. Ginnane, a former member of the Solicitor General's Office, was general counsel to the ICC from 1955 to 1970. He and Margolin surprised friends by announcing in 1981 they planned to marry, revealing a clandestine romance that had started more than two decades earlier. Ginnane died in 1984, never having married Margolin and only just beginning to enjoy their public life together. *Courtesy of Ellen Ginnane Gambrell.*

In January 1972 more than two hundred coworkers, family members, and friends as well as dozens of prominent judges and government officials attended a formal dinner at the Washington Hilton to mark Margolin's retirement. Retired chief justice Earl Warren (*seated*), before whom Margolin argued fifteen times, was one of many who sang her praises. Her great contribution to millions of American working people, said Warren, was the "flesh and sinews" she developed around the "bare bones" of the Fair Labor Standards Act. *U.S. Labor Department photo. Courtesy of Malcolm Trifon.*

Margolin took the opportunity at her retirement dinner to acknowledge the people who had supported her throughout her career, including Justice William O. Douglas, seated at table 6 and turned to face the lectern, with his wife, Catherine, to his left. U.S. Fifth Circuit judge John Minor Wisdom, who shared history with Margolin going back to their student days at Newman School and Tulane Law School, sits next to Mrs. Douglas. Wisdom partially obscures Justice Goldberg, seated at table 7, with white hair and glasses, who had served as secretary of labor from January 1961 to September 1962. *U.S. Labor Department photo. Courtesy of Malcolm Trifon.*

At her retirement dinner, Margolin introduces Justice Abe Fortas, whom she met at
Yale Law School in 1930, and his wife, Carolyn Agger, to Carin Clauss. Before Margolin
retired, she groomed the talented Clauss to take over as associate solicitor. In 1978
President Carter appointed Clauss solicitor of labor, the first woman to hold the post.
U.S. Labor Department photo. Courtesy of Malcolm Trifon.

Four veteran Supreme Court advocates catch up at Margolin's retirement dinner. *From left:* Daniel Friedman, first deputy solicitor general; Oscar Davis, judge, U.S. Court of Claims; Bea Rosenberg, criminal appeals chief, Justice Department; and Margolin. Mabel Walker Willebrandt (29 arguments), Rosenberg (28), and Margolin (24) set the record for the twentieth century as the top three female advocates with the highest number of Supreme Court arguments. *U.S. Labor Department photo. Courtesy of Malcolm Trifon.*

Margolin in Berkeley, California, 1980. *Courtesy of Malcolm Trifon.*

6

WAGES AND HOURS
1939–1946

On March 16, 1939, Bessie Margolin began her job as a senior litigation attorney at the Labor Department's fledgling Wage and Hour Division, making a lateral move from TVA that reflected her eagerness for a new opportunity back in Washington, D.C. There labor secretary Frances Perkins, the first woman appointed to a cabinet position, had just begun to implement the Fair Labor Standards Act of 1938 (FLSA), legislation she proudly nurtured from a draft locked in her desk drawer until President Roosevelt was ready to press for it.[1] Although Perkins left no clear imprint on Margolin's hiring, over the next six years Margolin's contributions to the FLSA's formative legal work would leave a distinct impression on Perkins.

When the FLSA was enacted in June 1938, President Roosevelt proclaimed it second only to the Social Security Act of 1935 as the most far-reaching and far-sighted program for workers ever adopted.[2] Prior to its passage, adults and children across the country, at least those lucky enough to find jobs during the Depression, often worked cruelly long hours to earn starvation wages. As he related the apocryphal story, Roosevelt's defining moment to press for Perkins's wage and hour law occurred as he campaigned for his second term. A young Massachusetts garment factory worker passed him a note about a recent wage cut that left her and two hundred other girls earning as little as $4 a week. "You are the only man who can do anything about it," the desperate girl wrote the president. "We cannot live on $4 or $5 or $6 a week."[3]

Despite public perception, Roosevelt explained at a 1936 press conference, the president had no power to set wages and hours or to eliminate child labor. Only Congress had such power and then only so long as the Supreme Court did not later invalidate Congress's action, as it had done earlier to federal efforts governing child labor and minimum wages.[4] Convinced of the wisdom and rightness of federal measures to address the miserable conditions facing countless Americans such as the Massachusetts factory worker, Roosevelt called on Congress to act: "A self-supporting and self-respecting democracy can plead no justification for the existence of child labor, no economic reason for chiseling workers' wages or stretching workers' hours."[5]

Congress responded by enacting the FLSA. The law banned products manufactured for interstate commerce by children under sixteen years of age and goods manufactured in hazardous industries by youths under eighteen. It also mandated a minimum hourly wage (to be increased from twenty-five to forty cents an hour by 1945) and set a maximum workweek (to be reduced from forty-four to forty hours per week by 1941), subject to an overtime wage rate at one and a half times the regular rate of pay. By restricting the number of hours an employee could work before being entitled to overtime pay, the FLSA was designed to reduce unemployment by forcing employers to hire more workers. Constitutionally limited to interstate commerce, the FLSA also reflected political concessions; it exempted the railroad industry and others from the overtime requirement and entirely excluded other categories of workers, such as domestic and agricultural workers. All told, as of April 1939, the FLSA covered about one-fifth of the nation's workforce, or about 13 million workers; of these the law promised immediately to increase the wages of some 700,000 workers and to reduce the hours or provide overtime pay to about 1.6 million workers, those numbers to increase as the wage and hour standards were phased in.[6] Despite its limitations, the FLSA represented a turning point in American public policy, endowing the federal government with a social responsibility for the nation's wage earners.[7]

As with TVA and other New Deal programs, new laws created jobs for lawyers. Despite her academic credentials and extensive legal experience at TVA, Margolin still had to prove her value to secure a job at the Labor Department's new Wage and Hour Division. She had asked for a salary of fifty-six hundred dollars, which Calvert Magruder, Wage and Hour's general counsel, thought was an awful lot "for a girl." John Lord O'Brian, Abe Fortas, and Larry Fly eagerly aided her negotiations, trying to help her convince Magruder that she was a seasoned attorney. Describing her familiar predicament in a letter to Herb Marks, Margolin asked, "Did I hear you laugh, Herb—or are you only smiling?"[8] With Magruder's assurances that she would receive responsible assignments, Margolin finally settled for the same five thousand dollars a year she had been earning at TVA.[9]

In her first week on the job, Margolin traveled home to New Orleans on business. She accompanied litigation chief Irving Levy to oppose a company's improper service of subpoenas on agency officials, one of the FLSA's many basic procedural issues being addressed for the first time. She and Levy divided the arguments, and both won favorable rulings, which the judge announced from the bench.[10] The case generated considerable publicity that focused as much on Margolin herself as the Wage and Hour victory. Celebrating her triumphant return to her hometown as a lawyer for the federal government, three New Orleans newspapers ran stories about her.[11]

Margolin loved her new job, where she was encouraged to take on as much responsibility as she wished to assume in enforcing a law that comported with her view of government as an institution of social justice. "I'm interested in labor and I'm a New Dealer," she told the press. Considering the large categories of jobs expressly excluded from the FLSA and the phasing in of the relatively modest minimum wage, Margolin described the FLSA as "pretty conservative" but a step in the right direction. She added a caveat, "Incidentally, I'm not a radical," likely distancing herself from a small but vocal group of TVA employees who had attracted attention by touting Communist sympathies in support of workers' rights.[12]

Although the press emphasized the exciting aspects of her job, Margolin also paid her dues, assisting in tiresome fact gathering that almost made her yearn for her old TVA condemnation cases. Dispatched to mill towns outside Boston to prepare Wage and Hour cases for trial, she quietly complained in a letter to Marks that she had never been in a "drearier dingier atmosphere." Although she expected she was getting helpful experience, she found the work very tedious and dull—mulling over endless time cards, piecework slips, payroll records, and invoices. "I didn't realize what a deadly bore the trial of some cases can be," she complained to Marks. Doubting that she could endure much more of the same, she decided to seek a transfer to opinion work.[13]

Within six months Margolin's case load greatly expanded, alleviating her desire to transfer. In her next press interview a few months later, Margolin described the practice of law as "exciting and as pleasant a way of earning a living as I can think of." Acknowledging the handicap women faced entering the legal profession, Margolin considered herself particularly fortunate. In her view government service offered women lawyers the best opportunity, compared to private practice, because there was less reluctance about hiring women for the abundant desk work that dominated the government's legal affairs. Recognizing that she enjoyed certain advantages in her own legal career, she added, "However, I have as much litigation as deskwork."[14]

Whether for desk work or litigation, Margolin went out of her way to share legal opportunities with other women. She sought to fill the void she left at TVA by recommending that Larry Fly and Herb Marks hire a top female Tulane law student she met while in New Orleans. Ironically, Margolin's recommendation sounded like the way she had been described by some of her own male supporters, well-meaning but sexist. She depicted the student as "bright and hardworking—well poised & attractive in appearance" yet "not disconcertingly so." Moreover, Margolin offered the young woman for nonlawyer work that may not have been asked of a man. "Seemed to me," Margolin wrote Marks, "she would be a good research person to have around Chattanooga & she might run your library, too—and finally I think you all should have at least one woman lawyer down there." Just as Richard Joyce Smith had characterized Margolin as one of the best if TVA had a place for a woman lawyer, Margolin offered the same limited praise for her female candidate. "She is the best qualified one I've seen in some time & heartily recommend her to you." Although the student's experience at the *Tulane Law Review* might not compare with Marks's work for Harvard's law review or her own for Yale's law journal, Margolin used Ivy League elitism in the young woman's favor: "I think you may be able to use her for tasks which these loftier ones might disdain."[15] Despite Margolin's recommendation, TVA did not hire the student; nearly a decade would pass before TVA hired another woman lawyer after Margolin left.[16]

Before 1939 ended, Margolin returned to New Orleans to attend a meeting with Fifth Circuit judge Rufus Foster and a Mississippi lawyer who represented fourteen southern textile mills. Judge Foster had convened the parties to discuss *Opp Cotton Mills v. Administrator,* one of two Supreme Court–bound cases filed by business interests to challenge the FLSA's constitutionality.[17] Margolin offered valuable connections; Judge Foster had served on the Fifth Circuit panel that presided over TVA's successful *Ashwander* appeal and was a former dean of Tulane Law School who remained involved with its law review while Margolin was an editor. Moreover, Margolin brought her experience from defending TVA to the *Opp* conference and helped write the brief the department later filed in the Fifth Circuit, which upheld the FLSA.[18]

By the time *Opp* reached the Supreme Court, where it was joined by a lumber mill's challenge to the FLSA in *United States v. Darby*, two significant events portended success for the law: the nation's highest tribunal had finally sanctioned a state's minimum wage legislation in *West Coast Hotel v. Parrish* (1937); and President Roosevelt's recent Court appointments had replaced progressive economic legislation opponents (Justices Willis Van Devanter, George Sutherland, and Pierce Butler) and supporters (Justice Benjamin Cardozo and Louis Brandeis) with justices sympathetic to the New Deal (Senator Hugo Black, Solicitor General Stanley Reed, Harvard professor Felix Frankfurter, Securities and Exchange commissioner and former Yale law professor William O. Douglas, and Attorney General Frank Murphy). In February 1941, not surprisingly, the Supreme Court upheld the FLSA in both cases, holding that Congress's power to regulate interstate commerce encompassed the production as well as the transport of goods and that the FLSA therefore could prohibit the shipment of goods in interstate commerce produced under its "forbidden substandard conditions."[19] Over the years that followed, the Supreme Court often revisited the FLSA to interpret its provisions. By Margolin's 1972 retirement from the Labor Department, *Opp* and *Darby* would number among the department's few Supreme Court FLSA cases in which Margolin did not materially shape the brief or present oral argument.

In July 1940, a few months after the *Opp* hearing at the Fifth Circuit, Harry Margolin died in New Orleans.[20] Although only sixty-three, Harry lived long enough to see his children succeed. By this time Jack, who had earned an MBA degree from Dartmouth, was starting a promising business career in Atlanta. Dora, after working as the Home's nurse, had married Dr. Harry Trifon, who practiced medicine in Shreveport, Louisiana, where they were raising their young boys, Rudy and Toby, with Malcolm to follow a few years later. As for Bessie, Harry's first American-born child, there is evidence, albeit scant, that she maintained contact with her father; in 1935 he provided her an affidavit to explain the errant spelling of her name on her birth certificate.[21] If she and her siblings did not keep their father apprised of Bessie's rising career, he needed only to read the local papers to know that she was earning a living as a New Deal lawyer who had defended the TVA and now enforced laws to protect workers in many industries, from mop makers and private security guards to furniture movers.[22] Those laws, however, could not help a peddler such as Harry improve his financial condition; his estate amounted to little more than a favorite enameled cigarette lighter he asked Dora to give one of his grandsons.[23] In spite of the tenuous role he played in his children's lives, Harry Margolin had every reason to be satisfied that he had done the right thing by entrusting his children's care to the Jewish Orphans' Home.

By October 1940 Bessie was promoted to supervising attorney, with an increased salary of fifty-six hundred dollars per year. In her new position she assumed a larger role in FLSA trial and appellate matters, including directing the work of other lawyers. Margolin was on her way to becoming known by all, and feared by some, as an equal opportunity perfectionist who held her staff to the same exceptionally high standards she set for herself. She conducted some of the most significant litigation for the labor solicitor's national and regional offices; she trained and reviewed the work of up to twenty regional attorneys, including one woman who headed the San Francisco office. She did this while continuing to directly supervise and encourage eight attorneys, including three women, in her Washington, D.C., office.[24]

Among her early trials, Margolin was particularly proud of her work in the department's successful test case over the FLSA provision that allowed employers to deduct from employees' wages the reasonable cost (which the department contended was actual cost without profit) of board, lodging, or other facilities furnished to employees.[25] The provision was enacted to prevent chiseling employers from using company stores and other devices to offset the minimum wage. The Peavy-Wilson Lumber Company employed 325 millworkers and log cutters in and around Holopaw, Florida, a company town seventeen miles from the nearest location of any consequence, where Margolin traveled to interview employees.[26] The government challenged as predatory the company's practice of issuing coupons, or "scrip," in lieu of wages, which the company cashed at only 90 percent of face value or exchanged at face value for groceries and other goods at the company store at inflated prices. After a lengthy trial in Shreveport, Louisiana, during which Margolin briefed numerous factual, accounting, and legal issues, the federal judge found that the lumber mill's practices violated the FLSA, a law he recognized had been enacted to prevent unconscionable employers from exploiting workers, thereby protecting not only their health and well-being but the financial well-being of their community as well.[27]

In another example of her early FLSA litigation, Margolin took to trial *Fleming v. Alterman,* the department's first case to test whether wholesalers

were engaged in interstate commerce—a prerequisite of the federal law—
when they distributed, wholly within one state, goods received from out-
of-state sources.[28] Within the Atlanta federal courtroom Margolin's trial
pertained to only sixteen employees of the Alterman Brothers' wholesale
grocery business; beyond that courtroom, however, the Labor Department
could use a favorable ruling to persuade federal courts across the country
to adopt the same interpretation, ultimately benefiting tens of thousands
of workers in similarly organized enterprises. As there was no definite and
unvarying formula to determine whether employees were engaged in commerce, Margolin had to marshal a compelling body of evidence, tailored to
Alterman's business, to prove that the goods it procured from other states
did not leave the stream of commerce simply because it took possession
of them before selling them locally. Through witnesses and documents
Margolin showed that Alterman increased its profits by quickly moving in-
ventory out of its warehouse, frequently delivered goods never stored in its
warehouse, and directly competed with out-of-state wholesalers. On these
facts and others she convinced the judge that Alterman engaged in interstate
commerce and therefore could not deny its employees FLSA protections.[29]

In those early days Margolin watched as cases she and her colleagues
had won at trial or on appeal went on to be argued at the Supreme Court by
more senior lawyers, all men, from the Solicitor General's Office or Labor
Department. In some of those cases her male superiors failed to prevail in
the high court, losing advantages Margolin and her colleagues had earlier
gained for the government. This happened in *Cudahy Packing of Louisiana,
Ltd. v. Fleming,* one of Margolin's earliest appellate successes.[30] After briefing almost every conceivable objection the company could raise, Margolin
convinced the Fifth Circuit to affirm the trial judge's order compelling the
meatpacker to testify and produce wage and hour records in response to
a regional administrator's subpoena. The company had challenged the
subpoena, arguing that the statute did not expressly authorize the Wage
and Hour administrator to delegate his subpoena authority to the regional
administrator.[31] The Supreme Court took the case and, after argument by
labor solicitor Warner Gardner, reversed the Fifth Circuit's favorable ruling
and held that the administrator lacked authority to delegate his subpoena
power.[32] In his memoir Gardner called the Court's five-four vote a "galling
defeat" that never would have been lost had he been able to convince just
one more justice that a statutory subpoena power necessarily implies the

power to delegate signature when hundreds must be issued across the nation each week.[33] However disappointing for Gardner, Margolin could look to this and other defeats in FLSA cases to counter occasional disparagements of her successes by those who claimed that winning an FLSA case at the Supreme Court required little more than showing up.

Walling v. Sun Publishing was the first major FLSA case in which Margolin was the department's chief trial counsel and also argued the circuit court appeal.[34] At the Sixth Circuit in Cincinnati, Margolin found herself opposing the immensely clever Elisha Hanson, one of the nation's most prominent media lawyers, who represented the American Newspaper Publishers Association.[35] Wearing a well-tailored suit that revealed her slender waist and a V-neck blouse trimmed with soft ruffles, Margolin entered the courtroom holding a handkerchief in one hand and her smart leather briefcase in the other. Hanson argued that freedom of the press, due process, and the limitations of interstate commerce shielded newspaper companies from FLSA's mandates. After argument he told reporters, "When regulation enters the door of the press, independence flies out the window," claiming that the trial court's judgment would effectively stop shipment of papers outside the state. In her argument Margolin called Hanson's objections "meritless," as the newspaper publishing business was indeed conducting interstate commerce. As for the claimed infringement of a free press, Margolin dismissed it as "almost a frivolous issue," adding that it was "so far removed from the intent of the First Amendment that it does not apply."[36] The Sixth Circuit agreed with Margolin and affirmed the trial court's ruling for the government.[37] Hanson sought review, which Margolin opposed and the Supreme Court denied, allowing the Sixth Circuit's ruling to stand.[38] Margolin had not only won a significant FLSA victory, but she had prevailed against Hanson, a formidable opponent who had earlier prevailed in an FLSA case against Solicitor General Francis Biddle.[39]

Throughout the *Sun Publishing* case Margolin was quietly pursuing a more personal fair labor case. As she continued to assume greater trial and appellate responsibilities, both personally and as a supervisor, Margolin sought to be considered for promotion to assistant solicitor, a position she had seen given to men with inferior qualifications than she had, in terms of education and length and quality of professional work.[40] Margolin presented her case directly to Frances Perkins, acknowledging in a cover letter that her request for Perkins's personal attention might appear presumptuous but that she was sure that if the labor secretary would read her memorandum, she would appreciate the propriety of approaching her directly. Margolin asked Perkins to face squarely the discrimination that prevented a woman from being considered for promotion to assistant solicitor. Despite the very limited number of these higher positions, to which no one could reasonably claim an absolute entitlement, Margolin asserted that the record strongly indicated that she had not been fairly considered.[41]

With the same cool logic she applied in her cases, Margolin offered as further evidence of discrimination not only the men chosen to fill the higher positions within the department but also the more advanced careers in other government agencies attained by her former TVA associates and fellow Yale Law School students, despite comparable training, standing, and experience. Margolin then urged Secretary Perkins to consider the relatively modest and justified advancement she sought in terms of its implications generally for women seeking professional careers in government service: "My situation, the record will show, has significance beyond the interests of one individual." Margolin also stressed that her failure to be considered for promotion was not because her superiors lacked confidence in her. To the contrary, they had given her responsible and interesting assignments and never questioned the quality of her performance. "For all practical purposes," she maintained, "in the day-to-day work, they have accepted me as one of them."[42]

"One of them"—and by *them* she meant the male attorneys with whom she worked—is exactly what Margolin wanted to be. She assigned no malice to the disadvantage she faced and took pains to emphasize that she was not claiming there had been intentional discrimination or that responsibility attached to any one individual. She believed it was a general, subconscious attitude. "A woman simply is not considered for the high ranking positions in the Solicitor's Office."[43] Labor's personnel director Robert Smith investigated Margolin's complaint and reported to Secretary Perkins that with only one possible exception he could see no justifiable basis for Margolin's claim of discrimination. Regardless, Smith suggested deferring Margolin's request until a new solicitor arrived so he could determine whether to recommend Margolin or some other qualified person as assistant solicitor.[44] Apparently, Secretary Perkins did not want to wait. In October 1942, just one month after Margolin pleaded her own case, acting solicitor Irving Levy recommended that she be made assistant solicitor, and Secretary Perkins promptly approved the promotion.[45]

Margolin's new position came with a nine-hundred-dollar increase in pay, raising her salary to sixty-five hundred dollars per year, equal to more than ninety-eight thousand dollars today.[46] Her responsibilities continued to grow. She was entrusted with overseeing the Labor Department's appellate work in state courts, circuit courts, and, under the solicitor general's direction, the United States Supreme Court. This included assigning and approving briefs and oral arguments to attorneys on the labor solicitor's staff and setting litigation policies, subject only to the approval of the solicitor or associate solicitor. Margolin took charge of preparing memoranda and collecting decisions, analyzing important opinions of trial and appellate courts, as well as making periodic reports to Secretary Perkins and the administrators of the Wage and Hour and Public Contracts divisions. Most important for Margolin's future career as a Supreme Court advocate, her new job brought her into frequent contact with the solicitor general and his staff at the Justice Department.[47]

Although Margolin did everything in her power to act like one of the male attorneys for purposes of pay, promotion, and other professional opportunities, she made no attempt to act masculine or even blend in. Instead, she used some of her increased earnings to make her wardrobe and hairstyle as elegant, dignified, and feminine as possible. While enforcing federal laws to protect America's poorest wage earners and children, she strode into courtrooms with the carriage and refinement of Hanna Stern and other genteel New Orleans women who had dedicated themselves to fostering the Home's wards.

Margolin's rise in responsibility and visibility in the Labor Department coincided with World War II and the dramatic influx of five million women into the labor force between 1940 and 1944. By the mid-1940s approximately eighteen million American women worked, with nearly one million of them working for the federal government.[48] It was patriotism and community service that employers and policy makers touted to welcome women during the war years, skirting the notion that women desired to work for its own sake and conveniently justifying their return to the home at war's end. Although professional women, represented by groups such as the National Federation of Business and Professional Women's Clubs, fared better than women wage earners in retaining wartime labor gains, all faced pressures to conform to prewar social roles.[49] After the war, women who wanted to work faced resentment from those who opposed giving jobs to women who did not need them.

Margolin could not be accused of neglecting a husband or children, but she still had to contend with pervasive notions that ambitious career women were dangerous or neurotic. A 1947 best-selling book, *Modern Woman: The Lost Sex,* urged women to avoid law or other fields that belonged to the "male area of exploit or authority." If women nonetheless entered such fields, the authors warned, they should expect the discrimination they received. Besides, such women were bound to be emotionally unstable, quarrelsome, and lacking in the focused imagination that makes a man work steadfastly on a long project.[50] These fears were bolstered by popular culture. Moviegoers of the mid-1940s watched Joan Crawford, an ambitious businesswoman, ruin lives and cause deaths in *Mildred Pierce,* and Ginger Rogers, who learned through psychoanalysis that her work as a magazine editor denied her femininity in *Lady in the Dark.*[51] Women who persistently ventured into a man's world were said to be "de-sexed" or to suffer from a deep illness that caused them to reject their natural instincts in a futile attempt to become men.[52] Meanwhile, concerns were being voiced about sexual and romantic relationships in federal government offices. Not only were men's unwanted sexual behaviors at issue, but women (especially those over thirty) feared losing hard-earned advantages to younger and more attractive women. That men surrounded themselves with attractive women was no surprise, but it was nevertheless seen as women's role to set moral standards and to keep men in line.[53] As a striking woman who rejected traditional roles by directly competing with men in a powerful career and who had once captured the heart of her married boss, Margolin walked a fine line between accomplishment and controversy.

Margolin forged ahead, performing high-quality work that continued to earn her recognition within and beyond the Labor Department. In December 1943 labor solicitor Douglas Maggs shared with Secretary Perkins solicitor general Charles Fahy's praise for Margolin's work in *Tennessee Coal, Iron & Railroad Company v. Muscoda.* Fahy considered the Supreme Court brief, "99 percent" of which Maggs attributed to Margolin, about the best brief that had ever been written for him outside the Department of Justice.[54] Margolin had argued the case, and prevailed, in the Fifth Circuit.[55] While preparing Fahy to argue the case at the Supreme Court, she mentioned that she had argued appeals in every one of the eleven federal circuits. An impressed Fahy promised to let her argue in the Supreme Court when the next FLSA case came up. Less than a year later the Supreme Court granted certiorari in an FLSA case, and Fahy honored his promise by assigning the oral argument to Margolin.[56] He chose Margolin, he later explained, because of "the excellence of her grasp of these complicated legal problems, coupled with her clarity of thinking and expression."[57]

Notwithstanding her intelligence and talent, Fahy's decision to choose Margolin to present argument at the Supreme Court was remarkable. Presenting the position of the United States government at the high court on behalf of a cabinet department, such as the Labor Department, was a responsibility and privilege reserved almost exclusively for lawyers in the Solicitor General's Office or elsewhere in the Justice Department. Where exceptions were made, they were often limited to the department's general counsel or top deputy.[58] Moreover, before Margolin only twenty-four women had ever argued at the Supreme Court, and two of them were parties to the litigation who were permitted to represent themselves. In fact, Margolin was one of only three women to argue at the Supreme Court during the entire 1945 calendar year, all well-respected federal government attorneys to whom the meritocratic Fahy had assigned argument.[59]

Preparing for Margolin's first Supreme Court argument involved more than law, as a close friend years later proudly recalled planning what Margolin should wear for her first appearance.[60] As with other pioneering women lawyers, including those who appeared at the high court, choice of apparel was a serious matter of form and function. When the *Women Lawyers Journal* asked in 1944, "What does the well dressed woman lawyer wear before the United States Supreme Court?" Helen Carloss, who had already argued twelve of her career total of twenty-one times, replied that protocol required either a dark dress with long sleeves or a coat suit. She had always worn a black suit with a plain white blouse simply because the attire made her feel more comfortable and less conspicuous.[61] Margolin left no record of her early Supreme Court attire, although she surely would not have deviated from the expected black outfit; much later in her career, however, one colleague recalls Margolin breaking the black color code, at least in the circuit courts, by wearing a "wonderful" bright blue suit.[62]

Margolin argued her first case, *Phillips v. Walling,* at the Supreme Court on March 2, 1945.[63] When she took her turn at the podium, she asked the justices to affirm the First Circuit's decision, in which associate labor solicitor Archibald Cox had prevailed in asserting that an FLSA exemption for employees of a "retail establishment" did not include warehouse and central office workers of an interstate grocery store chain.[64] Margolin's opponent in the Supreme Court was former Massachusetts governor Joseph B. Ely, who, after losing the 1944 Democratic presidential nomination, had demonstrated his contempt for Roosevelt and his New Deal by supporting Republican Thomas Dewey. Although there is no audio recording of Margolin's first argument (or of her other pre-1955 arguments), her former Yale law professor William O. Douglas, by then a Supreme Court justice, later described Margolin's argument style: "She was crisp in her speech and penetrating in her analyses, reducing complex factual situations to simple, orderly problems." Douglas deemed Margolin's argument in *Phillips v. Walling* as typical of the "worrisome but important issues" that she argued at the Supreme Court.[65] Douglas was in a position to know; he would serve on the bench for all twenty-four of the arguments she presented throughout her career.

After what must have been a lively argument with an active bench, Justice Robert H. Jackson, who had earlier proved an outstanding oral advocate as solicitor general, marked the occasion with a handwritten note: "You have every reason to feel satisfied with the way you took care of yourself under fire. I'm sure there would be no dissent from the opinion that you should argue here often. One always feels low after an argument—at least I always did. But you need not."[66] Although Jackson typically encouraged younger lawyers, this and later notes he sent to Margolin reflected a special connection.[67] Not only was Margolin one of the rare women to argue in the Supreme Court, but Jackson had heard only good things about her from their mutual mentor and friend John Lord O'Brian. Jackson, who was admitted to the Supreme Court bar on O'Brian's motion, succeeded O'Brian as assistant attorney general in charge of the Antitrust Division.[68] Touched by Jackson's note, Margolin promptly thanked him: "Nothing could have served better to lift that 'low' post-argument feeling of which you speak."[69]

Just three weeks later Margolin learned that she had won *Phillips v. Walling* and in so doing established the fundamental principle that any exemption from the FLSA's humanitarian and remedial legislation must be narrowly construed.[70] The news quickly reached Secretary Perkins, who sent hearty congratulations. Perkins was pleased to learn that Margolin had made an "unusually good argument, so much so that the Justices asked a lot of questions, which always denotes an unusual interest and an intelligent presentation."[71] Her victory and the good wishes from Justice Jackson and Secretary Perkins buoyed Margolin's confidence as she prepared to argue the next case Fahy assigned to her, *10 East 40th Street Building, Inc. v. Callus,* which was less than two weeks away.

When the day arrived, Margolin unexpectedly learned that she would be presenting not one but two arguments to the Supreme Court.[72] Although she had also worked on the brief for *Borden Company v. Borella,* Fahy had assigned oral argument to Chester Lane, a senior attorney in the Solicitor General's Office. On the morning of the argument Lane lost his voice—he could hardly whisper. At 10:30 a.m., as Margolin was making last-minute preparations to argue *Callus* at noon, assistant solicitor general Bob Stern called Margolin. Solicitor General Fahy wanted Margolin to argue *Borden,* too, because she knew more about the case than anyone else besides Lane. Stern gave her the courage to go on, saying that she had nothing to lose because the Court would know the circumstances. Indeed, when the case was called, Lane rose and hoarsely whispered to the Court that Margolin was pinch-hitting on very short notice. Years later she recalled making a pretty lousy argument in *Borden,* as she was overwhelmed with fear and nervousness.[73] As it turned out, the Court ruled in her favor in *Borden* (by a seven-two decision) but ruled against her in *Callus* (by a five-four decision), the case she had prepared to argue that day.[74] In any event Margolin's incipient career as a Supreme Court advocate certainly did not suffer.

With her Supreme Court record at two wins and one loss, Solicitor General Fahy again acknowledged Margolin's qualifications by assigning her two more FLSA Supreme Court arguments in 1945, *Roland Electrical Company v. Walling,* which she argued on October 8, and *Boutell v. Walling,* which followed the next day. She earned favorable rulings in both cases. In *Roland Electrical Company* the Court adopted the department's view that the FLSA's coverage of Roland's employees (who repaired equipment for industrial and commercial customers) was premised on the fact that their work was necessary to the production of commodities produced for commerce by Roland's customers and that Roland was not entitled to the exemption for "service establishments," which were limited to local merchants, local grocers, or filling stations whose customers buy for personal consumption.[75] Douglas Maggs, a former labor solicitor who was now teaching law at Duke University, recognized Margolin's victory in *Roland* as an important narrowing of FLSA's section 13(a)(2) exemption. "What a victory!!" Maggs enthusiastically wrote. "Not only in this case, of course, but in all 13(a)(2) matters. And a unanimous court! And what an opinion! Sure you didn't write it?"[76] In Margolin's other case, *Boutell,* the Supreme Court affirmed the Sixth Circuit's conclusion that the mechanics employed by a business that repaired transportation equipment used in interstate commerce by another business were themselves engaged in interstate commerce and were therefore protected by the FLSA.[77]

Sandwiched between Margolin's arguments in *Roland* and *Boutell* was *Martino v. Michigan Window Cleaning Company,* an FLSA suit by window washers who cleaned industrial plants.[78] The government, which had filed an amicus brief in support of the window washers that Margolin helped write, declined to present oral argument in the case. Nevertheless, when Margolin reached the podium to argue *Boutell,* several justices bombarded her with questions on *Martino* until the five-minute warning light came on. Seeing her predicament, Bob Stern slipped Margolin a note suggesting that she request extra time. Margolin's deferential plea for a few extra minutes to argue the case assigned to her was futile; Chief Justice Harlan Stone curtly replied, "You have only four minutes left to complete your argument, Miss Margolin." Justice Douglas then posed a tough question, her answer to which consumed the remaining time.[79] Although an apparently unsatisfied Douglas dissented in *Boutell,* the Court's rulings to extend FLSA coverage in all three cases further enhanced Margolin's reputation as a Supreme Court advocate who could think on her feet.[80]

As Margolin was making her first appearances in the Supreme Court, she was also focusing her efforts and those of the regional attorneys on convincing trial judges not only to find that employers had violated the FLSA but also to issue injunctions to prevent future violations. The FLSA empowered courts to issue injunctions for cause but left that determination to the court's discretion. Even after finding that an employer had violated the act, some judges, particularly in the South, where there was distaste for the law, looked to the employer's contrite demeanor on the witness stand or his general good reputation in the community and refused the government's request for an injunction. Judge Sidney C. Mize, for example, sitting in a Mississippi federal district court, refused to issue the requested injunction, even though he found that two vegetable-packing companies, Kemp & Pitts and Hazlehurst Mercantile Company, had repeatedly violated the child labor provisions by employing children under age fourteen, employing children between the ages of fourteen and sixteen beyond the maximum workday and workweek, and assigning them prohibited jobs such as constructing packing crates. "Having seen the defendants on the stand and in the court-room, and knowing their general standing and reputation as substantial, outstanding citizens of the state," wrote Judge Mize, "I cannot believe that these men will violate this law in the future."[81]

A judge's refusal to grant an injunction after finding that an employer had violated the law posed a serious problem for Margolin and her lawyers. Under the FLSA at that time the administrator had no power to compel the payment of, or bring an action for, unpaid wages or overtime. The act gave this remedy only to the employee, who often lacked the money or ability to bring an action. Through contempt proceedings, however, the administrator could enforce a Court's order enjoining future violations of the act, often coupled with provisions for payment of wages. Without the injunction the department had little recourse with a repeat offender other than to start the process anew, losing the powerful incentive for compliance provided by the threat of contempt. Margolin realized that if standards were not imposed on courts that refused to use their discretionary authority, the FLSA would be rendered toothless.

Just four days before Judge Mize issued his ruling in the *Kemp & Pitts* case, Margolin convinced the Eighth Circuit to reverse a Kansas City federal trial judge who had refused to issue an injunction despite having found that a bakery violated the child labor laws at its plant, where children between the ages of fourteen and sixteen used mechanical jacks to move four hundred–pound barrels of milk and worked longer than eight hours per day. The Eighth Circuit held that the trial court had abused its discretion by denying the injunction where the company's officials offered no testimony to explain repeated violations or to identify steps they would take to comply in the future.[82]

Margolin was eager to use the Eighth Circuit's decision to persuade the Fifth Circuit, where many FLSA cases arose, and decided to take an active role in the appeal of Judge Mize's decision, drafting the *Kemp & Pitts* appellate brief herself. The court had sidestepped the evidence in the record, she wrote, to avoid the obvious conclusion that an injunction was needed to prevent repeat future violation. In her looping handwriting Margolin recited the trial court's errors, finally concluding, "We submit that the Court below misconceived the nature of its discretion in ruling that the court's personal knowledge of defendants' 'general standing and reputation as substantial and law-abiding citizen' outweighed the plain evidence in the record that an injunction was required to prevent repetition of violations."[83]

Margolin's strong draft sentences made their way into the brief and into her oral argument at the Fifth Circuit, where she urged that Judge Mize had abused his discretion. In January 1946 the Fifth Circuit agreed. In reversing the trial court, the Fifth Circuit noted that law books abound in cases of laws violated by outstanding citizens, generally reputed to be law abiding. "Lip service to a law, with a background of violations," cautioned the appellate court, "does not guarantee future compliance."[84]

"I need not tell you how happy the Children's Bureau people are," Margolin wrote to a former colleague, who a year earlier had lost a similar case.[85] It was an important victory, proclaimed by one newspaper as "a significant blow against exploitation of child labor in Dixie."[86]

Six months earlier, following the death of Franklin D. Roosevelt, Frances Perkins had resigned her position as secretary of labor. Margolin marked the occasion by sending a letter to Perkins. Whatever Margolin wrote elicited this touching response from the nation's first woman cabinet secretary to her first woman assistant solicitor: "It is kind of you to tell me, and perhaps only a woman would have thought to say this, that the job that I have had to do has been at times very delicate and very difficult, and that keeping one's mouth shut, while sometimes hard, has truly been the better part of wisdom. At any rate, I had the deep satisfaction of seeing the program of legislation and administration, which I came here with the intention of doing, accomplished and put into effect, and that ought to be enough. Also I have had the deep comfort of having the warm support and affectionate friendship of the people in the Department who have done the work. We have lived through great days together and can all take satisfaction in the contribution we made to civilization."[87]

7

AN INTERESTING ADVENTURE IN NUREMBERG
MAY–DECEMBER 1946

When Margolin presented her fourth and fifth Supreme Court arguments in *Roland* and *Boutell,* Justice Robert H. Jackson was not on the bench. He was in Nuremberg, Germany, leading the United States's prosecution of major German officials accused of Nazi atrocities and war crimes before the International Military Tribunal (IMT). He had taken what would turn into a sixteen-month leave of absence from the Court to carry out President Harry Truman's appointment.[1] Jackson had distinguished himself for the post by publicly calling for fair trials constituted under principles of international law, instead of summary executions.[2]

Margolin was intrigued by this unprecedented historic legal event. The day after Jackson's appointment, she sent him a letter asking to join his staff. Although she had no specialized knowledge in the field, she was keenly interested in the undertaking and willing to participate in a useful capacity.[3] He would be delighted if there were an opportunity to put her on his staff, Jackson replied, but the great pressure to get the work done in the shortest possible time was forcing him to rely chiefly on military personnel who were already at work assembling the evidence. Beyond those individuals, Jackson explained, he was hiring only a few civilian trial lawyers. Although he had developed a form letter for efficiently rejecting the dozens of lawyers who volunteered for his war crimes staff, Jackson's response to Margolin was unique. He ended his polite rejection by telling her that their mutual friend John Lord O'Brian "always speaks of your work with admiration."[4]

By April 1946 Margolin's ongoing interest to join the American effort to prosecute war crimes in Nuremberg intersected with an opportunity born from a developing shortage of qualified personnel. The outrage and demand for bringing Nazi criminals to justice that existed at the end of the war were already dimming. Even those most passionate about the cause—including Jackson and his Americans lawyers who remained in Nuremberg after most had returned to the United States—were growing weary.[5] Jackson made it clear to President Truman that he planned to resign as chief prosecutor and return to the Supreme Court when the first trial concluded.[6] He and his staff had spent the last year preparing and prosecuting one case before the IMT against two dozen of the most famous surviving Nazi war criminals, including Gestapo founder Hermann Goering, deputy führer Rudolf Hess, and Albert Speer, Hitler's minister of war production.

Composed of judges and prosecution teams from the United States, Britain, France, and the Soviet Union, the IMT was a costly and cumbersome undertaking, requiring diplomatic, legal, logistic, and linguistic coordination among the Allies and their personnel, with the United States funding much of the enterprise.[7] Even after the IMT trial concluded, which would not occur until the fall of 1946, there was still much more to be done. Beyond the top Nazis prosecuted in the first trial, there were many other potential defendants, although the Allies had not yet determined which defendants would be tried and for what crimes, nor had they determined whether to convene the proceedings jointly before another international military tribunal or separately before new tribunals to be established by each Allied country's military authority.

Whether to lead another IMT or a new American military court, Jackson needed to identify his successor. In March 1946 he appointed Telford Taylor, a top prosecutor in the ongoing IMT trial, as his deputy chief of counsel, to take over as chief of counsel when Jackson resigned. Jackson charged the thirty-seven-year-old Taylor with organizing, planning, and prosecuting what became known as the "Subsequent Proceedings"—all war crimes proceedings other than the main trial still under way before the IMT. Before prosecuting new cases, Taylor faced the daunting task of constructing a new American administrative and judicial machine that would mete out justice to the yet unprosecuted German army leaders, industrialists, jurists, and concentration camp doctors accused of criminal acts ranging from waging aggressive war, slave labor, and plundering to human experimentation and extermination.[8] Taylor's first order of business was to return to the United States to recruit lawyers to travel to Nuremberg for the Subsequent Proceedings.

Although it is possible that Jackson remembered her earlier interest, it is far more likely that Margolin once again initiated inquiries through any number of her contacts in the close-knit world of Washington lawyers. As Charles

Horsky, a Washington lawyer, reported to Jackson in April 1946, "General Taylor (as he is since yesterday) is going to have a fearful time because he has been signally unsuccessful in obtaining adequate assistants. The best that he has gotten so far is probably Bessie Margolin, the Assistant Solicitor of the Labor Department, who is extremely competent but probably [will] not be able to handle much of the kind of work that will have to be done."[9] There is no obvious explanation for Horsky's opinion that Margolin was not equipped to prepare and try cases; she had conducted several civil trials, assisted in criminal proceedings under the FLSA as a specially appointed assistant U.S. attorney, and had already argued five times at the Supreme Court and more than a dozen times in the circuit courts. Whatever reluctance Horsky had about Margolin was apparently not shared by Taylor, who promptly hired Margolin as a war crimes attorney, on a five-month loan from the Labor Department, and would assign her a range of important policy and legal matters during the organizational phase of the Subsequent Proceedings.[10]

On May 11, 1946, Margolin received her orders to fly to Nuremberg. Making her first trip to Europe, she flew from Washington, D.C., to Paris.[11] Already a seasoned and intrepid traveler within the United States, Margolin was thrilled by the overseas flight.[12] Seeing how accessible the United States was to Europe, Margolin could not understand how anyone who had taken the same flight could retain any isolationist tendencies.[13] Before continuing to Nuremberg, Margolin spent several days in Paris. She walked along the Avenue des Champs-Élysées, looking in shop windows, disappointed to find the fashionable stores closed. The people she saw looked very sad and despairing, with a dazed, dreary stare in their eyes, which she attributed to prolonged hunger and deprivation. In the midst of Paris's beautiful spring weather and foliage, to Margolin the city looked alive but not the people.[14]

By the time Margolin reached Frankfurt a few days later, she felt no sympathy for the hardships of the German people but instead was disgusted by their comparatively healthy and robust appearance. The Germans, Margolin wrote Kate, "will never catch up with the suffering they have inflicted on the people of other countries, however badly battered their cities. And battered they are, Kate—beyond all imagination!" She found Frankfurt and later Nuremberg, though still beautiful even in complete ruins, were destroyed block after block, mile after mile. She did not disagree when an American general told her: "They asked for it. They resisted with all their armed power to the limit on these towns."[15]

It was nearly impossible to escape the dust, devastation, and the smell of death. Margolin's friend Dorothy Owens, who was in Nuremberg as a secretary, years later vividly remembered the horror of seeing buildings with rooms and bathtubs hanging halfway out.[16] Even the relatively intact Palace of Justice, which housed the courtrooms and offices used for the IMT and later for the Subsequent Proceedings, still had bomb damage in certain hallways, leaving them open to wind and rain.[17]

American civilians were assigned a range of accommodations, scattered throughout the city. Owens was billeted with other women, all secretaries and court reporters, in a once-grand home that was now a barely furnished guesthouse, with a neglected swimming pool and tennis court. Along with other American lawyers and staff, Margolin was billeted at Nuremberg's Grand Hotel, which had suffered serious damage and was still being repaired.[18] Tarpaulins flapped over holes in the structure of one wartorn wing, and bags of water, chemically treated for drinking, lined the corridors.[19] Fortunately, the hotel's elaborately furnished lobbies, dining rooms, and main ball-room were intact, providing a focus of social life for civilian employees and military officers. According to Telford Taylor, who, like other officers and judges, was individually lodged in a large house, the Grand Hotel offered cheap and reasonably good food and liquor, and its Marble Room featured a dance band and often a floor show.[20] One of the hotel's unpleasant features, however, was that the dining room had a large window to the street. German townspeople, many of whom lacked adequate food, clothing, and shelter, pressed their noses against the window, making mealtime uncomfortable for the hotel's diners.[21]

While the living and working conditions were not ideal, Margolin never regretted her venture, finding every minute of it interesting and stimulating.[22] She had arrived in time to witness the testimony of the last seven defendants in the IMT trial, beginning with Grand Admiral Erich Raeder, Germany's highest-ranking naval officer, followed by Baldur von Schirach, the head of Hitler Youth. With the defense presentations under way and the Allied participants eager to conclude what had already been a long trial, the tribunal was typically in session from ten in the morning to five in the evening five days a week and often on Saturday mornings. The lawyers and staff spent far longer hours at work, as needed.[23]

Whatever Margolin understood before she arrived in Nuremberg about the Nazis' atrocities and the complicity of the German people gave way to a

profound awakening during her assignment. From reading case files, conferring with new colleagues, and observing IMT courtroom proceedings, Margolin quickly absorbed the enormity of the Nazis' "shocking and nauseating
doctrines and crimes." Even her most abusive wage violation and child labor
cases did little to prepare her for what she saw and heard at the Nuremberg trials. "Certainly it has been a revelation to me," she wrote O'Brian.
She heard conservative estimates that the Nazis had "exterminated outright
(exclusive of military killings) about 5 million people including many little
children—and they made slaves of about 10 million more from various
parts of Europe and Russia." Margolin, the daughter of Russian-born Jews,
soon concluded about the Nazis, "Human life apparently was the cheapest
commodity on earth in their view—and human dignity non-existent."[24]

Margolin's responsibilities and senior status gave her access to ranking
officials, allowing her to seek out their views on the trials and share her opinions
with them. Justice Jackson told her he feared the Nazis had been victorious
because in the long run, through sheer force of numbers, Germans were
bound to dominate the population. In a conversation with David Maxwell-
Fyfe, the British prosecutor who skillfully cross-examined Goering, she
worried that she might sound bloodthirsty, as she wanted to "prosecute at
least five million and impose the death penalty freely on all that had any
connection with the mass murders and atrocities." Maxwell-Fyfe assured
her that he wanted to prosecute and execute or give long foreign labor sentences to twice that number. This was not mere vengeance, he reasoned, but
the only way to prevent the revival of Nazism. Early on Margolin resolved
to use her position to improve the odds: "So my first two weeks here have
brought me to the conclusion that any little weight I may carry should be
thrown in the direction of increasing the number of Nazis to be prosecuted
for murder."[25]

Within Margolin's first month Taylor outlined the organization of his
Subsequent Proceedings staff. He assigned most of his recently arrived
lawyers and researchers to teams that would assess and prepare evidence
for the cases. But his assignment for Margolin was much broader. He put
her in charge of legal research and assigned her to draft opinions, orders,
and rules and regulations arising out of the Allies' fundamental agreements,
including the August 8, 1945, London Agreement that established the IMT;
Control Council Law No. 10, which authorized each Allied nation to establish
its own military tribunal; and the Denazification Law, which codified the

Allies' efforts to remove active members of the former National Socialist Party from positions of power. His most specific directive to Margolin, and the one to which she applied most of her efforts over the next five months, was to prepare the necessary orders to establish American military courts and their rules of procedure.[26] Although she described her assignment to O'Brian as "quite limited," Taylor was looking to Margolin to propose a basic structure for the Subsequent Proceedings—whether tried by another international court or by each country alone—with fundamentally fair procedures. She was excited that her work would entail considerable travel and interesting associations.[27]

During the summer of 1946 the decision to forgo another IMT was inevitable to the United States but had not yet been officially accepted by the rest of the Allies. Margolin thus worked on alternate proposals, spending some of her time in Germany attending meetings of the multinational board that oversaw the IMT and acquainting herself with the laws and legal procedures of the four countries, so that she could synthesize their laws into another international proposal, if necessary.[28] To prepare for subsequent trials conducted solely by the United States, Margolin also drafted an order establishing American military tribunals, which took shape by mid-August.

Taylor, anticipating that he would be ready to file the first indictments by early October, was anxious to get Margolin's draft order finalized so that he could recruit and transport the necessary personnel and ready the equipment and facilities for the American military proceedings. He sent Margolin to Berlin to meet with American military officials to expedite the order's approval.[29] While there on several trips over the next two months, Margolin was accorded a level of courtesy that reflected her professional stature. In addition to her meetings, she was hosted at cocktail and dinner parties also attended by an elite group, including Taylor and his wife and high-ranking lawyers visiting from the United States as part of the postwar efforts.[30]

On October 18, 1946, Gen. Joseph T. McNarney, the United States military governor of occupied Germany, issued the final order establishing the new war crimes courts: "Military Government—Germany, United States Zone Ordinance No. 7, Organization and Powers of Certain Military Tribunals." In addition to stylistic changes (such as replacing Margolin's original references to "war criminals" with the more impartial "persons accused of offenses" or "defendants"), the final version revealed substantive changes, including requiring (instead of permitting) the tribunal to set forth its reasons for its judgments. One of the most significant revisions to the draft concerned the extent to which IMT legal rulings bound the American tribunals in the Subsequent Proceedings.[31] The express language of the early draft would have bound the American courts to both the IMT's factual findings and legal rulings; the final version retained the requirement that the American courts were bound, with certain exceptions, by the IMT's factual findings but dropped the language requiring that IMT legal rulings be given binding effect. Neither Margolin nor her colleagues documented why or precisely when they made this change, thus leaving open the question of whether they were attempting to limit the impact on the Subsequent Proceedings of potentially adverse legal rulings by the IMT.[32]

On September 30 and October 1, 1946, Margolin was among the hundreds of people who packed the main courtroom of the Palace of Justice, eager to hear the results of the trial that had begun nearly one year earlier and had concluded at the end of August. She had spent the greater part of four months following the main IMT trial, observing the courtroom proceedings and conferring with the trial lawyers while she drafted the order establishing the American military tribunals.[33] Not surprisingly, Margolin had become emotionally invested in the outcome: "Time and time again we heard the defense that they were simply carrying out orders (orders to murder millions of innocent men, women and children). And those who did not actually participate in the murders purported to have no knowledge of what was happening in the concentration camps within a few miles from their homes."[34] Even two decades later, Margolin readily recounted the verdicts and sentences rendered for the "top 21 Nazis" that day, each of whom she could still list by name. The IMT acquitted three defendants and found eighteen guilty on at least one charge, sentencing eleven of them to death, three to life imprisonment, and four to prison sentences ranging from ten to twenty years.[35]

The general reaction in the courtroom to the verdicts was that the court had considered the issues thoughtfully and punished most of the guilty people appropriately. Some expressed surprise at the relatively light twenty-year sentence given to production czar Albert Speer and the complete acquittal of Hjalmar Schacht, but generally the verdicts and sentences seemed fair to the expectant public.[36] Moreover, for most people, the recital of the verdicts meant that the Nuremberg trial was over and done. But for the prosecutors who were readying the future cases, and for Margolin who had another month of duty to help them prepare, the IMT judgment marked a beginning. In several respects the logistics of the Subsequent Proceedings would dwarf the IMT; instead of the IMT's single multinational panel, which presided over one trial of 24 defendants for eight months, the Subsequent Proceedings ultimately encompassed six American military tribunals (each comprising three judges and an alternate), which presided over twelve separate trials of a total 185 indicted defendants, spanning more than two years.[37]

Like other American civilians in Nuremberg, Margolin seized opportunities to escape her complex and often disturbing work. She immersed herself in Nuremberg's international social scene, often rubbing shoulders with officials, all of whom she found lively and enjoyable. When there was room for another lady guest, Justice Jackson invited Margolin to several parties, including one for officials of the French delegation and another for Belgian officials. Taylor and his wife invited Margolin to cocktail parties, where she became acquainted with British and Russian officials. "So you see," she wrote to O'Brian, "it is quite an interesting adventure for me."[38]

Just before Margolin left Washington, the press had reported that the U.S. Army was beginning to supply armbands to soldiers' wives and daughters stationed in Germany to protect them from "wolf calls" by GIs.[39] Yet Margolin saw little evidence of any such demoralizing atmosphere and found the soldiers were pretty well behaved in the places she had been. "At any rate," she told O'Brian, "I haven't felt the need of an armband to protect me as the newspapers had led me to believe."[40] But it was not Margolin's encounters with American soldiers that would cause concern. Her favorable impressions of Russian military officials she met during social gatherings caught the attention of the Army's Military Intelligence Corps, which investigated Margolin's character and loyalty. Apparently unaware that she would soon return (or had already returned) to the United States, the army reportedly recommended that "Miss Bessie Margolin be separated from the Government Service and be returned to the Zone of the Interior."[41] Independently, the FBI learned during its investigation of connections between American officials and alleged Communist spy Nathan Gregory Silvermaster that Margolin "spoke very favorably regarding the Russian officials she met in Germany."[42] Although Margolin then suffered no ill consequence and may have been completely unaware that her Nuremberg conduct was in question, the allegations regarding her Communist sympathies would resurface several times over the next two decades.[43]

On Monday, July 29, 1946, Justice Jackson gave another large dinner party at the Villa Schickedanz, a grand manse that housed visiting dignitaries.[44] The event marked the conclusion of the closing arguments by the Allies' chief prosecutors. Just three days earlier Margolin sat in the courtroom at the Palace of Justice, listening to Justice Jackson deliver his final summation of the evidence marshaled over the previous eight months. She had been so moved by Jackson's eloquent denunciation that she immediately wrote: "Your argument was powerful, stirring, and thrilling—not to mention unanswerable. . . . I feel greatly privileged to have been able to hear it."[45] In one of the many disorienting contrasts of her Nuremberg experience, in which the horrors of Margolin's work yielded to playful diversion, here she was, days later, looking smart in a black dress with a deep neckline, a large white flower adorning her hair, sharing a lively evening in the villa's ballroom, seated with Dorothy Owens and members of the British prosecution team.[46]

Margolin also took advantage of opportunities for travel, a pastime she enjoyed with Edith Simon, a German-born graduate of the University of California at Berkeley who interpreted for the IMT. Margolin relished Simon's sense of adventure, and their trips together sparked a lifelong friendship and love of foreign travel. On one memorable excursion Simon "liberated" a military vehicle by hot-wiring it so the pair could take a whirlwind tour of Switzerland and Italy.[47] In October, soon after the IMT rendered its judgment, Margolin took a five-day trip to Paris that featured a cocktail party hosted by the French deputy prosecutor and a shopping spree in which she returned to some of the boutiques that had been closed when she first arrived in May. Upon Margolin's return to Nuremberg from her Paris sojourn, she made a triumphal entry into the Grand Hotel to conduct an impromptu show of the latest French fashions.[48]

Margolin's experience of being invited by Justice Jackson as a single woman to a party to even up the number of men and women at social gatherings was not uncommon at the time. Unlike a young female staffer who spoke about being invited to Nuremberg's social events only "when they need some female 'bodies,'" Margolin seemed to take no offense at being asked to be "the lady guest" to fill an empty seat, especially when it provided an interesting opportunity. By 1946 she had grown comfortable being the only woman among men in professional settings or the only single woman among couples socially. Gender bias in social and professional affairs was a fairly universal phenomenon in 1946, so it is not surprising that it also existed in Nuremberg, and some American women considered it more pervasive there.[49] Even after Taylor allowed personnel to bring wives and dependents to Nuremberg to aid recruitment, the war crimes community included very few married couples. As Taylor explained, "Most of the senior personnel, including the lawyers, were married men, while most of the women were single and young and not a few very attractive." Obviously speaking from a male perspective, Taylor candidly added, "This gave the society a relaxed, tolerant, and philanderous ambience which many of us found agreeable."[50]

Notwithstanding any philandering that may have occurred after hours, the Subsequent Proceedings afforded women lawyers relatively more job opportunities than were available in the United States at the time. Of the estimated 130 lawyers Taylor brought to Nuremberg for the Subsequent Proceedings, no fewer than 12 were women, most of whom he assigned to prosecution teams or, in Margolin's case, to high-level policy work.[51] The proportion of women Taylor hired as lawyers on his Nuremberg legal staff was one and a half times greater than their presence among lawyers employed by the federal government, more than three times greater than their presence among all American lawyers, and two and a half times greater than their presence among American lawyers working on the IMT in Nuremberg during Jackson's tenure.[52]

As Margolin's original tour of duty was ending, Taylor realized that she could greatly aid the effort to recruit judges for the tribunals she had helped to create. Having argued appeals in every federal circuit and having participated in trials in dozens of district courts, Margolin knew many judges. Moreover, she was well equipped from her work drafting Ordinance No. 7 to explain jurisdictional and procedural issues. In late November, Taylor extended Margolin's tour of duty for an additional thirty days.[53] She traveled to Atlanta, New Orleans, Shreveport, and Houston, carrying a copy of the IMT judgment, Control Council Law No. 10, and Military Government Ordinance No. 7. While interviewing highly recommended members of the bar and bench, Margolin answered their many questions and emphasized the importance and prestige of the post.[54]

Supreme Court chief justice Fred Vinson's refusal to permit federal judges to serve on the Nuremberg Military Tribunals was undermining her recruitment efforts, Margolin reported to Taylor, because it unfortunately eliminated many highly qualified candidates. Nevertheless, she was pleased that some very good people were still available. Although a few disparaged the alleged ex post facto nature of the trials—claiming the proceedings retroactively criminalized certain conduct, such as "crimes against humanity" —Margolin reported that most of the thirteen judges and lawyers she visited on her recruitment trip were "favourably interested and impressed" with the program. This was especially true with Judge James V. Allred, former governor of Texas. Although Allred was not available to serve in Nuremberg, in the middle of his December 1946 meeting with Margolin he telephoned his colleague Mallory B. Blair, a former Texas appeals judge, who eagerly accepted the assignment.[55] Within three months Judge Blair was in Nuremberg, one of three judges comprising Military Tribunal III, determining the fate of sixteen German jurists and lawyers charged with committing "judicial murder and other atrocities" by usurping German law and justice to persecute, enslave, and exterminate a vast number of Jews and Poles.[56]

More than just an interesting adventure, Margolin's time in Nuremberg and her hand in creating Ordinance No. 7 would remain a source of pride. In his 1949 official report to the secretary of the army, Taylor expressly acknowledged Margolin's role in creating the ordinance, under which the bulk of the Nazi war crimes were tried.[57] When he wrote to thank labor secretary Lewis Schwellenbach for loaning Margolin to the army, Taylor told him she had made a "very distinct and important contribution to our work here."[58]

Despite numerous jurisdictional and procedural challenges during the twelve trials of the Subsequent Proceedings, including a direct attack on the legal basis for Ordinance No. 7 and its allowance of hearsay evidence and civilian judges, each tribunal upheld the ordinance.[59] Margolin's work in Nuremberg contributed not only to ensuring fair trials for individuals accused of violating international law but also to creating a historical record of evil that would otherwise seem unimaginable but for the sworn evidence of the proceedings.[60] Moreover, she had helped establish the courts that greatly increased the number of Nazis who were prosecuted, as she had set out to do.

Nuremberg also became an experience Margolin shared with Justice Jackson, strengthening their collegial relationship and similarly informing their views on certain issues. In one memorable example, in May 1949 Justice Jackson wrote an emotional dissent, castigating the majority for reversing the disorderly conduct conviction of a racist and anti-Semite whose public invectives at a meeting whipped to a frenzy not only his supporters but also his rock- and bottle-throwing opponents. Drawing upon his Nuremberg experience, Jackson noted that the defendant's speech closely followed the tactics of European fascist leaders, citing evidence he had introduced at the IMT to establish Hitler's strategic use of mass demonstrations. Nothing in the Constitution restricted local government from imposing a civil fine to maintain order in its streets, reasoned Jackson, so long as it was not invoked in bad faith to censor or oppress.[61]

Margolin, who was in the Supreme Court when Jackson read his dissent, agreed. She wrote Jackson to congratulate him on his "stirring and incomparably eloquent dissenting opinion." Quoting a radio commentator, she wrote that "perhaps we can have faith that ultimately Truth will not be 'put to the worse in a free and open encounter,' but the six million Jews of Europe could not await the outcome of the encounter and that it would have been well at some point before their slaughter to 'misdoubt her strength' a little."[62] Jackson fondly acknowledged Margolin's letter, briefly noting, "No other letter that I received, and no comment from any source, about the *Terminiello* case touched the spot the way yours did."[63]

On a more personal level, Margolin's Nuremberg experiences connected her for years with a close circle of public-minded and intellectual friends, many Jewish, all of whom had played supporting roles in the war crimes trials. Their contributions would go unrecognized by history, but the events they witnessed had indelibly marked their lives, leading many to undertake other humanitarian endeavors. Margolin's travel companion, Edith Simon, returned to San Francisco, where, after raising money for Jewish war refugees, she spent her career with the Asia Foundation, promoting human rights and economic development in twenty-four countries; she always made time for Margolin when both were in Washington, D.C., or on the West Coast, and they kept tabs on each other's pioneering ventures.[64] Margolin also cherished her relationship with Morris Abram, which began when he came to Nuremberg during his Oxford summer recess to assist the IMT prosecutors.[65] Regarding his war crimes experience as a turning point in his life, Abram committed himself to civil rights and Jewish causes, becoming the Peace Corps's first general counsel, the U.S. representative to the United Nations Commission on Human Rights, president of Brandeis University, and president of the American Jewish Committee.[66] He would later lend his considerable support to Margolin's candidacy for a federal judgeship.[67]

Margolin also maintained a lifelong friendship with assistant French prosecutor Henri Monneray.[68] Before Monneray died in 1974, they saw each other when Monneray visited Washington, and he hosted a dinner party in Margolin's honor when she traveled to Paris in the early 1960s.[69] He always let Margolin know when he crossed paths with other "old Nuernbergers," and when she had been a topic of conversation. After one such evening in 1948, Monneray wrote Margolin, "We talked of course about you and agreed on this remarkable feature of yours to be a first class dancer as well as a first class lawyer."[70] Monneray was also delighted, he wrote Margolin, when Abram reported that he had argued a Wage and Hour case at the Fifth Circuit —with Margolin on the other side.[71] As Abram good-naturedly recalled his unsuccessful legal encounter with Margolin, he received some scars but learned a very good lesson from his able adversary.[72]

For more than a year after Margolin returned to the United States, she worried about Monneray's access to necessities amid the rations and black markets in postwar Paris, sending him food packages and offering to send woolen underwear and an electric heater, all of which he gratefully acknowledged as his "private Marshall plan."[73] In turn, through the *valise diplomatique* of a French intelligence officer, Monneray sent Margolin flacons of her cherished Chanel No. 5.[74] But Monneray, the French lawyer and lover of democracy who for many years actively mourned FDR's death, most appreciated Margolin's thoughtfulness in sending books he treasured, including Jackson's collection of IMT evidence, *Nazi Conspiracy and Aggression,* and later Robert Sherwood's colossal work *Roosevelt and Hopkins: An Intimate History.*[75]

Although Margolin's Nuremberg colleagues would go on to successful careers, their war crimes work would always hold unique significance. Years after their time together in Germany, Monneray admitted to Margolin that his private law practice, while lucrative, failed to provide him with even the "slightest illusion of shaping human destiny."[76] For a brief time in their lives Margolin and her circle of "old Nuernbergers" had played a role in shaping human destiny, a rewarding experience that they sought to recapture in later professional pursuits.

8

RETURN TO THE LABOR DEPARTMENT
1947–1961

A Glamorous Career

When it first hit newsstands in 1939, the magazine *Glamour of Hollywood* promised to show its readers "The Hollywood Way to Fashion, Beauty, Charm" by focusing on the lives of movie stars: their mansions, limousines, and elegant evening clothes.[1] But in the aftermath of World War II, ideals of glamour shifted, reflecting more attainable visions, the austerities of war, and the fact that women had become and would remain a significant presence in the workplace.[2] Even the namesake magazine recognized this societal shift. By 1943 *Glamour of Hollywood* became *Glamour—For the Girl with a Job.*[3]

Sporting a popular "Victory roll" hairstyle and a lace-collared blouse that peeked over her smartly tailored jacket, Margolin appeared in the January 1948 issue of *Glamour,* illustrating fresh opportunities that awaited women in law, a field of employment long biased against admitting women. Choosing Margolin to represent the tiny fraction (0.01 percent) of America's eighteen million workingwomen who were lawyers and judges, the article lightly described the assistant labor solicitor's job as tracing cases in legal history, preparing litigation, and sometimes pleading cases in the U.S. Supreme Court. The magazine made no promise that other women lawyers could expect their voices to be heard, as Margolin's was, in the nation's most powerful legal venue. Although the war's demand for women lawyers had subsided, the article noted that the government continued to welcome them as hearing officers in domestic and juvenile matters. Or they could use their legal training in the private sector, doing administrative or research work or perhaps serving as executive secretaries to corporation officers.[4]

Any evidence that Margolin ever considered a legal career in the private sector had disappeared by the time she completed her bankruptcy studies at Yale, and it remains unclear whether she would have pursued the opportunity if it had been offered to her. Instead, she dedicated herself to government service. From the time she returned from Nuremberg, she would not again significantly interrupt her work at the Labor Department until 1961, when she enjoyed a one-year sabbatical awarded to recognize a career of outstanding service and contribution. Before then, Margolin would devote herself to building a body of law to make the FLSA as powerful and far-reaching as Congress had intended it to be, thereby protecting the greatest number of American workers possible. Much of it she would accomplish through hard work and painstaking attention to documenting the gritty details of the quotidian jobs of wage earners. But the image she projected for the work, the law, and herself was one of prestige, fascination, and even glamour.

Developing a Body of Law

Margolin owed her career as an appellate advocate to Congress's decision in the FLSA to withhold general rule-making authority from the Labor Department. As a result, the courts, including the Supreme Court, were frequently called upon to clarify the act's imprecise language unaided by administrative decision or regulation to which it should defer for subject matter expertise.[5] In the first five years after the FLSA took effect, the Supreme Court decided more than thirty FLSA cases.[6] After the Court upheld the constitutionality of the act in *Darby* and *Opp Cotton Mills,* the litigation focused on how the act was interpreted, and Margolin served for three decades as the principal architect of that litigation.[7]

In simplest terms Margolin's goals were to make sure the courts' interpretation of the FLSA was faithful to the letter and humanitarian spirit of the law and to provide the broadest allowable coverage for employees with the narrowest exemptions. Because the statute's protections were limited to employees who engaged in or produced goods for interstate commerce, Margolin's FLSA litigation encompassed a never-ending litany of factual scenarios that tested the meaning of *employee, engaged in commerce, goods,* and every other operative phrase in the law. Recognizing the limitless ways in which American businesses created, transported, and distributed their products and services, Congress left many FLSA terms undefined, providing little guidance on how to apply the provisions to particular jobs and industries, prompting Margolin and other lawyers in the field to mine the legislators' debates and reports for evidence of their intent. Each FLSA trial in a federal district court, each appeal to a circuit court, and ultimately each decision by the Supreme Court contributed to the growing body of law that protects the wages and hours of America's workers.

Margolin employed two important techniques to influence the Court's interpretation of the statute. The first was her Case Analyses, a series of legal memoranda that she started writing shortly after she was promoted to assistant solicitor and which, by the time she retired, numbered nearly two hundred.[8] Margolin personally wrote or oversaw the writing of these legal commentaries, which she distributed to her staff and to the regional attorneys. Ranging from one to ten pages, some of her analyses summarized the status of the law on fundamental FLSA issues such as interstate commerce and the employment relationship, but most followed each new Supreme Court and significant circuit court ruling, reviewing the decision's impact, providing advice on its implementation, and setting forth guidance to identify future cases to achieve what had not yet been accomplished.[9] Considered the FLSA "bible," Margolin's Case Analyses were crucial to the Labor Solicitor's Office not only for writing appellate briefs but also in deciding whether regional offices should bring a particularly tough case involving a novel issue of law.[10]

Margolin's second technique was in working closely with her colleague and good friend Harold Nystrom to prepare interpretative bulletins on which the federal courts placed a great deal of weight. Lacking statutory authority to promulgate regulations, the Wage and Hour administrator issued the bulletins to inform the public about the agency's legal conclusions regarding the meaning and application of the FLSA and its amendments on matters the courts had not yet determined. Occasionally, Margolin and Nystrom argued about the bulletins, especially when she—who was looking to use the bulletin later to persuade a judge or justice—felt he was pushing the limits of the interpretation. "You can't get from the statute to there without litigation," she would warn him. "The Court won't make that big a jump."[11]

In April 1947, just four months after returning from Nuremberg, Margolin again presented argument at the Supreme Court. The case, *Rutherford Food Corporation v. McComb,* centered on the FLSA's meaning of *employee.* Margolin argued that meat boners (the workers who removed beef from the bones of slaughtered cattle) were entitled to FLSA protections because they were the employees of the slaughterhouse operator and not independent contractors.[12]

Although no recording exists of Margolin's argument, the department's brief, which she principally drafted, traced the assembly line operations—from the slaughter and skinning of the cattle through the boning and trimming of the carcasses to the collection of the trimmed meat in large barrels that were then sent to the loading dock—all to show that the boners were an essential part of the slaughterhouse's "integrated continuous process."[13] She captured the attention of Justice Jackson, also back from Nuremberg, who marked the occasion with a playful note from the bench. He toyed with the word *boner,* then commonly understood to mean a costly mistake: "Cheer up. You are in an historic case. One side or the other has often been the beneficiary of 'boners' in Court but you are first in this Court's history to urge that 'boners' are beneficiaries!"[14]

Margolin's urgings were successful. Justice Stanley Reed, who as solicitor general had sponsored her 1935 Supreme Court admission, authored the opinion for the unanimous bench, agreeing with Margolin that Rutherford Food's meat boners were entitled to FLSA protections. More important, the decision established a precedent that FLSA's test for distinguishing a protected employee from an unprotected independent contractor depended upon the totality of work circumstances, despite any contractual limitations.

With the fate of the boners and other low-wage workers in her well-manicured hands, Margolin was committed to making even the messy business of cattle carcasses, meat hooks, and leather aprons decidedly dignified and pertinent. She applied the same care to learning and explaining the details of the jobs performed by the wage earners in all of her cases, including the manufacture of wet storage batteries, the bulking of tobacco, knife sharpening by meatcutters, commercial warehousing, and the freezing and packaging of vegetables. With this attention to detail and belief in the FLSA, Margolin would win the next thirteen Supreme Court arguments that the next four solicitors general assigned to her from 1948 to 1959.

The first such assignment, by Solicitor General Philip Perlman, involved the Jacksonville Paper Company, a large distributor of paper products, for whose branch office employees Margolin recovered wages the company had failed to pay in violation of a prior court order. In so doing, she also established a far broader principle: an employer who violated any section of the act covered by the terms of a court injunction previously secured by the Labor Department is to be adjudged in contempt, whether his violation was willful or innocent, and the federal court has the power to order restitution of the unlawful underpayments. In rejecting the employer's claim that the injunction was too broadly phrased, the Supreme Court recognized that injunctions must not be so narrow as to invite easy evasion or experimentation with disobedience of the law and validated the Labor Department's injunctions in hundreds of other FLSA cases.[15]

Margolin's successes were well known within Washington and in the field of labor standards, and she enjoyed an admirable reputation as a serious and capable advocate. She also sought advice from other attorneys and appreciated the kudos she received from them. In December 1949, for example, she presented the government's position as amicus curiae in *Powell v. U.S. Cartridge Company,* urging that the FLSA protected employees of private wartime munitions firms who worked under government contracts.[16] Although it was her eighth argument at the high court, when Margolin returned to counsel table from the podium, she jotted a quick note to assistant solicitor general Robert L. Stern, an experienced Supreme Court advocate, asking for his appraisal of her performance: "Bob—Did I give away too much—or not enough?" He wrote on the back of her note, "I don't think anyone could have done any better or said anything different."[17] Stern's positive assessment of Margolin's argument was shared by at least two other spectators. A private attorney who argued later that day said it was the best argument he had ever heard.[18] Supreme Court justice Tom Clark, who recused himself from her case due to his prior involvement as attorney general, was sufficiently impressed to send a note relating how pleased he was with her argument.[19] On May 8, 1950, the Supreme Court issued its opinion, reversing the judgments from the lower courts, as Margolin had advocated.[20] Labor secretary Maurice Tobin publicly lauded Margolin for winning the Court's recognition that the preservation of America's great social gains are just as important to national defense as physical armament itself.[21]

Beyond offering praise, the Labor Department also recognized Margolin's remarkable achievements by awarding her honors and bonuses. In July 1953 she received the department's Distinguished Service Award. She had won eight of the nine cases she had argued at the Supreme Court and all of the last thirteen cases she had argued in the circuit courts. For Margolin these were not simply notches on her professional record. She understood that the welfare of literally millions of workers depended on the FLSA's protection and that her work could increase the number of workers protected and the degree of protection they received.[22] The award recognized that Margolin's skill and devotion during her eleven years as assistant solicitor of labor had produced a success rate in the department's litigation "phenomenally beyond those normally to have been expected," especially because she most frequently sought to reverse a lower court decision.[23]

Three years later, in November 1956, Margolin received a four-hundred-dollar Special Performance Award recognizing that in 1955 alone the department had the largest number of cases, twelve, before the Supreme Court of any year over the previous decade. Six of the cases were heard on the merits, and the rest were resolved on petitions for review. Although an attorney's competence cannot be judged on the basis of whether he wins or loses a particular case, labor solicitor Stuart Rothman recognized that Margolin's unusually impressive record of 100 percent success consecutively in such a substantial number of Supreme Court cases unquestionably reflected the exceptional quality of her performance.[24] Solicitor General Simon Sobeloff considered his office fortunate to have a lawyer of Margolin's caliber on whom to rely in the Labor Department's litigation in the Supreme Court, noting her persuasive briefs and effective oral arguments in complex and difficult cases.[25] Such appraisals were not news to Margolin's staff. In March 1956, when the Supreme Court announced two of her Labor Department victories on the same day, Sylvia Ellison, a talented lawyer on Margolin's staff, wrote her boss a quick note, "People are again saying, 'It's Bessie Margolin Day in the Supreme Court.'"[26]

Her Supreme Court record was unusually impressive. After her first loss, in *Callus* in 1945, Margolin prevailed in every case she argued at the Supreme Court until 1959. In *Mitchell v. Oregon Frozen Foods,* Margolin's twentieth Supreme Court argument, she sought to reverse the Eighth Circuit's decision that applied the FLSA's exemption for "first processing of perishable or seasonal fruits or vegetables" to employees who repackaged bulk frozen corn and carrots after the season ended. As can happen, the Court decided after argument that there were ambiguities in the record over the department's position regarding the proper scope of the exemption.[27] Despite supplemental briefing and without ever reaching the merits, the Court dismissed the writ of certiorari as improvidently granted, allowing the Eighth Circuit's ruling to stand.[28] In several lists she compiled of her Supreme Court arguments, Margolin never included the case, perhaps because it did not represent a ruling on the merits, although it was nonetheless an unfavorable outcome for the department.

Margolin's third and final loss at the Supreme Court followed her 1959 argument in *Mitchell v. H. B. Zachry*,[29] in which the Court upheld the Fifth Circuit's ruling and decided that the construction of a dam by a contractor hired by a water supply district was not "closely related" or "directly essential" to production of goods for commerce and therefore the FLSA did not cover the contractor's employees. Despite the Supreme Court's ruling, which Margolin always noted she had lost by only one vote, she claimed victory to the extent the decision repudiated much of the Fifth Circuit's reasoning, which would have had far-reaching negative implications on the scope of the act's "production" coverage.[30]

Margolin's 24 Supreme Court arguments pale in comparison to the numerous circuit court arguments she presented. Of the 150 circuit court cases, Margolin received favorable rulings in 114; only one ruling was later reversed by the Supreme Court, and it was argued by someone other than Margolin. Of the 36 circuit court arguments she lost, 7 were reversed by the Supreme Court—6 of which Margolin argued.[31]

Margolin's frequent appearances at the Supreme Court also allowed her to get to know the Court's members—so much so that she was able, when she deemed the circumstances appropriate, to employ humor when addressing the justices. Her first use of humor, however, occurred rather unexpectedly during her 1947 argument in *Rutherford Food*. Justice Frankfurter was expressing great irritation that Margolin could not satisfy his repeated demand for a precise standard under the FLSA to determine whether an employment relationship existed. With her time quickly dwindling, Margolin surprised herself by saying, "Well, Your Honor, the only other specific test I can think of is one Your Honor suggested in another case involving a question of coverage of the Act." Despite the risk of seeming impertinent, she drew upon the rather vague standard he had articulated in *10 East 40th Street Building, Inc. v. Callus*, in which in ruling against her two years earlier, he had been satisfied with what "spontaneously satisfies the common understanding." Although she drew hearty laughter from all of his brethren, Justice Frankfurter became and remained silent for the rest of the argument but later joined the unanimous *Rutherford* decision in her favor.[32] Thereafter, she was more confident in deploying humor. In her November 1955 argument in *Steiner v. Mitchell* she urged that battery plant workers were entitled to wages for time spent changing clothes and showering to remove caustic and toxic chemicals. Justice Frankfurter rapidly fired questions at Margolin, reflecting his ongoing dislike of the "line drawing" burden Congress had imposed on the Court by the FLSA. While acknowledging the complexities of the case, Margolin replied, "[You've] many times said to me the Court should leave the question for Congress, and not for the Court. But, after all, Congress has 4 or 500 people that they have to get into agreement on language, and the Court has just nine—which is enough!"[33] The audio recording does not capture Frankfurter's response, but the audience's laughter is quite clear.

Later that day Margolin returned to the podium to argue a different case, *Mitchell v. King Packing Company*. Now her goal was to persuade the Court that the time meatcutters spent sharpening knives before their regular workday was part of their "principal activities" and therefore was compensable. Frankfurter quickly resumed his disdain for the FLSA's inexactitudes, pounding the bench for emphasis as he admonished Congress for "legislation like this that throws the burden upon the courts and not make some administrative agency the determiner of facts in so many different cases." Justice Black, the former senator from Alabama who staunchly supported the TVA, jumped into the fray to challenge Frankfurter, noting the frequent and sound interplay of judicial and legislative processes, whereby the Court's interpretation of legislation occasionally "brings up a difference that Congress wants to change." Margolin playfully added to Justice Black's point, "Well, I think I heard one of the justices on this court say once that there wouldn't be much need for lawyers if that . . . job were taken away from us." Amid laughter in the courtroom Justice Frankfurter tersely shot back, "You underestimate the tenacity of lawyers."[34] Margolin prevailed in both cases, winning unanimous votes.

Margolin's preeminence in the FLSA also allowed her to be bold with the justices, engaging them in ways that would have been rejected as impertinent or foolish from a less experienced advocate. Take, for example, her exchange with Justice Charles Whitaker during her 1960 argument in *Mitchell v. H. B. Zachry Company*. In addition to principal issues regarding the act's coverage, Margolin also wanted the Court to address the trial court's authority to order back pay when an employer breached a prior injunction against violations of the act. Margolin was again greatly concerned about the growing number of trial judges—such as the one in this case—who refused to grant injunctive relief even when they found FLSA violations, thereby preventing the department from seeking back pay for repeat violations and in turn encouraging employers to contest FLSA coverage, while withholding wages, without financial disincentive. When Justice Whitaker complained that the government favored employees at the expense of their employers, Margolin directly challenged him, "Oh, you think that this law was intended to put them on an equal basis as to minimum wages?" Despite the seeming audacity of counsel to question a member of the Court in this way, Whitaker replied, "The government throws its weight to one side." Margolin sharply reacted: "Well, I think, the government, certainly Congress, intended the government to throw its weight on the side of . . . the substandard wage earners in this country when it passed this law. I think that is certainly clear beyond doubt, Mr. Justice Whitaker."[35] Confidence notwithstanding, the injunction issue was not one for which Margolin could claim even a partial victory in this case; the Court affirmed the lower court's ruling for the employer.[36]

With only a handful of women who argued at the Supreme Court—no more than seven women (compared to more than two hundred men) per year throughout the 1950s—each who appeared attracted considerable attention; although many reactions pertained to their legal skill, women advocates were also subject to critiques about their appearance and deportment.[37] Even after twenty arguments at the high court, Margolin's gender was often made an issue, with Justice Frankfurter implying that her successes were aided by "the deft use of her feminine charms," to his apparent delight.[38] Margolin was not the only woman whose attractiveness became a topic at the Supreme Court. Beatrice Rosenberg was a brilliant lawyer at the Justice Department, who by the end of 1959 had argued at least sixteen times before the Court and was well on her way to a career total of twenty-eight arguments.[39] That year Justice Frankfurter took the time to write about Rosenberg's hairstyle on three different occasions. After some disappointment that she had let herself go a bit, Frankfurter complained in a note, "I HAVE TO LOOK AT HER."[40] When her appearance once again met his approval, he wrote with relief of her vastly improving hairdo.[41]

Whether it was "feminine charm" or not, Margolin's style of argument was calm and measured. Her honeyed voice was engaging, and though her New Orleans accent was unmistakably southern, somehow "drawl" does not adequately convey the sound of her speech. In southern fashion she extended her vowels, but she did so in ways that seemed absolutely necessary, much like the way a spoon must move more slowly through a thick gumbo than a watery broth. *Exclusively* became *eggs-clooziv-ly*, while *highly* and *court* softened to *hah-ly* and *cawht*. She also had a gift for choosing simple words and phrases to recite facts and explain complex statutory provisions.

Despite these strengths, Margolin was no great orator. Judges and justices paid attention because they knew she spoke with authority and meticulous preparation. She addressed their questions directly, conversationally, and did not shy away from admitting on rare occasions when she did not have an answer to a question. "I've never looked up the legislative history on that," Margolin candidly replied when Justice Frankfurter, during the oral argument in *Mitchell v. Lublin, McGaughy & Associates*—a case that turned on whether draftsmen, clerks, and stenographers in an architectural and engineering firm were "engaged in commerce"—asked why Congress had included a parenthetical reference to "marine equipment" in the definition of *goods*.[42] She often edited herself as she spoke, making verbatim transcripts of her arguments difficult to follow due to the fragments of sentences she started and then abandoned. But listening to the recordings of her arguments, the logic in her presentation is clear. The lively fluctuations in her tone of voice and her simple descriptions prevent the listener from getting lost along the way. Take, for example, her effective way of denigrating opposing counsel's argument that the 1949 amendment to the FLSA broadened the "retail and service establishment" exemption to include personal loan companies. She described how a respondent's case went too far by claiming in effect that "Congress opened up the whole exemption and just granted a field day and open season to every employer that could possibly be subject to the Act."[43] She also pointed out the far-reaching consequences of generally exempting small loan businesses from the FLSA: "The small loan business is not small business. That's big business. It's a billion . . . dollar a year annual business. And the bulk of it is in the hands of 20 huge chains, nationwide chains, closely integrated."[44]

Margolin's clearheaded and moderated approach did not conceal her passion for her work. In *Mitchell v. Robert DeMario Jewelry,* for example, after finding that the employer had unlawfully fired three employees in retaliation for filing an FLSA complaint, the trial judge granted the department's request to reinstate the employees but refused to reimburse their lost wages, interpreting the FLSA's 1949 amendment as authorization to bar such relief in an action brought by the department and not by the employee.[45] After spending most of her argument time explaining the amendment's legislative history, Margolin devoted the few remaining minutes to shift the justices' attention away from the particular employees. It was the broader public interest, Margolin urged, that demanded employees be protected from suffering financial loss if they aid the act's enforcement. "The act depends necessarily on their cooperation and if employees learn or think, as they will if the decision below remains in force, that they cannot be protected from loss of wages . . . they certainly are not going to have much assurance under [the law] that they're free to come in and complain."[46] As Margolin's time expired, she cautioned the Court that absent recovery of lost wages, the FLSA's protections would be limited to "only the most courageous if not foolhardy employee." Justice Harlan, writing for the majority, agreed: "We cannot read the Act as presenting those it sought to protect with what is little more than a Hobson's choice."[47]

In the circuit courts, too, Margolin drew assurance from her extensive experience; she was unflappable before difficult judges or opposing counsel, as there was little that she had not done or come up against already. For a 1949 argument in the Second Circuit, Margolin had requested only twenty minutes because she thought that her recent Supreme Court victory in *Jacksonville Paper* would be decisive. Instead, for forty-five minutes the illustrious panel of judges persistently questioned Margolin about two issues neither party had briefed because she was unwilling to concede on those points.[48] Margolin was also known for her ability to put facts before the circuit court that were not always in the record and to respond to similar tactics by opposing counsel. A circuit judge recalled how Margolin had argued an appeal like "a game of judicial blackjack." She urged his court to take notice of publicity (not part of the appellate record) to find that an employer knew or should have known about his workers' entitlement to FLSA overtime to support her position that the trial court had abused its discretion in denying injunctive relief. The judge colorfully described Margolin's rather unorthodox but effective performance: "Bessie opened with an article from an engineering journal. Her opponent replied with the bond offering prospectus out of his briefcase, and Bessie hit the jackpot on rebuttal with an article from the Saturday Evening Post!"[49]

Margolin could also stand her ground with hostile judges. Margolin appeared before a panel on which the presiding judge was no fan of the FLSA, the federal government, or anything spawned by the New Deal. Her case was the last to be argued that day, and the judge summarily cut Margolin off mid-argument. Undeterred, when she appeared the following morning to argue another case, she began right where she left off: "Your Honor, as I was saying yesterday afternoon when we adjourned."[50]

Margolin demonstrated the same tenacity outside the courtroom. Whether driven by stubbornness or a sense of justice, Margolin equally stood her ground in an impasse with another motorist over a parking space to which she asserted a claim as well as in a letter to the *Washington Post* to denounce an ambulance driven recklessly on its supposedly humane errand.[51] In 1959 she complained to the chairman of the Civil Aeronautics Board and the president of Trans World Airlines that a steward had nearly caused her to miss her cross-country flight apparently to make room for a military official who had no reservation. She was particularly incensed that as one of only three women on the flight, and the only one traveling alone, she had been "selected as the victim for this subterfuge because I appeared to be the passenger who was most defenseless and susceptible to intimidation without recourse."[52] Little did the steward know with whom he was dealing.

Margolin's courtroom successes were often viewed not just as personal victories but as symbolic victories for women. Fifth Circuit judge Elbert P. Tuttle, who first met Margolin when she worked at TVA for his former law partner, William Sutherland, recognized that Margolin "contributed very much . . . to the much too slowly awakening realization that high professional competence may be demonstrated equally well by women as by men advocates."[53] Similarly, Fifth Circuit chief judge Brown proclaimed Margolin as "the original woman's liberationist." She was a very able advocate, as he witnessed from her frequent appearances in his court, "but when the going gets tough on the legal arguments, at that moment she liberates the woman and turns on all of her charms."[54] Margolin, the accomplished attorney, was a role model not only for women lawyers in Washington but also for young women in her hometown of New Orleans, whose mothers encouraged them to grow up to be like Bessie Margolin.[55]

She took her image, and that of female government lawyers, seriously, as Jerry Kluttz, a *Washington Post* columnist, learned in April 1953. Kluttz wrote about an unnamed "brilliant but alcoholic" female government attorney who got in a cab and asked to be driven to Union Station to catch a train to Dallas to try an important case. En route, Kluttz wrote, she pulled out a bottle and took a drink.[56] Just hours after the paper hit the newsstands, Margolin started receiving facetious inquiries about the story and fired off a letter in protest. She castigated the columnist for "subjecting a limited and rather readily identifiable group of women employees to further unjustified indignities and slander."[57]

At the Supreme Court, Margolin's self-assurance continued to rise not only because she argued there often but also because each appearance further enhanced her expertise as a Supreme Court advocate with firsthand knowledge of the growing body of FLSA decisions she cited. She frequently invoked cases she had earlier argued to several of the same justices. During Margolin's 1957 argument in *Mitchell v. Bekins,* for example, involving the meaning of *establishment* for purposes of the FLSA's retail and service establishment exemption, she referred repeatedly to the Court's 1945 ruling in *Phillips v. Walling,* a case four of the justices had heard her argue. The audiotape, left running after Margolin had left the podium, captured Justice Harlan's otherwise off-the-record comment. "Two good lawyers," he said, apparently referring to Margolin and her formidable adversary that day, William French Smith, then in private practice and later U.S. attorney general under President Ronald Reagan.[58]

Margolin took great pride in her Supreme Court record. She was deeply offended by what she considered "downright disparaging" and "scornful" claims that all one had to do to win a Fair Labor Standards Act case in the Supreme Court was to stand up and say, "Your Honors, this is a case arising under the Fair Labor Standards Act," and then sit down. She was aware of certain detractors, perhaps envious of her winning record, who viewed FLSA cases, which were largely limited to statutory interpretation and whose New Deal origins had long ago stopped provoking hostility from the bench, as easier to win than Supreme Court cases that posed heady and politically divisive constitutional questions. When she recounted this perspective at a Federal Bar gathering in the presence of Judge Charles Fahy, he vehemently remonstrated and reminded Margolin that he in fact had lost a Fair Labor Standards Act case in the Supreme Court when he was solicitor general.[59] The truth was, and still is, there are no easy cases at the Supreme Court.

Margolin also sought to enhance the reputation of the FLSA as a subject worthy of recognition by lawyers and law schools, despite its complex exemptions and circuitous definitions, all susceptible to frequent amendment. As late as 1967, she opined, "Specialization in FLSA and related wage legislation has not, thus far, achieved any comparable 'bread and butter' interest, and perhaps may never do so, but the widespread and important impact of the FLSA upon employees and businesses would appear to be at least equal to that of Federal Taxation and Labor Relations Law."[60] She wanted other members of the bar to recognize the FLSA as she knew it, as one of the nation's most vital pieces of social and economic legislation.[61]

Because she so valued the FLSA and her time in court, Margolin had a vaulted view of her work within the hierarchy of the Labor Solicitor's Office. She considered the Litigation Division, and particularly the appellate section, to be without peer not only in the Solicitor of Labor's Office but also in the federal government, with the exception of the Solicitor General's Office within the Justice Department. She was viewed by lawyers in other divisions of the Labor Solicitor's Office as single, totally work driven, a perfectionist, and an elitist.[62] Although one young lawyer's office was right around the corner from hers, it was not until after he had written a brief that Margolin ever recognized his existence and started to speak to him in the corridor by name.[63] Others agreed with Margolin's high appraisal of her work. When Judge Simon Sobeloff, a former solicitor general, was asked in the mid-1960s by a recent law graduate to recommend the best offices in the federal government to practice appellate law, he offered only two suggestions: the Office of the Solicitor General and the office of Bessie Margolin.[64]

Paying a Price for Federal Employment

Although Margolin was grateful for her rewarding and high-ranking legal career in the federal government, her public service did not come without a price, especially for someone who supported workers' rights and other liberal social causes. In March 1947, to address criticism that his administration was lax in protecting the government from Communist infiltration, President Harry Truman instituted a far-reaching employee loyalty program. Executive Order 9835 required each executive department to create a "loyalty board," to ferret out disloyal employees largely on the basis of membership in groups deemed subversive by Attorney General Tom Clark. Employees for whom "reasonable grounds for belief in disloyalty" were established, through confidential proceedings, were to be dismissed. The program had many flaws, including the use of anonymous informants, reliance on arbitrary and inconsistent lists of subversive organizations, and repeat investigations of employees that often revisited the same accusations.[65]

When the Labor Department commenced its loyalty program in September 1947, Margolin dutifully listed all organizations to which she belonged.

Neither her membership in Kappa Beta Pi, a women's legal sorority, nor her donations to the American Red Cross raised any concern. Her intermittent membership in the National Lawyers Guild and modest contributions to the Southern Conference for Human Welfare, however, prompted the Labor Department to request that the FBI investigate Margolin's loyalty.[66] The FBI, after cross-checking its files, learned that Margolin's parents had been born in Russia and that she had once contributed ten dollars to the United American Spanish Aid Committee, a group identified as a "Communist-front." The FBI also discovered that Army Military Intelligence, after investigating Margolin during her service in Nuremberg for speaking "very favorably regarding the Russian officials she met in Germany," had recommended earlier that she be separated from government service and returned to the States.[67] Finally, the FBI also uncovered allegations that Margolin, in the late 1930s, had been a member of the Communist Party's "Tennessee Valley Authority Branch" and that she had been the mistress of Larry Fly.[68]

After notifying Attorney General Clark of the information it had collected about Margolin, FBI director J. Edgar Hoover authorized a thorough and discreet investigation. Conducted by a half-dozen field agents in New Orleans, New Haven, Knoxville, Chattanooga, and even Coral Gables, Florida (where Yale professor Lorenzen then lived), Margolin's loyalty investigation offers a glimpse of the postwar hysteria and rumormongering then pervading Washington, D.C., in the name of national security.[69] The agents interviewed no fewer than thirty-nine people, including four confidential informants, work colleagues, janitors, receptionists, managers of Margolin's various residences, and even the hairdresser she visited weekly. The vast majority of these people consistently praised Margolin as a dedicated and hardworking public servant. Joe Swidler, then TVA's general counsel, described Margolin as a humanitarian who was sympathetic to appeals for help from underprivileged groups, while John Lord O'Brian called her intensely patriotic. Everyone who was willing to have their statements attributed to them vouched for Margolin's loyalty, despite risks to their reputations. When one former labor solicitor stated he had no reason to doubt Margolin's loyalty, the FBI noted that he himself had belonged to the National Lawyers Guild and that his wife had belonged to the Washington Committee for Democratic Action, both suspect groups. Two confidential informants expressed the only concerns about Margolin, one of whom claimed that she had hired the Labor Department's most liberal employees.[70] Although the FBI ultimately found plenty of evidence that Margolin was a liberal who desired to improve the lot of the workingman, it found no evidence that she had ever been disloyal.[71]

In late March 1948 the FBI closed its investigation and forwarded its report to the Labor Department for review. Eight months later, the Labor Department's Loyalty Board notified Margolin that it had no reasonable grounds for believing that she was disloyal to the government and allowed her to retain her position. Other "liberal" federal employees who had entered government service for New Deal jobs that promoted social democracy through economic reform were less fortunate. By the end of the first year more than 2 million federal workers underwent loyalty screening, and at least 6,000 were subject to similar full-field investigations. Of these an estimated 86 federal employees were fired, and 619 resigned.[72] Although Margolin was luckier than many, her investigation was not without consequences. For more than a year she had been the subject of extensive, stigmatizing scrutiny, which carried the threat of dismissal and intruded on her relationships with friends, colleagues, and acquaintances.

Moreover, each time a question was raised about Margolin's loyalty, as occurred several times, the FBI revisited its earlier investigations. Twice in 1950 and once in 1955, Margolin would come to the attention of the FBI as it investigated others. In each instance—"literature of a Communistic nature" had reportedly been spotted in her apartment, her name had been found on an accused Communist's telephone list, and she had provided a housing reference for a coworker who reportedly associated with Communist sympathizers—the accusations were unproven or deemed inconsequential, and the FBI discontinued its inquiry.[73]

Meanwhile, Joe Swidler, still TVA's general counsel, was also defending himself against a wide range of disloyalty accusations. During the summer of 1951 the FBI received reports that he had attended meetings sponsored by Communist organizations, socialized with "concealed Communist" James Lawrence Fly, and had years earlier closely identified with other individuals in TVA's Legal Department, namely Fly, Herbert Marks, Melvin Siegel, and Bessie Margolin, who were "regarded as extreme left wing pro-Communists." Although the principal informant was a former TVA employee who blamed Swidler for his discharge, the FBI's report prompted the TVA Loyalty Board to proceed against Swidler, threatening discharge if it found evidence to reasonably doubt his loyalty.[74] Swidler had little choice but to treat the specious charges very seriously and filed a voluminous response countering each accusation, including dozens of affidavits he obtained from colleagues and community leaders.[75] Swidler's notes reflect that he considered but ultimately decided against obtaining an affidavit from Margolin to explain the nonpolitical nature of the regular poker evenings they and their colleagues enjoyed throughout their TVA years together. That Swidler relied on affidavits from Fly, Fitts, O'Brian, and others no longer employed by the federal government suggests that he did not want to subject Margolin to further loyalty scrutiny.[76] By the end of 1951 the TVA Loyalty Board had cleared Swidler of all charges.[77]

Even without being involved in Swidler's loyalty case, in December 1954 Margolin faced a second Labor Department Loyalty Board inquiry. For the first time she was asked to supply detailed written answers to a series of questions, which not only revisited her memberships that had prompted the 1947 investigation but also sought the "degree of her association" with the United Federal Workers of America and any other pro-Communist organization on a list compiled by the attorney general. Finally, she was asked to explain her relationship with three federal employees, one of whom also had figured prominently in the charges against Swidler. Three months after receiving Margolin's detailed response, in which she categorically denied having any Communist sympathies, the Labor Department's personnel security officer advised her that her continued employment had been found "to be completely consistent with the interests of national security."[78]

In 1964, when the White House requested a name check for Margolin as a prospective nominee for federal judgeship, the FBI rehashed its 1948 report once again, specifically including its account of her "illicit love affair" with Larry Fly.[79] Although Margolin's relationship with Fly had ended years earlier, her connection to him could still negatively impact her. No stranger to controversy in his protection of personal liberties, ACLU board member Fly in 1947 had urged Attorney General Clark to increase protections for federal workers subject to loyalty inquiries; in 1949 had defended Communist Party member Harry Bridges against one phase of his lengthy prosecution by the Justice Department; and in 1950 had vigorously attacked the Justice Department's and FBI's use of wiretaps in the espionage trial and conviction of alleged Soviet spy Judith Coplon.[80] The FBI first opened its file on Fly in September 1943 and added to it every year between 1949 and 1957, mostly to track and assess his public criticisms of the agency. Not surprisingly, Bessie Margolin's name found its way into Fly's FBI file. In 1951, in response to an unexplained White House request for a name check on Fly, FBI agents recounted the 1943 allegations of his affair with Margolin, alternately referring to their association as "notorious," "illicit," and "immoral."[81]

Pursuing a Professorship

Perhaps on account of Loyalty Board scrutiny or the fear that a possible Republican victor in the 1948 presidential election would curtail FLSA enforcement efforts, Margolin launched a campaign to become a law professor that lasted for the next five years. As she revealed to one prospective dean, "Teaching was my original choice for a profession, but I was unable at the time I completed the work for my JSD to convince any of the deans that it was a good profession for a woman."[82] Now more than fifteen years later, Margolin's appetite for teaching law had been whetted anew, but she found little had improved for women.[83] One law school dean after another regretted that he had no position to offer her.[84] Although she received consistently positive assessments of her character and qualifications, Margolin was fighting a losing battle; before 1950 only five women ever held positions as full-time, tenure, or tenure-track law professors at accredited law schools.[85]

With no teaching prospects and growing demands on her time at the Labor Department, Margolin refocused her efforts on finding a part-time position, preferably teaching labor law in a Washington, D.C., or Maryland law school.[86] Finally, in June 1953 American University invited Margolin to teach a course in the fall semester.[87] Instead of labor law, however, Margolin—the assistant labor solicitor celebrated for her vigorous enforcement of the Fair Labor Standards Act with nearly two decades of experience in federal procedure, evidence, and administrative and constitutional law—was assigned to teach a course in wills. If Margolin was insulted or disappointed, she did not reveal it, even as she wrote to a friend, "Since the subject is quite far removed from any of my specialties, I am finding the preparation rather difficult but quite stimulating."[88] After two semesters Margolin gave up teaching (and the additional income) to devote herself to her increasing responsibilities at the Labor Department.

Effectively barred from full-time academia, Margolin found other teaching outlets. She eagerly accepted an invitation to return to Yale in 1960 to present a lecture on appellate advocacy to first-year students as part of their moot court program.[89] She also intensified her training efforts within the Labor

Department, where for many years she played a significant role in the professional development of its lawyers. Despite the dry titles of her presentations, such as "Organization and Functions of Appellate Litigation Division" and "Historical Background of Wage and Hour Legislation," Margolin seized these opportunities to impart her enthusiastic and encyclopedic understanding of the FLSA and its importance as a body of law. She recognized how easy it was to become immersed in day-to-day problems and isolated cases involving technical, refined aspects of the law. She was determined to awaken the department's lawyers to "the dramatic struggles behind and the economic and social principles underlying the legislation with which we are spending our working days." Margolin firmly believed the FLSA's rich and colorful history did and should influence the content of the department's interpretations, legislative reports, and legal briefs.[90]

Through her in-house training sessions Margolin also shared her considerable expertise in appellate advocacy, extending her impact beyond the lawyers she supervised or consulted on a daily basis. As the Labor Department attracted lawyers early in their legal career, many straight from law school, she covered basic principles and offered commonsense instructions she had learned, such as "Be respectful but don't be afraid" and "Talk loudly enough." After explaining the wise adage that "oral argument alone won't win your case—but can lose it for you," she warned her pupils not to engage in obvious oratory and insisted that simple speech makes the most powerful appeal. Drawing from her personal tactics, she stressed the importance of knowing one's weaknesses and how to overcome them. "Personally, I find myself dull, tongue-tied and dumbfounded without questions," she told her staff. "When I learned this about myself I deliberately started my arguments in way to provoke and encourage questioning." She prodded her students to keenly observe and learn from other lawyers—if for no other reason, she explained, than often an adversary's argument "will advance your contentions better than your own argument will."[91]

Aunt Bess

Known primarily for her professional life as a single and ambitious woman, Margolin also enjoyed a full and active personal life. Although she enjoyed other people's children, she could not see herself changing diapers or otherwise involved in the messy business of babies and toddlers.[92] She was, nevertheless, a beloved and important member of her extended family, which included four nephews. And they all came to know and admire Aunt Bess, the career woman.

Margolin and her sister, Dora, remained very close, in spite of the geographical distance between them. Margolin's relationship with Dora's husband, Harry Trifon, however, was tested at times. His conventional attitudes about women conflicted with Margolin's liberal ideas, especially the priority she gave her career. Harry had not only dated Margolin before realizing they had little in common, but he had introduced her to his friend Bob Butler, who also ultimately lost to Margolin's ambition. Over the years their love for Dora forced Margolin and Harry to get along, their accord subject to occasional disagreements and heated exchanges, most often about politics and women's role in society.[93]

From the Trifon boys' earliest memories, Aunt Bess was a glamorous, almost exotic figure. Seeing articles about her in newspapers and magazines, they were proud to have a famous aunt in the family.[94] She wore a fox stole, its head and tail still on, enough to fascinate any young boy, and called her nephews "darling."[95] When the Trifons drove from Shreveport to New York, they stopped in Washington, D.C., to visit Margolin. Although Dora, too, hired maids to clean and help with cooking, the Trifons acknowledged the special relationship Margolin enjoyed with Maude, her full-time housekeeper and trusted companion, generously offering financial and other assistance over their nearly four decades together. Margolin's beloved Cavalier King Charles spaniel, Chucky, and her well-appointed apartment with a television and chic pink bedroom enchanted the boys.[96]

Aunt Bess was affectionate, genuinely interested, and involved in the boys' lives. She was also generous and fearless when it came to entertaining her adolescent nephews, each of whom spent a summer with her when they reached twelve or thirteen—as Malcolm later conceded, "the worst possible age to take on a young boy for the summer."[97] And what summers they were, eagerly anticipated and then thoroughly enjoyed. Margolin treated her young nephews as if they were small adults, introducing each of them to Washington, D.C., as she knew it. During the day Margolin saw no need to babysit her nephews while she went to work, on at least one occasion letting Toby entertain himself by touring the FBI headquarters, much to his delight.[98]

In early 1955 Dora was diagnosed with leukemia. Seeking a better climate and Stanford University's medical care, Harry moved Dora and the boys to

Palo Alto, California. Margolin's work regularly took her to the West Coast, enabling frequent visits with Dora and her family. When experimental treatments put Dora into a coma, surgery relieved the swelling in her brain but impaired her mobility and speech.[99] As a result of her sister's illness and early death in 1960, Margolin assumed a greater role in her nephews' lives, especially with young Malcolm.

Malcolm's visit with Aunt Bess in the summer of 1956 was much like his older brothers' trips had been, including visits with legal luminaries. Margolin took him to the Supreme Court to visit Justice Frankfurter, reflecting the cordial relationship the two enjoyed outside the courtroom. She carried two copies of Frankfurter's recent book, *Of Law and Men,* a series of essays, including advice to young men interested in pursuing a career in law. In Malcolm's copy Frankfurter inscribed, "It cheers me to think that you want to have this book—for I assume that your Aunt Bess is too good to force it on you."[100] In Margolin's copy he wrote, "For Bessie Margolin, who pleases me more often than I—through no fault of mine—please her."[101] As they were leaving the Supreme Court building, Margolin asked Malcolm what he thought of the great jurist. Malcolm remembers his aunt's disappointment when he expressed his surprise over Frankfurter's wrinkled seersucker suit.[102]

Malcolm's visit with Solicitor General Simon Sobeloff was more memorable. Sobeloff asked Malcolm how he was enjoying his summer. Margolin interjected, "Well, his one disappointment is that the All-Star Game is here and he would really like to go, but there are no tickets available." To Malcolm's amazement Sobeloff opened his desk drawer and pulled out a ticket. Malcolm went to the All-Star Game on his own, a thrilling experience for a young teen. Looking back, Malcolm credited his aunt with arranging in advance for Sobeloff to present the ticket; she was not a sports fan and would not otherwise have had any reason to mention Malcolm's interest in the game.[103]

Social Life

As Toby learned, his Aunt Bess enjoyed an active social life. She liked hosting cocktail parties, often inviting her regular crowd, which included Dorothy Owens, the Swidlers, the Fowlers, and the Horskys. She was a good poker player and loved to bet on horses at the track. She came home late one evening after Toby was, or pretended to be, asleep on the foldout couch in her living room. She was accompanied by a gentleman, who, spying her young guest, hesitated about entering her apartment. According to Toby, his aunt said, "Don't worry, he's asleep," before they disappeared behind her bedroom door. The man left before morning, and the subject was never discussed. On other occasions when Toby inquired about various men in Margolin's life, she quickly dismissed his questions, saying, "He's a friend of mine." Years later Toby again witnessed his aunt's penchant for partying. After an evening of blackjack on a trip to Lake Tahoe, an exhausted Toby entreated, "Bess, it's getting late." His aunt shooed him away, telling him, "You can go ahead, I'm fine," and continued playing cards, enjoying her cocktail, cigarettes, and gambling companions until four in the morning.[104]

In the mid-1950s Bessie endeared herself to Ted Clifton, a charismatic and talented military man who later served as a top aide to Presidents Kennedy and Johnson. Clifton's letters to Margolin while he was stationed in Germany and France suggest their relationship ranged somewhere between flirtatious and intimate, certainly closer than he would have disclosed to his wife. In one letter Clifton told Margolin how very much he missed her and that he planned to go shopping in Paris "for some liquid reminder of afternoons and evenings gone by." He asked his "beautiful, passionate" correspondent to tell him "which particular essence you now choose to touch behind your ears, and between . . . uh, oh . . . anyway, what kind of perfume would you like?"[105]

Three months later Clifton chastised Margolin for being so "frugal with words," assuring her that he, and no one else, opened all of his mail. He thanked her for sending him a book about the importance of simple words but was disappointed that *love* was omitted. He believed it could "convey an idea from one mind to another, and in one specific case I know of, may convey it exactly, n'est-ce pas?"[106] He next wrote from Paris, pleased about Margolin's recent work achievements and the high esteem she enjoyed, and asked whether she wanted the same perfume, "Femme, or some Griffe, or even something more scintillating?"[107] Since her affair with Larry Fly, she had learned the importance of discretion and avoiding romance with direct reports. But Clifton's letters suggest that she attached less significance to avoiding intimacy with a married man. And Clifton would not be the last married man Margolin captivated.

9

EQUAL OPPORTUNITIES, PERSONAL
AND PUBLIC, 1961–1972

View from Abroad

In January 1961 Margolin's successes earned her the Labor Department's coveted Career Service Award, granting a year of paid leave for pursuits to further her work. Under the award's generous terms she spent four months the following fall at Harvard's Graduate School of Public Administration studying labor relations, followed by seven months in Europe, primarily at the International Labor Office in Geneva, with visits to Belgium, Italy, France, Great Britain, and the Scandinavian countries, hosted by American labor attachés in each locale.

Although she submitted a formal report in October 1962, at the end of her journeys, Margolin also captured her work and leisure experiences abroad in a series of letters to Robert W. Ginnane, who had served since 1955 as general counsel to the Interstate Commerce Commission (ICC), after a distinguished career in the Solicitor General's Office. "I simply feel the need to record some of the many beauties I am seeing, lest I forget them as I had most of what I saw in 1946," she wrote to him, referring to her scant records of Nuremberg. Margolin's letters also reveal an intimate involvement with Ginnane, which had blossomed at least four years earlier, despite the fact that he was married and had a teenage daughter.[1] Although Ginnane's ICC office was located in the same building as the Labor Department, his relationship with Margolin is best evidenced by their long-distance correspondence. In twenty-four letters written on ninety onionskin pages, Margolin expressed her feelings for Ginnane, both in her greetings ("Dear, Dear Robert") and in her dramatic closings ("As ever" and "Remember"). She signed all of them the same way, "Marc," either as a pet name or an alias, reminiscent of the discreet and solitary "L" Larry Fly had used to sign his love letters nearly twenty years earlier. Margolin's letters to Ginnane also reflect a whimsy and flirtatiousness in her character that were hidden, if they existed, in the one-sided remnants of her correspondence with Burton, Fly, Monneray, and Clifton. In one letter, after querying whether Ginnane was still bemused by the "crazy little women" of a popular song, she described herself as one crazy little woman who yearned to see him when she returned.[2] She ended another letter writing that she was unable to convey the most important things she wanted to say and would save them for when they saw each other again.[3] He apparently felt the same way, reflected by Margolin's comment "The thoughts and sentiments you expressed are completely reciprocated on this side of the Atlantic Ocean."[4] Margolin also shared news of late-in-life marriages, including that of her dear and now widowed friend Kate, reflecting her comfort in discussing the subject with Ginnane, if not also dropping a hint about her desires for their future.[5]

Aspiring to the Federal Bench

In April 1962 Margolin set her sights on a bold new professional goal. After President Kennedy appointed one of her close colleagues from the Solicitor General's Office to the U.S. Court of Claims, she, too, wanted to become a federal judge.[6] Even more audacious than her 1927 decision to attend law school, Margolin now wanted to join the nation's nearly four hundred lifetime federal judges, of which there were still only two women.[7] Bolder yet, Margolin wanted one of ninety-seven federal appellate judgeships, which, since Florence Allen retired in 1959, no woman had held.

From Europe, Margolin set her plan in motion. She wrote to Louisiana congressman Hale Boggs, a friend and fellow Tulane alumnus, and assistant labor secretary Esther Peterson, a top woman in federal government, and requested their help in getting a judgeship on Washington's U.S. Court of Appeals or the U.S. Court of Claims.[8] Although there was no vacancy, several circuit judges were nearing retirement. Boggs and Peterson pledged their considerable support, which Peterson immediately demonstrated by writing to Attorney General Robert F. Kennedy to recommend Margolin's appointment.[9] Joe Fowler, now assistant Treasury secretary, soon joined her campaign. Margolin "combines nearly thirty years of outstanding service as a Federal attorney with a record in the trial and appellate area that is unusual, if not unique," wrote Fowler to deputy attorney general Nicholas Katzenbach, adding that her appointment to the bench would acknowledge both the service and the role of a woman lawyer in the judicial system.[10] Notwithstanding her qualifications and influential backers, Margolin's judicial campaign would be neither swift nor certain.

During her travels Margolin received word about extensive changes under way at the Labor Department. She was to be promoted to associate solicitor, one of only three, and as part of a general reorganization would assume responsibility for trial litigation in addition to appellate work. Despite this great recognition of her abilities and the increase in grade and pay that went with it, Margolin was averse to the added administrative duties. Just three years earlier, despite being gratified by a newspaper's favorable report that she was Stuart Rothman's likely and worthy successor as labor solicitor, she told a close colleague that she did not want the supervisory duties that would interfere with her true passion: "I love practicing law—I love arguing cases in the courts."[11] Now faced with a more definite promotion, Margolin again expressed little excitement. She was not at all certain she would be happy with the additional administrative and personnel duties that the new hierarchical arrangement would impose but reasoned that there was nothing she could do about it from Europe.[12] Margolin returned to the Labor Department in October 1962 and, without objection, immersed herself in her work.

Although her duties as associate solicitor swelled considerably, she made time to quietly resume her judicial campaign, meeting with Hale Boggs to plan strategy. By January 1963 she armed him with her latest accolade— nomination by the labor solicitor for a National Civil Service League Career Service Award and a growing list of other influential supporters. Justice Arthur Goldberg, who had served as labor secretary for twenty months before taking Felix Frankfurter's seat on the Supreme Court, had pledged his wholehearted endorsement, as had Justice Douglas, Solicitor General Archibald Cox, and Morris Abram, her Nuremberg friend who had recently won a Supreme Court voting rights case in which Attorney General Kennedy personally participated. Other federal judges and leading members of the bar were ready to vouch for her qualifications.[13]

Timely and favorable public recognition made it hard for the White House to ignore Margolin. In May 1963 she was one of six women to receive the Federal Woman's Award, the only lawyer among them, created just two years earlier to recognize outstanding women in federal government. The elaborate black-tie ceremony, where she was honored for her exceptional competence and significant contributions in handling cases before the Supreme Court, followed a meeting with President Kennedy in the Oval Office. After complimenting their looks, Kennedy praised the winners' achievements, hoping women across the country might follow their example by entering public service.[14] Margolin acknowledged to a colleague some misgivings about the segregated recognition but eased her conscience by allowing, "Perhaps discrimination against women has not disappeared to the extent of denying a little discriminatory recognition in favor of women."[15]

Six months later President Kennedy's assassination shocked the country. Immediately following the tragedy, one dramatic image seared into collective memory validated the role of women judges. The photo depicted Texas federal district judge Sarah Tilghman Hughes, who had been urgently called aboard Air Force One, administering the oath of office to Lyndon B. Johnson.[16] Ted Clifton, Margolin's affectionate correspondent, now a major general, was also aboard in his role as Kennedy's top military aide; he served Johnson in the same capacity until he retired in July 1965. Shortly after Johnson took office, Clifton offered to help Margolin's judicial quest by putting in a good word for her.[17]

Yet Johnson's earliest judicial appointment was not a woman. In January 1964 he responded, instead, to the push for qualified African Americans on the federal bench by appointing Spottswood William Robinson III to Washington's federal district court. Just two months later Margolin's campaign shifted into high gear following news of three upcoming vacancies on the Washington federal courts she most wanted, one on the circuit court and two on the court of claims. The vacancies nicely coincided with *Time* magazine's brief but positive mention of Margolin in a story about the progress being made by prominent women lawyers to succeed in a still male-dominated profession.[18]

Margolin continued to enlist well-connected supporters and did not mince words about her qualifications. She quickly convinced Katie Louchheim, deputy assistant secretary of state for public affairs, who had been instrumental in creating the Federal Woman's Award, with this self-confident appraisal: "There are very few men attorneys, and I know there is no other woman attorney, with as much experience in federal appellate practice as I have been privileged to acquire."[19] The well-connected Louchheim wrote directly to Ralph A. Dungan, special assistant for presidential appointments, endorsing Margolin.[20] John Lord O'Brian, Margolin's loyal mentor, threw his considerable weight behind Margolin with a strong recommendation that Attorney General Kennedy personally acknowledged.[21]

The campaign was successful enough to advance Margolin to the next stage of official consideration. In March 1964 the Justice Department asked her to complete its lengthy questionnaire.[22] At the same time, the White House began to compile information about her, beginning with a memo that favorably noted O'Brian's backing. As for her age, the memo emphatically read, "*She won't tell.*"[23] Elsewhere in the White House, Bill Moyers, Johnson's special assistant and later press secretary, noted that Hale Boggs was "strongly behind this woman."[24]

It was another good sign that Margolin was invited to interview with John B. Clinton, who served as executive assistant to Dungan and to another top Johnson talent scout, Civil Service Commission chairman John W. Macy Jr.[25] Margolin impressed Clinton, who summarized their March 20, 1964, meeting. Driven by her love of practicing law and her extensive Supreme Court experience, Clinton learned, she was most interested in a judgeship on the circuit court or court of claims and had little interest in an administrative position on a regulatory commission. He noted Boggs's support but was even more impressed by her widespread backing from lawyers and judges around town including some Supreme Court justices. Clinton summed up Margolin as "a mature, self possessed, self-confident woman of somewhat flamboyant appearance."[26]

Within his overwhelmingly positive and accurate appraisal, Clinton's comment about Margolin's "somewhat flamboyant appearance" is noteworthy. Its negative connotation contrasts with contemporaneous and later assessments of her elegant and fashionable appearance. Clinton may have been struck by Margolin's dramatic hairstyle, which featured white streaks at her temples and forehead, in stark contrast with her otherwise surprisingly black hair. At the same time, he may have considered her high-fashion wardrobe out of the norm in conservative and male-dominated Washington, D.C. Whatever the reason, Clinton's unexplained comment tarnished the assessment of a woman who wanted a seat on the almost exclusively male federal bench.

The next day Margolin's name was discussed in the Oval Office. President Johnson called labor secretary Wirtz to grill him on several issues, including the progress being made on Johnson's pledge to put women in high-level federal positions. By this point the president had appointed or promoted some fifty women, but none had been judges. When Wirtz mentioned Margolin as a judicial candidate, Johnson asked her age and whether she had "any political assets." Wirtz's uncertainty prompted Johnson's impatient demand: "Don't you be hesitant about this! This is what I want! I want you to push me on some of these things. I don't know about them if you don't tell me. . . . I'm looking for women, so just get that woman's biography over here. . . . Get her picture, get her biography, get four or five copies of it, and then get this record on cases, and let me have it."[27]

Within the hour Johnson called Dungan to ask about Margolin. "She's a very able woman," Dungan replied, describing her as one of the department's best lawyers "for years and years." They discussed her possible appointment to the District of Columbia's Juvenile Court, but Dungan pointed out the seat offered neither the prestige nor intellectual challenge of a federal judgeship or even of Margolin's current work arguing before the Supreme Court. Taking a longer-range view, President Johnson directed Dungan to "put a name check on her right quick."[28] One week later Margolin remained on the president's mind. "What about this Jewish woman for this Court of Claims?" Johnson pressed Dungan, and then queried without further explanation, "Is she a little dangerous on that?" Dungan replied only to remind the president, "She's really hot for the circuit court."[29]

In the meantime Margolin submitted her questionnaire to the Justice Department.[30] She detailed her impressive career, listing all of her appellate cases and summarizing her most noteworthy litigation. She also explained that virtually all of her work was of national importance, as judicial acceptance or rejection of the Labor Department's interpretations determined the wage and hour rights of an estimated 27.5 million workers employed by more than one million employers and set the labor standards for eighty-five thousand government contracts annually.[31]

Two more influential backers soon contacted the White House on Margolin's behalf. "If I had to list the ten best advocates who have appeared before us in the last 25 years that I have been on the bench," wrote Justice Douglas directly to President Johnson, "I would put Bessie Margolin down as one of the ten. She is tops."[32] On her husband's congressional stationery Lindy Boggs, a fellow Newcomb alumna and Hale's savvy wife, who would later assume his seat in Congress, hand-wrote a letter to Liz Carpenter, Lady Bird's chief of staff and LBJ's confidante. Margolin was "eminently qualified by temperament, training and experience for a Federal judgeship," wrote Lindy, adding that her childhood in an orphanage would inspire young people struggling to remain in school.[33]

A month passed without judicial nominations. Fearing her candidacy was losing momentum, Margolin sent Peterson her latest media attention—an article in the Federal Bar Association's magazine that featured Margolin in a series on distinguished women attorneys, noting her "beauty and brains."[34] Peterson forwarded the article to Clinton and Dungan, reiterating her unwavering support for Margolin.[35]

In the meantime a White House aide requested that the FBI check its files for information regarding Margolin, as President Johnson had directed. The FBI's prompt response summarized its 1948 loyalty investigation of Margolin, which "failed to establish Communist Party membership" but disclosed allegations of her "illicit love affair" with Larry Fly.[36] Whether Margolin's thirty-year-old affair with Fly hurt her bid for a judgeship is unknown; the last time a female federal court nominee had faced allegations of an improper relationship with a married man was in 1951, when Congress refused to confirm Frieda B. Hennock's appointment.[37] At a minimum a wider circle of people knew about Margolin's romantic scandal. If President Johnson learned about the FBI report, he might have recalled that he, in 1943, along with Sam Rayburn, had prevented Congressman Eugene Cox from questioning Fly about his adulterous relationship with Margolin. Regardless, over the next six months President Johnson filled both vacancies on the court of claims with men.[38]

A disappointed Margolin redoubled her efforts for the circuit court, where there were now two vacancies. She again asked Peterson for help. Although Margolin recognized that "the masculine competition would be much stiffer" for the circuit court, the two vacancies improved her chances.[39] In a letter to the White House, Peterson asked Clinton and Macy to give Margolin "any attention you can."[40] Over the next six months, however, President Johnson announced five nominations to Washington's federal bench—all men—filling the two seats on the circuit court and three on the district court.[41]

Following these appointments, a not-too-subtle reference to Margolin appeared in a May 1965 *Washington Post* article, asking "Where Are the 'Can-Do' Women?" Featuring John Macy, "the President's No. 1 talent scout," the article bemoaned the dearth of qualified women's names being submitted to the White House. Hardly a day passed, it reported, that the president did not ask someone—sometimes asking a dozen people a day—to send him the name of just one woman qualified for a top job. And then, undoubtedly referring to Margolin without naming her, the article described a quiet campaign then under way to win a lower court appointment for a lady lawyer in the Labor Department as a stepping-stone to the Supreme Court.[42]

Despite the White House's reported searching and the nod to Margolin's judicial aspirations, all federal judgeships in Washington had been filled. During that time Margolin finally told her backers that she might consider a nonjudicial appointment.[43] Following her lead, in July 1965 Hale Boggs wrote to Macy, expanding the scope of Margolin's possible interests for some higher post that could put her exceptional talents to even greater use than her current role as associate solicitor.[44] When Katie Louchheim called to test Margolin's interest in any of six administrative positions for which the Civil Service Commission was seeking female candidates, however, Margolin declined them all, citing her lack of interest and qualifications. She knew she was making herself a hard case, but she refused to settle for just any appointment.[45]

In late November 1965 another federal appellate vacancy emerged.[46] Boggs, now assistant majority leader in the House, again contacted John Macy on Margolin's behalf, as did Esther Peterson.[47] In his reply to Boggs, Macy provided a glimmer of hope for Margolin: "She does indeed make an interesting candidate for this post."[48] Margolin also asked Joe Fowler and labor secretary Wirtz to resume their efforts. "If the appointment of a woman is in the cards," wrote Margolin, "it would be appropriate to advance my name for consideration."[49] Fowler, O'Brian, former labor solicitor William S. Tyson, and others strongly recommended Margolin for the vacancy, some of whom noted that she gave the president the opportunity to appoint a highly qualified woman.[50]

Throughout her campaign Margolin directed the Labor Department's trial and appellate litigation, continuing personally to brief and argue significant appellate cases. When she flew out to Los Angeles for an argument at the Ninth Circuit, her nephew Malcolm met her at the airport. She was prepared for her argument, as always, recalled Malcolm, but awaiting word about the judgeship kept her on pins and needles. She expected to get the appointment and soon.[51] When she returned to Washington, however, there was still no news. Margolin focused on preparing for her twenty-fourth Supreme Court argument, a record previously achieved by only two other women lawyers and relatively few men.[52] On December 8, 1965, she argued *Wirtz v. Steepleton*

General Tire Company, seeking to reverse the Sixth Circuit's acceptance of industry standards to determine an employer's entitlement to the FLSA "retail or service establishment" exemption. *Steepleton* turned out to be Margolin's last Supreme Court argument and, as she learned in February, when the Court announced its unanimous decision, another victory for her career tally.[53]

The same day Margolin argued at the Supreme Court, Macy wrote to Clinton. Amid rumors that a woman would fill the circuit court vacancy, Margolin's name was being "bandied about."[54] Recognizing the value in considering a woman, Macy suggested they should prepare a slate of "prominent lady lawyers with appellate experience" before the first of the year.[55] When 1966 began, however, Macy's first mention of Margolin was not as a judge but as a candidate for the newly created Equal Employment Opportunities Commission (EEOC).[56]

By late January 1966 deputy attorney general Ramsey Clark sent President Johnson a memo identifying the candidates the Justice Department was evaluating for the circuit court vacancy. Topping his list was district judge Spottswood Robinson, described by Clark as a capable scholar whose talents would be better utilized on the appeals court than on the trial court. Since Thurgood Marshall became solicitor general, Clark added, there had been only one African American judge on the U.S. Courts of Appeals. Of all circuits, Clark reasoned, it would be "most appropriate to have a Negro on the District Circuit where the population is predominantly Negro and the Court is large."[57] Clark then listed, in alphabetical order, fifteen additional people who had been proposed for the vacancy. Although there were no women on the U.S. Courts of Appeals, Margolin was the only woman on Clark's list.

In June 1966, while Margolin anxiously awaited word on the circuit court judgeship, President Johnson urged delegates to the National Conference on the Status of Women to aid his search for women judges, scientists, ambassadors, and other professionals to occupy leadership posts in federal government. While moderating a panel discussion the following day, John Macy, too, emphasized the need for more women in public service.[58] Despite the promising rhetoric for women, on October 6, 1966, President Johnson elevated Robinson to the circuit court.[59]

From 1963 through LBJ's last appointments in 1968 Margolin watched as men filled fifteen seats on Washington's federal courts.[60] When Johnson finally appointed a woman to Washington's federal bench in 1968, he did not increase the number of women federal jurists but only filled the vacancy created when district judge Burnita Shelton Matthews retired.[61] Although Margolin never pressed to become a federal trial judge, a woman's appointment to any federal bench relieved the pressure on the president to appoint other women judges. Johnson's pledge to put women in top federal positions did not benefit Margolin, but nationwide he increased the number of women on the federal bench to four, including his 1968 appointment of a woman to the Ninth Circuit.[62]

Margolin was deeply disappointed over not getting a judgeship and was left wondering why she could not win the president's approval. While there were ample reasons given for Johnson's nominations, the only reason recorded for not nominating Margolin was her age, coupled with her gender. In January 1967 Macy agreed with a staff recommendation "that her age (58) would tend to preclude her from consideration. One does not get the impression from perusing her record, that she outshines some of the younger feminine candidates that we have."[63] Margolin was younger, however, than several of the male judges Johnson had nominated, and she was only four years older than the woman he appointed to Washington's federal district court.[64] But Margolin never saw the memos in the White House or FBI files and therefore would never know that her appearance, age, and past love life were all part of her dossier. If she believed that she personally had been denied a judgeship for any of these reasons, or her gender, she neither recorded it nor shared her view with anyone who can shed light on the subject today.[65] Moreover, she knew she had been considered for the appointment, which had not happened three decades earlier until she asked Secretary Frances Perkins to address the gender discrimination that prevented her from being considered for promotion to assistant solicitor.

Instead, Margolin had a different theory. Three close friends from her days at Yale wielded considerable political influence. Justice Douglas and Treasury secretary Joe Fowler had stepped forward to lend their support, while Justice Abe Fortas, the most influential of those three men from his role as President Johnson's personal lawyer and longtime confidant, was conspicuously absent from her team of backers. Margolin privately speculated that Fortas and his wife, Carolyn Agger, with whom she socialized, may have quietly sabotaged her efforts with their silence or by expressing concern about her drinking. Margolin's alcohol theory was tenuous, however, as neither Fortas nor Agger, a prominent tax lawyer with a penchant for cigars and bourbon, were teetotalers.[66] Margolin's nephew Malcolm, who spent a good deal of time with his aunt during her judgeship campaign while he attended law school in Washington, recalled that she regularly enjoyed a few gin and tonics or glasses of bourbon before dinner. He considered her generous alcohol consumption consistent with liberal social drinking habits at the time but never a problem.[67] For whatever reason, the fact that Margolin never listed her longtime colleague Fortas, one of the president's closest advisors, among her references strongly suggests that she believed he would offer little support for her judicial campaign.[68]

Discovering the Principles of Equal Pay and Equal Opportunity

Margolin's failure to win a judgeship yielded a gleaming, albeit ironic, silver lining: for the last decade of her career she remained at the Labor Department, where she enforced the Equal Pay Act of 1963 (EPA) and the Age Discrimination in Employment Act of 1967. Prior to the passage of these laws, Margolin's work had focused on neither gender nor age. She came to these responsibilities late in her career, when her own gender and age challenged her bid for a judgeship, and only after the subjects of sex and age discrimination had piqued her professional interest for the first time during her sabbatical.

While examining European collective bargaining processes, Margolin had also explored those countries' compliance with the Common Market's requirement that men and women receive equal pay for equal work.[69] She summarized her research in a report on the "Status of Women in European Countries Visited," the first women's rights project she had undertaken since her summer job for Doris Stevens three decades earlier. She learned that the term *equal work* was susceptible to evasive interpretations and began questioning the effectiveness of merely eliminating pay differentials when most women held lower-wage jobs than men. She noted the lack of job opportunities and training programs for older people as well. Margolin was learning that the ultimate goal of equality in employment required equality not only in pay but also opportunity. Using a portion of her sabbatical to consider sex and age discrimination in employment turned out to be a wise investment of her time.[70]

In December 1961, one year before Margolin's European travels, President Kennedy established the President's Commission on the Status of Women

(PCSW), the brainchild of assistant labor secretary Peterson, who, with the Labor Department's Women's Bureau, oversaw its administration. Broadly charged with recommending ways to improve women's lives, the PCSW supported federal equal pay legislation, which had failed in Congress every year since 1945.[71] But in June 1963, pushed by the PCSW's findings, Congress finally took action. President Kennedy signed the EPA, outlawing, in his words, the unconscionable practice of paying women lower wages than men.[72]

Far less foreseeable than a federal law against sex-based wage differentials was Congress's decision to add the EPA to the Fair Labor Standards Act and assign its enforcement to the Labor Department. Once this happened, the EPA's court enforcement naturally was entrusted to Margolin in her expanded role as associate solicitor for litigation. The EPA was premised, as Margolin learned and later informed courts and conferences, on stark social and economic facts that had shocked Congress into taking the federal government's first step to safeguard the right of women to hold jobs on the same basis as men. Women workers constituted more than a third of the nation's labor force and had become an essential and permanent part of the modern industrial economy. Three out of five workingwomen were married, many had school-age children, and with a median age of forty, few were simply earning pin money or marking time until marriage. Most of these women worked for the same reasons as men—to support themselves and their dependents and to improve their economic conditions. At the same time, however, they were the victims of an appalling and growing wage gap: women were earning only 59 percent of the median wage paid to men.[73] Nevertheless, the act's basic purpose was not simply one of fairness and justice to women workers, Margolin stressed, but would produce far-reaching social and economic benefits for the nation.

Although Margolin considered the EPA's passage, after eighteen years of unsuccessful legislative attempts, an epic milestone that portended epochal significance, she confessed her initial misgivings.[74] Reflecting considerable compromise by women's organizations and labor groups, the law guaranteed equal pay for "equal" rather than "comparable" work and required equal skill, effort, and responsibility performed under similar working conditions. The law also exempted wages set by seniority or merit systems and permitted pay differentials based on "any factor other than sex," which Margolin called a "blunderbuss" of an exception.[75] Moreover, the EPA was also subject to the FLSA's interstate commerce requirements for coverage and its complex definitions and exceptions.[76]

By 1966 Margolin happily admitted she had underestimated the law, pointing to sizable sums already recovered by thousands of employees as tangible evidence of the Equal Pay Act's significance.[77] She stressed in public speeches and papers, however, that the EPA's full potential was possible only in tandem with Title VII of the Civil Rights Act of 1964, a far broader mandate, which President Johnson had signed one year after Kennedy signed the EPA. Title VII outlawed not only sex-based wage differentials but virtually all discriminatory employment practices in hiring, discharge, and other terms of employment on the basis of race, color, religion, national origin, or sex.[78] The two laws, Margolin explained, reinforced and enhanced each other. Employers who considered evading the EPA through wholesale firings of one sex, segregating women employees, or gerrymandering job duties would find themselves running afoul of Title VII's broader mandates. By the same token the Equal Pay Act's enforcement mechanisms strengthened Title VII's prohibitions against sex-based wage discrimination.[79]

Although Congress created the EEOC to aid Title VII's administration, it gave the agency no enforcement authority, other than any voluntary compliance the EEOC could induce after receiving a complaint.[80] In sharp contrast, the EPA benefited from the Labor Department's explicit enforcement authority, a large and well-trained investigative force, and an extensive body of judicial decisions authoritatively interpreting the FLSA's application. Perhaps one of the EPA's greatest strengths was that its judicial enforcement was entrusted to Margolin, who for more than two decades had shaped the FLSA's court decisions and now turned her attention to the legal, if not moral and personal, fight for equal job opportunities for women. It is difficult to imagine anyone who was better equipped than Margolin to champion through the courts the FLSA's new prohibitions against sex-based wage discrimination while modeling a powerful image of a professional woman.

By the mid-1960s Margolin had perfected her elegant and formidable persona. "A handsome woman of 58, who maintains a fashionable, small apartment in the District and drives a sporty European automobile," began the article in Tulane's alumni magazine, "Miss Margolin unveils camouflaged feminine traits of sensitivity once she permits herself to relax. An air of subtle, polite charm, telegraphed by hesitant smiles, reveals her apparent dislike for trifle and small talk."[81] A courtroom veteran with few equals among women attorneys in Washington, Margolin was by then considered one of the most effective and highly respected lawyers in the entire federal service. One of only thirty-six women in federal government earning at least twenty-five thousand dollars as a GS-17, the second-highest salary grade available for nonpolitical employees, Margolin directly supervised a staff of thirty-five attorneys and dozens of clerical employees in Washington while marshaling a workload of nearly two thousand cases. Litigation had been Margolin's life for more than three decades, and she continued to find it as satisfying and rewarding as ever, especially now that she was tackling the tough problems confronting workingwomen.

Considered a tough but fair administrator by her staff, Margolin was proud that ten of her thirty-five lawyers were women, several of whom she enabled to work part-time to accommodate family obligations—an arrangement she considered quite successful, as she quipped that her part-time women attorneys turned out just as much work as the division's full-time male attorneys.[82] Long before the EPA and Title VII, Margolin had modeled equal opportunity among her own staff; she welcomed women and was equally tough on all of them. For this her subordinates uniformly credited her with starting or enhancing their careers in litigation and appellate law. They also cited Margolin's consistent practice of acknowledging staff for good work yet making sure any blame stopped with her. She encouraged and relied on her capable employees, rewarding them with challenging cases and assignments. Most chafed, however, under the demands Margolin made on their time, as she expected them to stay as late as she did just to find the perfect word, fact, or legal authority for a brief. They did not dispute the end product had been improved as a result; they simply saw a woman who was married to her work and required that they pledge the same allegiance.[83]

Margolin kept an unorthodox work schedule. Former labor solicitor Laurence Silberman humorously recounted at her retirement how he had first learned about her unusual routine. Soon after his 1969 appointment, for days he telephoned her office around eight or nine in the morning, only to have his calls go unanswered. Once informed about his calls, according to Silberman, Margolin said it was inconvenient for her to be in the office before eleven o'clock and that he was undermining the morale of her staff by ringing into her office before that time.[84] Margolin's late-hour arrivals, as her staff also well knew, were due to her recurring hair appointments at the nearby Elizabeth Arden salon. As a concerned supervisor, however, Margolin did not want her subordinates to adopt this aspect of her work habits. As she cautioned a junior lawyer: "Every day I run the risk of receiving a call from the Secretary and getting fired. I don't want that to happen to you."[85]

Speaking Out for Women

The Equal Pay Act cast Margolin as a voice of the Labor Department, a role she had rarely played for the FLSA. Between 1966 and 1972 Margolin addressed no fewer than fourteen conferences, which were organized by bar associations and industry groups across the country. She cogently explained the EPA and Title VII to labor lawyers, corporate counsel, and their industry clients and urged their compliance.[86] She published papers in conjunction with several of her speeches, greatly expanding the reach of her words and furthering her reputation among a national audience.[87] A 1968 Chicago Bar Association conference organizer feared its seminar on the EPA would be incomplete without her, while her invitation to address corporate executives at a 1971 California meeting favorably cited "the fear of god" her EPA litigation track record had put into certain West Coast companies.[88]

Margolin's experiences speaking about sex discrimination at legal conferences and seminars offer a window into being a professional woman in the 1960s. Her appearances generated a buzz that came from the sheer novelty of having a woman who was an accomplished litigator and senior governmental administrator addressing these nearly, if not exclusively, all-male gatherings. Her presence at these events was still such an anomaly that her hosts often made an awkward point of it, such as welcoming her to attend a fashion show or sightseeing tour arranged for the attendees' wives or touting the recent addition of the organization's first female member.[89]

It is not surprising that Margolin, while speaking to mostly men about women's equality in the workplace, contended with a fair share of unenlightened attitudes. The 1967 Atlanta Corporate Law Institute organizers specifically requested, for example, that she address "the question of Amazons," presumably referring to large or powerful women, and the problems involved when one man works among a large group of women, a situation they dubbed as the "Tail Wagging the Dog."[90] Margolin, disturbed by the requested topics, which were repeated in the printed program, seized the occasion as a teachable moment. While she was not averse to a little humor, Margolin explained to the almost all-male audience, "We have not yet reached the stage of public understanding that sex discrimination in employment is both economically and morally wrong to afford the luxury of discussing the subject in a light or humorous context—at least not by a responsible public official." She laid out for them the economic realities that had impelled Congress to pass the EPA, of which a surprising number of otherwise responsible and knowledgeable people were either ignorant or unmindful. Although these facts had not been as widely or as militantly publicized as the facts on race discrimination, Margolin said that widespread sex discrimination in employment and its far-reaching implications, if seemingly not urgent, were equally important to the nation's welfare.[91] After a 1968 speech in Dallas, Margolin warned that the Labor Department and the federal courts did not view sex discrimination as humorous or banal.[92] In spite of the joking attitudes she encountered, Margolin remained optimistic about women's rights. "It'll take time," Margolin told a reporter after her Atlanta speech, "but I think things are looking bright."[93]

Margolin was also developing a more decidedly feminist position as she read widely to prepare for her speeches. She wielded a red pencil as she reviewed articles and government reports to underscore ideas that captured her attention and colorfully challenge or embrace contentions that she read. She scribbled references to feminist writers, including Betty Friedan, Alva Myrdal, Alice Rossi, Simone de Beauvoir, and perhaps for the first time since annotating Bob Butler's book of quotations, Virginia Woolf. On one article Margolin qualified a remark about workingwomen's multiple roles as wives, mothers, and homemakers by writing, "Many are not, however."[94] She demonstrated agreement with the view that women would remain underrepresented in society unless they avoided the mistake of thinking that women as a sex have some special contribution to make. Margolin scribbled in accord there and elsewhere that each woman must be valued for her individual contribution as another human being—not as a sex group but, rather, as men are judged. She recorded other observations, such as "People who attack discrimination on the basis of race often see nothing wrong with discrimination in same way on basis of sex" and "Title VII reached so deep into social policy that for many people it seemed easier to laugh than to think."[95]

Margolin used her speeches as effectively as her litigation to secure compliance from America's employers. Conferences typically gave her a nonadversarial forum to persuade corporate lawyers to abandon specious and unfounded assertions and offered them legal arguments to convince their clients to comply with the new law rather than risking litigation to defend a sexist business practice. She explained the department's consistent position, founded upon the EPA's legislative history, that "equal work," notwithstanding Congress's rejection of the phrase *comparable work,* did not mean "identical work." The law required only that the work be "substantially equal," while insubstantial differences in skill, effort, and responsibility did not render the work unequal. She pointed out the futility of evasive schemes such as transferring higher-paid men and replacing them with lower-wage women or reclassifying duties assigned to men and women, respectively, into "light" and "heavy," rather than the blunt "female" and "male" differentiation.[96] As she stood before them, listing and then refuting employers' most common excuses for paying women less, she was the best evidence of a reliable, career professional who coolly recited statistics and quoted studies to debunk her audience's tired myths.

Expectably, Margolin's public appearances were not free of confrontation or controversy. The most significant of these issues arose at New York University's Annual Labor Conference in April 1966, Margolin's first major opportunity to speak publicly for women's rights. Events transpired that put her at the center of a bigger controversy about the EEOC's failure to treat Title VII's prohibition against sex-based job discrimination seriously, stemming from its last-minute addition to the prohibitions against discrimination based on race, religion, color, and national origin. Sex was added, according to a widely held but disputed view, for the specific purpose of killing the entire civil rights bill by making it unacceptable or a joke.[97] Regardless of intent, the bill's sex amendment prompted immediate and compelling endorsement by female legislators and thus was written into the Civil Rights Act.

At the conference Margolin's remarks immediately followed those of Herman Edelsberg, the EEOC's first executive director. In his presentation Edelsberg, conveying the popular view, said that Title VII's prohibition against sex discrimination was "something of a fluke" and had been "born out of wedlock," with no legislative history to support it. Moreover, Edelsberg asserted that sex discrimination did not carry the same moral overtones as race discrimination and lacked similar protest organizations to sway public attitudes. Coming from the government official entrusted with the law's administration, Edelsberg's remarks stunned Margolin, who abandoned her prepared outline. She immediately challenged Edelsberg and opened her talk by declaring, "The sex provision is not a fluke." She pointed out that the Equal Pay Act's extensive legislative history had paved the way for Title VII's sex provision, which therefore deserved to be treated as an integral part of the civil rights legislation and not as an orphan. The EPA, said Margolin, was only the first step toward job equality, and Title VII was the next step. The fact that Title VII was a giant step and came sooner than expected afforded no basis for taking it lightly or ignoring the Equal Pay Act's history behind it. Title VII's sex discrimination provision, she stressed, "must and will be pushed with equal vigor."[98]

When the conference ended, Margolin believed she had sufficiently rebuffed Edelsberg to improve his attitude. She was therefore dismayed a few weeks later to read that Edelsberg had made similar remarks to another national audience. Although this time Edelsberg refrained from characterizing Title VII's sex discrimination provision as a fluke, he continued to exaggerate the difficulties of interpreting the provision, claiming that its "virtually blank" legislative history left it "shrouded in doubt."[99]

There was only so much that Margolin, a federal government employee, could do to restrain Edelsberg, the head of an independent federal agency, from publicly discrediting Title VII's sex provisions. She reached out, personally and unofficially, to Marguerite Rawalt, an attorney who served on the PCSW and had presided over the Federal Bar Association, the National Association of Women Lawyers, and the National Federation of Business and Professional Women's Clubs. Margolin urged Rawalt to use her considerable prestige to counteract Edelsberg, who was undermining Title VII's sex provision by suggesting that industry could expect lax enforcement. Margolin insisted that every possible effort be made to induce women's organizations to overcome their lack of numbers by more articulate, aggressive, and persistent protests. Margolin offered to assist in any appropriate way she could.[100]

Margolin followed up her offer by using the paper she published following the New York conference to lambast Edelsberg and anyone else who dared claim that Title VII commanded any less authority to prohibit discrimination on account of sex than race. "Only ignorance or thoughtless oversight of the pertinent legislative background, if not simply 'entrenched prejudice' 'rooted in a psychological downgrading of women generally,'" wrote Margolin, "can explain the view that inclusion of 'sex' discrimination in Title VII was no more than a 'fluke' not to be taken seriously."[101] She warned that minimizing the problem of sex discrimination would mislead employers and unions into complacency and deter voluntary constructive measures. Instead, she urged that the objective of sex equality should be joined with the more militant movement for race equality, which would illuminate the reasonableness and justice of the women's cause.[102]

Before Margolin's paper was published, the information she shared with Rawalt about Edelsberg's remarks found its way into several public arenas. In addition to Edelsberg's comments, the EEOC had angered women's rights advocates by issuing a controversial guidance document that allowed publishers to continue running separate male and female "help wanted" ads. In June 1966 Congresswoman Martha Griffiths, speaking on the House floor, sharply criticized the agency's help-wanted guidelines and repeated Edelsberg's comments at the New York conference as evidence of the EEOC's negative attitude toward Title VII sex provisions, which cast ridicule and disrespect on the law.[103] Later that summer Rawalt published an article in the Women Lawyers Journal in which she quoted Griffith's speech and Edelsberg's remarks, and challenged the organization's members to take action. Moreover, just two months after Margolin wrote to Rawalt, the National Association of Women Lawyers, over which she formerly presided, invited Margolin to address its annual conference that summer, themed "Women in Government."[104]

Margolin accepted the invitation. She used her platform to criticize the EEOC for condoning gender-specific help wanted ads and undermining compliance with Title VII's sex provisions. But she directed most of her remarks to reviewing the federal government's progress in promoting job opportunities for women lawyers, boasting that the Labor Department employed the government's greatest percentage of women attorneys, 18 percent, while highlighting dark spots in the glowing picture. Margolin noted the pitifully small percentage of women hearing examiners throughout federal government (7 of 546), a statistic she described as "particularly difficult to explain on any basis other than sex discrimination." Without lodging a similar claim of discrimination, she also cited the dearth of women federal judges (2 of 445), a poignant fact she was then privately citing to advance her candidacy for a federal judgeship.[105]

Becoming a Feminist, Reluctantly

Just as Edelsberg's remarks had pushed Margolin to intensify her public rhetoric about the social, economic, and moral underpinnings of the EPA and Title VII's sex provision, the EEOC's overall lethargy in enforcing Title VII's sex discrimination provisions spurred bold action by leading women's rights advocates. By the summer of 1966 Mary Eastwood, a Justice Department lawyer, and Catherine East, the Labor Department's executive secretary to two federal committees on women's issues, reached out to Betty Friedan, whose 1963 best seller *The Feminine Mystique* had been a rallying manifesto, to organize a feminist action group. Unhampered by official connections, the new group could pressure government to enforce Title VII's equal opportunity for women provisions. At a June meeting of the State Commissions on the Status of Women, they and other like-minded individuals, frustrated by the lack of progress evidenced at the conference, walked out, committed to forming such a group, which Friedan named the National Organization for Women. They agreed to conduct a fall meeting to organize the group, to be known by its urgent acronym, NOW.[106]

The organizing meeting took place in the community room of the Washington Post Building, beginning early Saturday, October 29, 1966. Although Eastwood issued three hundred invitations, Margolin was one of only thirty-two people who attended.[107] Friedan opened the meeting, sharing her hope that their work would be historically comparable with the Seneca Falls Convention of 1848, which had launched the women's rights movement.[108] After robust discussion, the group enthusiastically approved NOW's Statement of Purpose: "To take action to bring women into full participation in the mainstream of American society *now,* assuming all the privileges and responsibilities thereof in truly equal partnership with men." Much of the five-page document reflected views that Margolin had demonstrated in advancing her own career, such as seeing women as human beings who deserve the chance to develop their fullest human potential. It also declared that too few women's organizations had been willing to speak out against dangers facing women, and too many women were restrained by the fear of being called "feminist." NOW would be a civil rights organization for women, akin to those for African Americans and other victims of discrimination.[109]

Never a morning person, Margolin arrived at the meeting more than two hours after it started. Veteran women's rights advocate Dorothy Haener, who was chairing the meeting while Friedan participated in discussions, interrupted the proceedings to welcome Margolin, who drew warm applause from the group.[110] Although Margolin had missed much of the lively debate over the Statement of Purpose, she arrived in time to discuss the proposed Targets for Action, including NOW's involvement in sex discrimination lawsuits, one of Friedan's priorities. Caruthers Berger, a woman lawyer on Margolin's staff who also attended the meeting, moved that NOW appoint a legal committee to file an amicus brief in the case of *Mengelkoch v. Industrial Welfare Commission,* which challenged California's law restricting women's work hours as a violation of the Fourteenth Amendment to the U.S. Constitution and Title VII. "Are they plant workers?" Margolin asked, explaining that the specific facts would determine whether the case could provide as broad a ruling as NOW wanted. She cautioned the fledgling group that there were many legal considerations that might make the lawsuit an undesirable test case and suggested that NOW generally empower its legal committee to determine whether to file an amicus brief but not instruct it to do so. Berger's motion, which she revised as Margolin suggested, passed.[111] Although Margolin had raised a narrow and technical issue, her contribution indicates that she was engaged in the meeting and offered her expertise to help NOW achieve its objectives, which aligned with her litigation goals at the Labor Department.

After NOW's October meeting, the media uniformly characterized the rapidly growing group, which included several men and a large number of prominent women, as a "militant organization."[112] Margolin never became a leader in NOW, but she made her membership part of her public profile. Speaking to a reporter in 1967, Margolin acknowledged that she was a NOW member. "Some people think it is too militant," she added, "but there are quite a few very responsible people in the group."[113] On the other hand, she remained reluctant to describe herself as a feminist even after she joined NOW and took several years to warm to the idea. During another interview the same year she denied ever being a feminist but related that her associates "accused" her of becoming one, as she was devoting at least half her time and that of her office to equal pay matters and related aspects of Title VII.[114] Margolin traced this transition to her growing awareness that she had benefited from job opportunities not available to most women and had been ignorant of what most women workers must contend with.[115] By 1968, after several years of hard-fought Equal Pay Act litigation and witnessing many competent, hardworking women suffer unjustified discrimination, she told a reporter, "I've never been a feminist, but I'm becoming one."[116] Even a wordsmith like Margolin never stopped to define the term *feminist* or to recognize that it described her personal demands for equal opportunity in her legal career. Regardless of what she called herself, Margolin was dubbed by the same reporter as "the nation's number one fighter for equal pay for women."[117]

Besides these larger fights and public platforms, Margolin seized opportunities to lecture misguided opinion leaders and colleagues individually about sex-based job discrimination. In August 1966 she learned that a former member of the Labor Solicitor's Office had published an arbitration award in which he found no sex discrimination by an employer who required physical examinations for female, but not male, employees who wanted work as janitors. "For shame!!!" Margolin chided her colleague, "I do beseech you to release that dynamic, discerning mind of yours from entrenched stereotyped assumptions about the characteristics and potentialities of women in general, and join the more enlightened movement of the mid-60s to recognize women as individual adult human beings."[118] Margolin was far less endearing in 1968 when she reprimanded a *Washington Post* editor for describing equal pay for equal work as a "once-burning problem." Citing her ongoing Equal Pay Act litigation across the country, she challenged the editor in a fiery missive: "I assure you that there are thousands, if not millions, of women workers in the United States who would vehemently dispute your statement that 'the memory of that once-burning problem' has almost been 'quenched.'"[119]

Breaking New Legal Ground

By June 1966 the Equal Pay Act litigation that fueled the passion in Margolin's speeches and letters and would eventually "put the fear of God" in her corporate audiences was beginning to mount. Unlike routine wage and hour cases, Margolin required the regional labor offices to obtain her approval before filing each new EPA case. With her personal involvement, the labor solicitor's field and Washington staff had already filed more than a dozen equal pay lawsuits in almost as many cities across the country, revealing employers' myriad artifices and excuses to justify paying women less than men for the same work. That month the department's lawsuit against Basic,

Inc., a Nevada manufacturer of refractory materials, became the first Equal Pay Act case to go to trial and, just one month later, produced the government's first victory. In his decision the judge quoted the company's plant manager, who, when warned of the act's passage, had scoffed that Congress would never pass such a foolish law. Only a few years later, wrote the judge, that "foolish" law was before the court for interpretation.[120]

Basic, Inc., paid a male laboratory analyst, who alternated between the day and swing shifts, fifteen cents an hour more than its two female laboratory analysts, who worked only the day shift. Mildred Lau, a junior attorney from the labor solicitor's California office, prevailed in urging the trial court to adopt the crucial legal standard, namely that "equal work" under the Equal Pay Act need only be substantially equal and not identical. Applied to the facts that Lau elicited from the witnesses, the judge found that the day shift work performed by all three employees was substantially equal and ruled that the female employees were therefore entitled to the higher wages that the male employee received for day shift work.[121] The next day Lau was in her boss's San Francisco office when Margolin called from Washington to offer hearty congratulations. "Give her a raise," cheered Margolin, obviously thrilled with the outcome. It was a small case, involving only two employees, but it represented a considerable sum of underpaid wages to those two women and portended great change for workingwomen around the country and the companies that employed them.[122]

By the summer of 1968 Margolin and her lawyers had approximately one hundred Equal Pay Act cases pending in trial courts in forty states directly involving an estimated five thousand women workers who were employed as tellers and clerks in banks, sales staff and managers in department stores, ticket agents and office accountants for airlines, and assembly line workers for manufacturers of goods ranging from toy rifles to air conditioners. The Labor Department's lawyers already had tried a total of ten Equal Pay Act cases, adding two more wins and six losses. "We shall probably appeal some of them," Margolin remarked matter-of-factly. The trial court losses did not discourage her; she well remembered similar setbacks in the early years of the FLSA that she had managed to reverse.[123] Margolin's long-range view of the department's EPA litigation was a prophecy she was determined to fulfill.

She personally briefed, argued, and won the first and principal appeals taken in EPA cases.[124] One of these may have been Margolin's single greatest legal victory of her entire career. Although not won on the merits at the

Supreme Court, but rather at the Third Circuit, the *Wheaton Glass* case was and remains a landmark EPA ruling. The first EPA case to be argued to an appellate court, *Wheaton Glass* marked the coming of age of the Labor Department's EPA enforcement program, likened in some circles to a "second *Brown v. Board of Education.*"[125]

The Wheaton Glass Company was one of the country's largest manufacturers of special-order glass containers, with principal plants in Millville, New Jersey. Male and female "selector-packers" inspected glass bottles and packed them into cartons, including bottles made for women's cosmetics giant Avon. Although the men and women worked side by side along the conveyor belt, doing identical work at least 80 percent of the time, Wheaton paid male selector-packers 21.5 cents (10 percent) more per hour than the women. The plant also employed "snap-up boys" who stacked, stored, moved, and swept, as needed, and who, even as the plant's lowest-paid men, received two cents per hour more than female selector-packers. At times male selector-packers, who the employer argued were more flexible and versatile than female selector-packers, performed the work of the snap-up boys and for this reason received the higher rate. Thus, the company contended, and federal district judge Mitchell Cohen later agreed, that male and female selector-packers were not performing equal work, and alternatively, even if they were performing equal work within the meaning of the EPA, the wage differential was justified by the males' flexibility, a "factor other than sex."[126]

Although lawyers from the labor solicitor's New York office conducted the sixteen-day trial in the Camden, New Jersey, federal courthouse, Margolin consulted on strategy, participated in pretrial conferences, and attended the trial. *Wheaton Glass* was one of the largest EPA cases on her docket, measured by the hundreds of female selector-packers and the amount of money at stake. It was also one of her most contentious cases. Even before the trial, Wheaton's lawyers' demands for a jury trial and disclosure of the informants' identities, although ultimately denied, required briefing and hearings.[127] Moreover, Judge Cohen demonstrated a heightened interest in the case, making two personal visits to the plant (when even one judicial site visit is rare) to familiarize himself with the technical aspects of the selector-packers' job. He was fascinated with what he colorfully described in his opinion as the "time-honored glass container industry, so rich in its early history of individual glass-blowing and down to the modern assembly line." Moreover, the judge gushed with admiration over Wheaton's plant manager, calling him an outstanding witness and "truly one of the giants of the industry [from whom] seldom has this Court had the benefit of such expert and credible testimony."[128]

In reaching his decision for the company, Judge Cohen reviewed the EPA's legislative history and concluded, despite the government lawyers' strong urgings, that Congress promised equal pay only when the work is "substantially *identical*." On that basis he found that snap-up boy duties performed by the male selector-packers constituted substantial differences from the work the women performed. Judge Cohen also found, apparently convinced by the plant manager's testimony, that the availability of male selector-packers to perform the snap-up boys' work was an element of flexibility, which was economically valuable to the company, and as such was a "factor other than sex" that legitimized the higher wage.[129]

Because Judge Cohen supported his ruling with a detailed recitation of facts, aided by his two site visits and his personal assessment of witness credibility, some of Margolin's lawyers reasonably feared his ruling would be reversal proof because an appellate court would be loathe to disturb the fact-finding province of a trial judge.[130] Undaunted and convinced of the legal, if not moral, correctness of her position, Margolin filed an appeal in the Third Circuit, challenging Judge Cohen's decision on three grounds, two of which focused on errors of law: first, that his construction of the term *equal work* rested upon an erroneous interpretation of legislative intent; second, that "male flexibility" was not a valid "factor other than sex"; and third, that in any event the evidence proved a violation to all the female selector-packers because at least some of the higher-paid men performed little or none of the extra duties that Wheaton claimed as the basis for the wage differential.[131]

Margolin traveled to Philadelphia to argue *Wheaton Glass* in May 1969, returning seven months later to address several specific questions that troubled the court. Margolin, who by this time had argued nearly 170 appellate cases, knew precisely what it took to be prepared and when she could allow herself to relax. A female staff lawyer recalled the evening before one of Margolin's *Wheaton* arguments. They were dining together when a waitress informed them that a gentleman wanted to buy them a drink. As Margolin lightly patted her impeccable coiffure, she said with a coy smile, "It's been a while since I had that offer."[132]

Within a month after her second *Wheaton* argument, Margolin received welcome news: the Third Circuit had reversed the district court, holding that the term *equal work* required only that the compared jobs be substantially equal, not identical. Additionally, the court rejected Wheaton's flexibility arguments. While individual differences in work capacity may be a proper basis for a wage differential, ruled the circuit court, sex-based group criteria are not acceptable. The court found the actual time spent by the males on the extra duties was minimal, but even if the time spent on the extra duties had been substantial, it reasoned there would still be no rational explanation why men who perform a job that typically earns 2 cents more per hour should receive 21.5 cents per hour more than females for the work they do in common. All of this was made possible because Margolin had succeeded in convincing the Third Circuit that it was not bound by the trial court's extensive recitation of evidence that did not constitute actual findings of fact nor by conclusions that were mere legal inferences from facts.[133]

Refusing to concede, Wheaton requested another hearing, which the Third Circuit denied. Wheaton then petitioned for Supreme Court review, a move that incited its women workers—who were impatiently awaiting their hard-fought back pay—to protest in a wildcat strike, hurling crude epithets traditionally considered off-limits for the fairer sex.[134] In May 1970 the Supreme Court denied Wheaton's petition, allowing the Third Circuit's ruling to stand. It sent the case back, instructing the trial court to enter judgment in the government's favor.[135] Wheaton still did not desist. It was willing to raise the pay scale for female selector-packers but refused to pay back wages and interest. Judge Cohen rejected Wheaton's latest arguments, and the company appealed anew.[136] In June 1971 Margolin returned to the Third Circuit for a third argument, prevailing once again.[137] Skirmishes over payments continued until mid-January 1972, when Judge Mitchell issued his final order.[138] After six years of litigation, dozens of briefs, and two appeals, the *Wheaton Glass* case was finally over—just ten days before Margolin retired from the Labor Department.

The Supreme Court would not hear its first EPA case until two years after Margolin retired, but she had blazed a trail through the lower courts with a stunning litigation record.[139] Her confidence that the appellate courts would interpret the law as she had advocated paid off. As associate solicitor, she had overseen the filing of three hundred EPA lawsuits, some in nearly every state. In addition to more than one hundred cases that were settled before trial, the department's lawyers had tried another fifty cases, obtaining favorable decisions on the merits in thirty. Of the twenty cases the Labor Department lost at trial, Margolin and her lawyers succeeded in reversing six on appeal, four of which Margolin had personally argued. In total the EPA litigation that Margolin oversaw resulted in payment of approximately four million dollars in back wages to eighteen thousand employees, with about ten thousand of those employees also receiving untold sums in wage increases.[140]

The Labor Department's leading EPA administrator said about Margolin: "A great many of us owe her a debt of gratitude for her courage and fortitude. . . . The work connected with the preparation for Equal Pay Act litigation has, of necessity, been both time-consuming and frustrating."[141] By the time she retired, the EPA was considered one of the leading and most effective pieces of equal employment opportunity legislation in the history of the United States, and Margolin had much to do with that appraisal.[142] One of Margolin's *Wheaton Glass* well-wishers wrote, "By almost a one-woman struggle, you have seen the Equal Pay Act through a most difficult infancy and placed it on sturdy legs." Phrasing the basic issue philosophically, he added, "It really gets down to a question of assuming the employees are all of one sex, and looking for a sensible explanation for differences in pay and employment treatment."[143]

Before Margolin retired, she also broke new ground for the Age Discrimination in Employment Act of 1967 (ADEA), enacted to promote employment of older workers and to prohibit arbitrary discrimination against them on the basis of age. Like the FLSA and the Equal Pay Act, Congress placed the ADEA's enforcement in the Labor Department, which was added to Margolin's litigation and appellate portfolio. In 1971 she argued the ADEA's first appeal in *Hodgson v. First Federal Savings & Loan Association*. The Fifth Circuit affirmed that the bank's refusal to hire a forty-seven-year-old woman was due to age discrimination, evidenced in part by an interviewer's note that she was "too old for teller." The Fifth Circuit also agreed with Margolin that the trial court had abused its discretion by enjoining the bank from future ADEA violations only in regard to bank tellers; the injunction should have protected all of the bank's job categories.[144] Margolin learned of her ADEA victory just three days before she retired.

It was difficult for Margolin to envision a future at the Labor Department that could be as rewarding as what she had already accomplished.

Her career had been launched by the New Deal, starting with bold social and economic programs embodied in the TVA Act and the FLSA. She then discovered a voice to advocate for women workers when President Kennedy added equal pay protections to his New Frontier initiative; her voice grew bolder under the broader civil rights Johnson guaranteed in his Great Society. To Margolin, Richard Nixon's Republican administration marked the end of an era of social and economic justice that she had championed since 1933. Bob Ginnane, who left the ICC for private practice in 1970, shared Margolin's gloomy outlook about Washington politics, dismayed by Nixon's looming reelection. But Ginnane also offered Margolin positive reasons to think beyond her government employment, writing her in 1972, "Without you, I would find living a stale business."[145]

While she would have been the first to argue that age was an illegal and irrelevant criterion upon which to deny employment opportunity, Margolin's longevity had begun to matter in her work. She had served under eleven politically appointed labor solicitors, each of whom had arrived determined to change the office—only to recognize their limitations when they bumped up against her. By virtue of her reputation, integrity, and persuasive power, Margolin pushed each new and ever younger and conservative solicitor to a more pro-worker stance, all in the name of administering and enforcing the statutes as Congress wrote them.[146] And while they were getting younger, she was not. Margolin's last three labor solicitors were all under thirty-five when Nixon appointed them; she had started her federal government legal career years before they were born.[147] With the financial security she had earned from federal retirement benefits, Margolin could move on and let a new generation of lawyers take over her work at the Labor Department. With an eye to this day she had already groomed her successor.[148]

10

RETIREMENT AND LAST YEARS
1972–1996

Bessie Margolin's January 1972 retirement affair, much like the woman herself, was elegant, gracious, and reflected careful attention to detail. It was no ordinary retirement party for a Washington bureaucrat. More than two hundred coworkers, family members, and friends, including dozens of prominent judges and government officials, crowded into the ballroom of the Washington Hilton Hotel to honor Margolin. During her four decades representing the federal government, a career she began at the dawn of Roosevelt's New Deal and ended just before Nixon's reelection, Margolin, as associate solicitor, attained the Labor Department's highest-ranking position for a nonpolitical lawyer. She served as the department's principal advocate in the United States Supreme Court, a distinction never before or again bestowed by the solicitor general on the Labor Department's lawyers.[1]

At sixty-two years old Margolin, widely admired for her sophisticated fashion sense, appeared as carefully put together as ever, except now thick shocks of white hair laced her sleek and improbably black coiffure. Long chandelier earrings framed her heart-shaped face, with its dark, arched eyebrows. She wore a delicately embroidered sleeveless white evening gown that shimmered against the dark and wintry formal attire of her guests. A reluctant feminist who yielded to vanity and old-fashioned social customs, Margolin had insisted on having an escort, a young male attorney, accompany her to the event. Although her celebrated guests, including four Supreme Court justices, represented more than a half-century of Margolin's personal and professional relationships, few if any of them knew the whole story of her remarkable journey from orphan to advocate. Her regal bearing and imperious professional demeanor belied the poverty, prejudice, and sexism she had overcome to achieve her distinguished career.

As master of ceremonies, labor undersecretary Laurence H. Silberman, later senior federal circuit judge for the District of Columbia, good-naturedly recalled his terror when, as a "callow, inexperienced youth," he had learned of three steps he had to climb a few years earlier when he become labor solicitor, a position that entailed supervising Margolin. "I had to be nominated by the President, confirmed by the Senate, and interviewed by Bessie. And she made it clear at the outset that the fact that I was a Republican would not make the interview any easier." He also used humor to convey the possessive pride she took in the Labor Department's Supreme Court litigation. He recalled discussing with Margolin whether to oppose the certiorari petition seeking Supreme Court review of the *Wheaton Glass* case. When he saw the "light in Bessie's eyes" as she envisioned her chance to argue the first Equal Pay Act case in the Supreme Court, he was concerned the outcome might not prove as favorable as the Third Circuit's sweeping decision, despite the effectiveness of her "avenging angel" style of argument. He figured out a way to deal with the problem. He leaned back in his chair and said, "Bessie, I've never argued a case in the Supreme Court." As he expected, Margolin could not abide letting him argue the case if she could not and immediately replied, "We'll oppose cert." Judging by the approving applause and friendly laughter that swept the ballroom, Silberman's anecdotes captured Margolin's essence.[2]

The room was a national legal constellation, past and present, with government luminaries distributed among the tables. In addition to the former and current members of the Supreme Court in attendance, many of those who came to pay tribute to Margolin had furthered her career. From Rufus Harris, the former dean of Tulane Law School who had recommended her to Yale Law School, to Judge Charles Fahy, the former solicitor general whose confidence in Margolin had paved the way for her Supreme Court career, all had helped open doors for her. The next generation of labor and employment lawyers was also well represented. Bob Nagle, Don Shire, and of course Carin Clauss, the daughter of Margolin's TVA friends and the talented protégée Margolin had groomed to become associate solicitor, all came to honor their mentor.[3] Although he attended without his wife, Bob Ginnane's assignment to the table directly in front of Margolin's seat at the dais raised no eyebrows; Ginnane's impressive Supreme Court career, having argued thirty-six times on behalf the government, earned him a place near Justice William O. Douglas.

For all, the highlight of the evening was Earl Warren, retired chief justice of the United States, before whom Margolin had appeared for most of her

Supreme Court career. Warren, the former three-term California governor who had served as America's fourteenth chief justice from 1953 through 1969, was the guest speaker, and he came to sing Margolin's praises. In her years at TVA and the Labor Department, said Warren, revealing his warm regard and admiration for Margolin, "she didn't always have a bed of roses." She authored hundreds of briefs and argued scores of cases, of which her Supreme Court arguments alone were a prodigious undertaking. But Warren then eloquently described Margolin's singular achievement at the Labor Department: "The Fair Labor Standards Act was not always popular in all quarters, and the flesh and sinews that were developed around its bare bones were her great contribution to millions of American working people. Many of these people do not know who Bessie Margolin is, or what a great service she rendered to them, but if they did know, they would praise her tonight. In their name, I would like to thank her tonight, because the bare bones of that Act would have been wholly inadequate without the implementation she forged in the courtrooms of our land."[4] Warren also honored Margolin's special contribution to women: "What a satisfaction it must be for her in this day and age when women are crying out for equality to realize that she had proved equality for them in a man's world, by prevailing in the highest courts of the land in a larger percent of her cases than any lawyer of modern times." Warren concluded by telling the audience, "[Margolin] has been a great public servant."[5]

Although Margolin's retirement gala marked the end of her full-time responsibilities as associate solicitor, she did not immediately relinquish her legal career or her influence on the law. For almost a year she returned to the Solicitor's Office, part-time, lending her expertise in several ongoing Equal Pay Act cases; Margolin helped draft the brief that convinced the Supreme Court to deny review of the Sixth Circuit's ruling she had won in *Square D*, which rejected an employer's attempt to cure its Equal Pay Act violations by merely making available to women, if there were vacancies, higher-paying jobs previously open only to men.[6] She also continued, at least for a few years, to use the bully pulpit to shape opinions. In the summer of 1972 she returned to New York University's Conference on Labor, where she had six years earlier challenged the EEOC's denigration of Title VII's sex provision. Now she was there to pose a provocative answer to the question "Who Discriminates against Women?" by saying: "It is difficult to find any appreciable number of companies—or unions—which do not engage in sex discrimination in some form or another."[7] Two years later she spoke about "Sex and the Equal Pay Act" at a seminar for lawyers and personnel managers, advising her audience what can—and what must—be done to avoid violations of sex discrimination laws.[8] For several years she shared her litigation expertise with attorneys, many women, who were representing clients across the country in equal pay and Title VII sex discrimination cases, reviewing their draft briefs and proposing strategy.[9]

During that time, on June 3, 1974, the Supreme Court handed down its first decision under the Equal Pay Act, *Corning Glass Works v. Brennan,* just one week short of the tenth anniversary of the date the act first took effect.[10] Faced with a direct conflict between circuit court decisions, the Supreme Court granted certiorari in *Corning Glass* to finally review, among other issues, the propriety of a corrective practice similar to the one in *Square D,* namely, allowing lower-paid female day shift workers to seek night shift jobs, when they became available, at the same higher wage paid to male workers. After the Court issued its opinion, ruling that the only proper remedy for an Equal Pay Act violation is to raise the lower wages to the higher, Margolin wrote a brief article for the *Women Law Reporter,* "The Impact of Corning." Although she was not surprised by the Court's ruling, wrote Margolin, she was hopeful that it, and the nearly million-dollar back pay award it validated, would put an end to the extensive and expensive case-by-case litigation over various schemes, devices, and half-measures pursued by some employers.[11] As Margolin described the decision's undoubtedly powerful impact on achieving the Equal Pay Act's goals, one aspect of the case went unmentioned. Although associate labor solicitor Carin Clauss and her lawyers conducted the trials, argued the appeals at the circuit courts, and helped write the Supreme Court briefs, the government's argument to enforce the Equal Pay Act had been presented at the Supreme Court by a male lawyer from the Solicitor General's Office.[12]

It was only in retirement that Margolin finally achieved a previously elusive career goal—teaching law in her field of expertise. Beginning in the spring of 1974, she taught a graduate course, Labor Standards and Equal Employment, at George Washington University Law School, which allowed her to share her knowledge of the Fair Labor Standards Act and the employment provisions of the Civil Rights Act. The Supreme Court decisions in cases she had briefed and argued provided a foundation for the course. To introduce her class to FLSA coverage, she assigned readings from *Jacksonville*

Paper and *10 East 40th Street,* while *Whitaker House* and *Rutherford Food* framed the discussion about the employment relationship. Half of the syllabus was devoted to equal employment, during which she reviewed the Equal Pay Act and Title VII.[13] In contrast to her own law school experience or even her lectures at bar conferences, where she was the only woman in the room, Margolin was teaching law, about equal employment opportunities, to classes in which at least one of every six students was a woman. At this later stage in Margolin's life, however, she was hampered by a loss of hearing, exacerbated by the vanity that prevented her from wearing a hearing aid. Afraid she would not hear her students' questions, she gradually stopped calling on them. Having reduced otherwise animated exchanges about employment rights to dry lectures, Margolin gave up teaching after only a few semesters.[14]

Impaired hearing, fortunately, did not impair Margolin from using her retirement to achieve another elusive career goal—rendering decisions in legal disputes, albeit as an arbitrator instead of a judge. By the summer of 1974 her name was added to the rosters of the American Arbitration Association's National Labor Panel and the Federal Mediation and Conciliation Service, and she promptly started receiving assignments in public and private labor disputes.[15] Over the next seven years Margolin arbitrated more than a dozen cases, covering a wide range of employee grievances filed pursuant to negotiated labor agreements. Performing some functions of a trial judge, she conducted hearings, usually one to two days long, analyzed case law and the parties' briefs, and issued binding opinions, ranging from twenty to forty pages, depending on the complexity of the matter.

As she had done in her hundreds of FLSA cases, Margolin immersed herself in the details of each job and industry that came before her. Shipyard sandblasters, machinists, secretaries, security guards, a baker, construction workers, and their employers all received her careful attention. Despite the fact that she had advocated exclusively on behalf of workers in her FLSA cases, her arbitration rulings appeared evenhanded. After hearing detailed testimony about the considerable grit and dirt to which naval shipyard workers were exposed, Margolin nevertheless rejected their claim to a 4 percent "dirty pay" differential for outdoor sandblasting because she found their work did not exceed conditions "normally to be expected for the job classification," as required by the collective bargaining agreement.[16] Margolin's desire for fairness was especially evident when she reviewed the severity of disciplinary sanctions. After finding that a federal agency had never clearly communicated its rules to security personnel and failed to adhere to its own deadlines, Margolin canceled a security guard's reprimand.[17] In another case Margolin reduced a discharge to a one-month suspension after considering a construction worker's otherwise unblemished thirty-year work history.[18] Notably, the only arbitration in which Margolin struggled to reach a decision was her last assignment in 1981; a female employee had filed a grievance alleging that her disciplinary suspension constituted unlawful retaliation for refusing her male supervisor's unwelcomed sexual advances. Whether Margolin's indecisiveness arose from the complicated and hotly disputed facts of a case that spanned five hearing days, her inexperience with a legal theory that did not exist during her career, or the administrative burdens she faced from not having regular secretarial support is uncertain. Also uncertain is how—or whether—Margolin ultimately ruled in the matter; the forty-three pages of the incomplete opinion she kept in her file reveals that she was leaning toward finding that the grievant was not suspended solely for refusing her supervisor's unlawful and improper requests but that her own misconduct warranted discipline.[19]

Before yielding her work as arbitrator, Margolin took great pride in an accomplishment that she had set in motion before she retired. In February 1977 President Jimmy Carter nominated Carin Clauss, who had succeeded Margolin as associate solicitor, to become solicitor of labor, the first woman to hold the position, putting her in charge of the enforcement of 135 labor laws and a legal staff of 750.[20] Clauss had won recognition for her achievements in precedent-setting litigation under the Equal Pay Act and the Age Discrimination in Employment Act and for her speeches and publications on civil rights litigation.[21] In September 1978 Clauss also received President Carter's nomination for a federal district judgeship in Washington, D.C.; although Carter later withdrew Clauss's nomination, at her request, after the American Bar Association's Judicial Selection Committee claimed she lacked personal trial experience, Clauss had attained the presidential recognition Margolin had not been able to achieve.[22] Clauss served as labor solicitor until March 1981, when President Ronald Reagan replaced her with a new appointment, and she began a distinguished career as a professor of labor and employment law at the University of Wisconsin Law School.[23]

As Margolin's professional activities waned, she dedicated more of her time to her cherished relationships with family and friends. Three of her four nephews, the sons of her siblings Dora and Jack, now had families of their own, and she delighted in traveling to California and Sweden to see them.[24] Toby's daughter Tracey, the only young girl in Margolin's family, loved spending time with her great-aunt and later recalled her stern but caring lectures about the importance of continuing her education.[25]

Margolin's closest friendships stemmed from her professional life. After Justice Hugo Black died in 1971, his wife, Elizabeth, moved into Margolin's apartment building. In 1986, when Elizabeth gave Margolin a copy of her memoirs, she inscribed it: "To Bess, Of whom I learned to share Hugo's admiration as a fine lawyer before the Court, and who later became my dear friend and neighbor."[26] For holiday dinners Margolin was welcomed in the homes of old friends, including Joe and Gretchen Swidler, who first met each other (and Margolin) when Gretchen worked as Joe's secretary at TVA.[27] Margolin also was a regular guest of Jonathan Marks, the son of her TVA friend Herb Marks, who died in 1960, and his wife. There Margolin was usually joined by Jonathan's mother, Rebecca Bowles Hawkins, who, despite her 1935 law degree, worked at TVA as a legal secretary and only began practicing law a decade later; Rita McParland, whose forty years as John Lord O'Brian's dedicated assistant also started at TVA; and Shirley Leva, a retired obstetrician and the widow of Marx Leva, Joe Fowler's law partner. Margolin and her pioneering contemporaries enjoyed lively debate about current events but often reminisced, taking great pride in their pathbreaking accomplishments.[28]

Retirement also gave Margolin more time to spend with Bob Ginnane, who had joined a private firm after leaving the ICC in 1970. Although he was still married, and apparently did not view divorce as an option, Margolin and Ginnane continued their clandestine romance. In a late 1972 letter he called her his "Beloved Bess" and wrote that her brief West Coast travels had left him "yearning for" her.[29] In 1981 Ginnane's wife died, dramatically changing the way he and Margolin could spend time together. The septuagenarians happily announced plans to marry, amazing their family and friends. The news delighted Margolin's nephews, who were as surprised to learn that Aunt Bess would ever marry as they were to learn for the first time about her twenty-year-old secret love affair.[30] Carin Clauss was equally stunned when Margolin called to share her marriage plans; Clauss had never before suspected the pair had a relationship, only then recalling that Margolin and Ginnane had particularly enjoyed competing for ever-greater recognition for their rising star junior lawyers, pitting Margolin's Clauss against

Ginnane's Betty Jo Christian. It now made sense to whom Margolin was speaking those times Clauss had entered Margolin's office only to find her engrossed in conversation on her private line, using an unusually soft and endearing voice.[31]

Margolin and Ginnane soon rented a larger apartment in her building, but they never got around to moving in together or setting a wedding date.[32] Ginnane faced increasing health problems, which could explain the foot-dragging on his side.[33] At the same time, despite being "in love for many, many years," Margolin later told her family that she and Ginnane were just too set in their ways and realized that they enjoyed their independence.[34] In 1984 Ginnane suddenly died of a heart attack, having only begun to share a public life with Margolin after so many years of secrecy. He was the last of her great loves.

Always proud of her accomplishments at the Supreme Court, Margolin enjoyed staying connected to the justices and the talented lawyers who appeared before them. In 1990 she attended a black-tie gala at the Supreme Court hosted by its historical society, just days before she was scheduled for cataract surgery. The aging but elegant Margolin was concerned that her clouded vision would prevent her from recognizing the justices and former colleagues who were standing at any distance. She need not have worried, recalled her nephew's wife, Charlotte, who accompanied her that evening. Old colleagues and admirers came up and warmly greeted Margolin, who was then able to tell Charlotte a fascinating detail about each of them.[35] It would be Margolin's last appearance at the Supreme Court.

Not long afterward, Margolin's health began to deteriorate. Her nephew Malcolm, who had joined the Labor Department's California office following law school, oversaw her care and arranged for her move to a nursing facility when the time came. Her former secretary, Eva Bowers Fitzgerald, who remained indebted to Margolin for encouraging her to become an award-winning paralegal at the Labor Department, often visited her former boss and brought her comforting gifts. On June 19, 1996, at age eighty-seven, Bessie Margolin died of a stroke. Honoring his Aunt Bess's wishes, in lieu of a funeral, Malcolm and his wife, Mary Catherine, organized a memorial later that summer. TVA colleague Joe Swidler and Nuremberg friend Dorothy Owens were among the small group of relatives, former colleagues, and dear friends who gathered to share stories and photos, express gratitude, and pay tribute to the remarkable life and career of Bessie Margolin.[36]

APPENDIX 1

Bessie Margolin's Arguments at the Supreme Court

Bessie Margolin presented twenty-four arguments at the United States Supreme Court, constituting twenty-seven separately docketed cases, set forth in the table that follows. Of these twenty-four arguments, she prevailed on the merits in twenty-one. Expressed as cases, she prevailed in twenty-four of twenty-seven. Of the three unfavorable outcomes, the Supreme Court ruled against her twice on the merits (*10 East 40th Street Bldg. v. Callus* and *Mitchell v. H. B. Zachry*) and dismissed certiorari after argument without reaching the merits in *Mitchell v. Oregon Frozen Foods*. When describing her Supreme Court record during her lifetime, however, Margolin and her contemporaries (including Chief Justice Earl Warren) consistently reported that she prevailed in twenty-five of the twenty-seven cases she argued. The tally Margolin kept, which corresponds with her reported twenty-five of twenty-seven record, differs from the following list in three ways: (1) it omits her November 1959 argument in *Mitchell v. Oregon Frozen Foods,* likely because Margolin counted only those cases the Supreme Court decided on the merits;[1] (2) it counts her February 1956 argument in *Mitchell v. Budd* as three cases, likely because the original trial involved FLSA actions against three separate companies; and (3) it counts the cross petitions she argued in March 1955 in *Maneja v. Waialua* as one case. By focusing on arguments, not cases, the following list employs a counting methodology that offers greater uniformity in comparing the historic records of Supreme Court advocates.[2]

1. Margolin's apparent counting of only those cases decided on the merits is not entirely without support. In 1954 Justice Frankfurter unsuccessfully tried to persuade the Solicitor General's Office to omit reference to "certiorari denied," the practical equivalent of "certiorari dismissed," arguing that the Court's decision to deny certiorari was legally meaningless. Stern, "Reminiscences of the Solicitor General's Office," 129–30.

2. Trestman, "Addenda to 'Fair Labor,'" 252–60.

DATES	CASES
1. Mar. 2, 1945	*A. H. Phillips, Inc. v. Walling* (No. 608), 324 U.S. 490 (1945
2. Apr. 6, 1945	*10 East 40th St. Bldg., Inc. v. Callus* (No. 820), 325 U.S. 578 (1945) [a,b]
3. Apr. 6, 1945	*Borden Co. v. Borella* (No. 688), 325 U.S. 679 (1945)[a]
4. Oct. 8, 1945	*Roland Electrical Co. v. Walling* (No. 45), 326 U.S. 657 (1946)
5. Oct. 9, 1945	*Boutell v. Walling* (No. 73), 327 U.S. 463 (1946)
6. Apr. 9–10, 1947	*Rutherford Food Corp. v. McComb* (No. 562), 331 U.S. 722 (1947)
7. Dec. 14–15, 1948	*McComb v. Jacksonville Paper Co.* (No. 110), 336 U.S. 187 (1949)
8. Dec. 8–9, 1949	*Powell v. United States Cartridge Co.* (No. 96); *Aaron v. Ford, Bacon & Davis, Inc.* (No. 79); *Creel v. Lone Star Defense Corp.* (No. 58), 339 U.S. 497 (1950)[a]
9. Feb. 2–3, 1953	*Alstate Construction Co. v. Durkin* (No. 296), 345 U.S. 13 (1953)
10. Feb. 4–5, 1955	*Mitchell v. Joyce Agency, Inc.* (No. 230), 348 U.S. 945 (1955)
11. Mar. 30, 1955	*Maneja v. Waialua Agricultural Co.* (No. 357), and *Waialua Agricultural Co. v. Maneja* (No. 358), 349 U.S. 254 (1955)[a]
12. Nov. 10, 1955	*Mitchell v. Myrtle Grove Packing Co.* (No. 44), 350 U.S. 891 (1955)
13. Nov. 16, 1955	*Steiner v. Mitchell* (No. 22), 350 U.S. 247 (1956)
14. Nov. 16–17, 1955	*Mitchell v. King Packing Co.* (No. 39), 350 U.S. 260 (1956)
15. Feb. 29– Mar. 1, 1956	*Mitchell v. Budd* (No. 278), 350 U.S. 473 (1956)
16. Feb. 26–27, 1957	*Mitchell v. Bekins Van and Storage Co.* (No. 122), 352 U.S. 1027 (1957)
17. Oct. 21, 1958	*Mitchell v. Lublin, McGaughy & Assoc.* (No. 37), 358 U.S. 207 (1959)
18. Mar. 3, 1959	*Mitchell v. Kentucky Finance Co.* (No. 161), 359 U.S. 290 (1959)
19. Nov. 16, 1959	*Mitchell v. Robert DeMario Jewelry, Inc.* (No. 39), 361 U.S. 288 (1960)
20. Nov. 17, 1959	*Mitchell v. Oregon Frozen Foods Co.* (No. 33), 361 U.S. 231 (1960), cert. dismissed
21. Jan. 11, 1960	*Arnold v. Ben Kanowsky, Inc.* (No. 60), 361 U.S. 388 (1960)
22. Feb. 25, 1960	*Mitchell v. H. B. Zachry Co.* (No. 83), 362 U.S. 310 (1960)[b]
23. Mar. 30, 1961	*Goldberg v. Whitaker House Cooperative* (No. 274), 366 U.S. 28 (1961)
24. Dec. 8, 1965	*Wirtz v. Steepleton General Tire Co.* (No. 31), 383 U.S. 190 (1966)

[a] Margolin argued as an amicus curiae.
[b] The Supreme Court ruled against Margolin.

APPENDIX 2

Program and Abbreviated Guest List for
Bessie Margolin's Retirement Dinner

Presiding
    Laurence H. Silberman, Undersecretary of Labor
Invocation
    Richard F. Schubert, Solicitor of Labor
Remarks and Introduction
    James D. Hodgson, Secretary of Labor
Guest Speaker
    The Honorable Earl Warren, Chief Justice of the United States, Retired
Honoree's Response
    Bessie Margolin
Presentation of Distinguished Career Service Award
    Laurence H. Silberman, Undersecretary of Labor

ABBREVIATED GUEST LIST

Attendees

Howard J. Anderson, editor, *U.S. Reports*
George T. Avery, Associate Solicitor, U.S. Department of Labor (DOL)
B. Harper Barnes, Regional Attorney, DOL, Kansas City, Mo.
Edith Barnett, Attorney, Solicitor's Office, DOL
Caruthers G. Berger, Attorney, Solicitor's Office, DOL
Beate Bloch, Attorney, Solicitor's Office, DOL
Fannie M. Boyle, Attorney, National Labor Relations Board (NLRB)
Isabelle Capello, Assistant General Counsel, Equal Employment Opportunity Commission
    (EEOC), former Attorney, Solicitor's Office, DOL
Joel Chasanoff, Attorney, Solicitor's Office, DOL

Carin A. Clauss, Counsel for Appellate Litigation, Solicitor's Office, DOL

Edith N. Cook, Associate Solicitor, DOL

Jean Saralee Cooper, Attorney, Solicitor's Office, DOL

Altero D'Agostini, Regional Solicitor, DOL, San Francisco

Oscar H. Davis, Judge, U.S. Court of Claims

Anna Johnston Diggs, former Attorney, Solicitor's Office, DOL

William O. Douglas, Associate Justice, U.S. Supreme Court

Anastasia Thannhauser Dunau, Attorney, Solicitor's Office, DOL

Bernard Dunau, Attorney, Private Practice

Catherine East, Executive Secretary, Interdepartmental Committee on the Status of Women and the Citizens' Advisory Council on the Status of Women

Mary O. Eastwood, Attorney Advisor, Office of Legal Counsel, Department of Justice

Donald Elisburg, Associate Counsel, Subcommittee on Labor, U.S. Senate Committee on Labor and Public Welfare

Sylvia S. Ellison, Chief Trial Attorney, Solicitor's Office, DOL

Charles Fahy, Senior Circuit Judge, U.S. Court of Appeals for the D.C. Circuit

Edith U. Fierst, Counsel, Solicitor's Office, DOL

Phyllis Fineshriber, Program Analyst, Training and Employment Service, DOL

Eva Bowers Fitzgerald, Administrative Assistant to Bessie Margolin, DOL

Abe Fortas, former Associate Justice, U.S. Supreme Court

Carolyn Agger Fortas, attorney, Arnold & Porter

Henry H. Fowler, Partner, Goldman, Sachs and Co.; former Secretary of the Treasury

Louise F. Freeman, Special Assistant for Manpower, Solicitor's Office, DOL

Daniel M. Friedman, First Deputy Solicitor General

Edward D. Friedman, former Deputy Solicitor, DOL

Sonia Pressman Fuentes, Attorney, EEOC

Samuel Ganz, President, President, Economic and Manpower Corp., New York

Robert W. Ginnane, Attorney, Galland, Kharasch, Calkins & Brown; former General Counsel, Interstate Commerce Commission

Arthur Goldberg, former U.S. Ambassador to the United Nations; former Associate Justice, U.S. Supreme Court; former Secretary of Labor

H. Stephan Gordon, Associate General Counsel, NLRB

Herman Grant, Regional Attorney, Department of Labor, Chicago

Marshall Harris, Regional Attorney, Department of Labor, Philadelphia

Rebecca Bowles Hawkins, Assistant Attorney General, State of Florida

James D. Hodgson, Secretary of Labor

Charles A. Horsky, Attorney, Covington & Burling; former Advisor to President on National Capital Affairs

Henry A. Huettner, Regional Director, DOL, Atlanta

Eugene R. Jackson, Attorney, Solicitor's Office, DOL

Leroy M. Jahn, Attorney, Solicitor's Office, DOL

Helen W. Judd, Attorney, Solicitor's Office, DOL

William J. Kilberg, Associate Solicitor of Labor for Labor Relations and Civil Rights; former General Counsel of the Federal Mediation and Conciliation Service

Ida Klaus, Executive Director, New York City School System; former Solicitor, NLRB

Dale B. Kloak, Chief, Child Labor Branch, Wage and Hour and Public Contracts Divisions, DOL

Harry M. Leet, Attorney, NLRB

Marx Leva, Attorney, Leva, Hawes, Symington, Martin & Oppenheimer; former Assistant Secretary of Defense

Shirley Pearlman Leva, Physician

Robert Levitt, Counsel, Western Electric Co.; former Attorney, Solicitor's Office, DOL

Morton Liftin, Attorney, Private Practice; former Assistant Solicitor, DOL

Herbert Eugene Longenecker, President, Tulane University

Katie Louchheim, former Deputy Assistant Secretary for Public Affairs, State Department

Adolph Magidson, Vice President, Bureau of National Affairs, Inc.

Morton J. Marks, Regional Attorney, DOL, Santurce, Puerto Rico

Rita McParland, Administrative Assistant to John Lord O'Brian, Covington & Burling

Ida C. Merriam, Assistant Commissioner for Research and Statistics, Social Security Administration

Robert Moran, Chairman, Occupational Safety and Health Review Commission

Donald M. Murtha, Attorney, Donald M. Murtha & Assoc.

Robert E. Nagle, General Counsel, U.S. Senate Committee on Labor and Public Welfare,

Peter Nash, General Counsel, NLRB; former Solicitor of Labor

Herman L. Neugass, District of Columbia Department of Economic Development

Harold Nystrom, Associate Solicitor, DOL

Arnold Ordman, former General Counsel, NLRB

Dorothy Owens, Administrative Assistant to Judge Gerard Reilly

E. West Parkinson, former Hearing Examiner, Division of Public Contracts, DOL

Thomas Phelan, Regional Director, DOL, Philadelphia

W. Scott Railton, Assistant Counsel, Occupational Safety and Health Administration

Joseph L. Rauh Jr., Attorney, Rauh, Silard & Lichtman

Arnold Raum, Judge, U.S. Tax Court

Jeter S. Ray, Associate Solicitor, DOL

Gerard D. Reilly, Associate Judge, D.C. Court of Appeals; former Solicitor of Labor

Kenneth C. Robertson, Regional Attorney, DOL, San Francisco

Helen Grundstein Rosen, former Attorney, Solicitor's Office, DOL

Howard Rosen, former Director, Office of Research and Development, Manpower Administration, DOL

Beatrice Rosenberg, Chief, Appellate Litigation, EEOC; former Chief, Criminal Appeals, Department of Justice

Stuart Rothman, former Solicitor of Labor, former General Counsel, NLRB

Richard F. Schubert, Solicitor of Labor

Donald S. Shire, Attorney, Solicitor's Office, DOL

Laurence H. Silberman, Undersecretary of Labor; Former Solicitor of Labor

Eldon Silverman, Attorney, Solicitor's Office, DOL

Morag McLeod Simchak, Special Assistant to the Assistant Secretary of Labor for Employment Standards

Bobbye Spears, Attorney, Solicitor's Office, DOL

John Stewart, President, Bureau of National Affairs, Inc.

Faye Blackburn Stone, Attorney, Solicitor's Office, DOL

Joseph M. Stone, Attorney, Private Practice; former Attorney, Solicitor's Office, DOL

Laurie M. Streeter, Counsel for Manpower, Solicitor's Office, DOL

Penelope H. Thunberg, Member, U.S. Tariff Commission

Marvin Tincher, Regional Attorney, Department of Labor, Nashville

Malcolm R. Trifon, Attorney, Regional Solicitor's Office, DOL, San Francisco

Ruth Van Cleve, Assistant General Counsel, Federal Power Commission

Ernest N. Votaw, Professor of Law, Dickinson College School of Law, former Regional Attorney, DOL, Philadelphia

Earl Warren, Chief Justice of the United States, Retired

Aryness Joy Wickens, former Deputy Assistant Secretary of Labor for Manpower and Employment

Richard S. Wilbur, Assistant Secretary of Defense for Health and Environment

Willard Wirtz, former secretary of labor

John Minor Wisdom, Circuit Judge, U.S. Court of Appeals for the Fifth Circuit

Irwin M. Wolkow, Economist, Wage and Hour and Public Contracts Divisions, DOL

Doris D. Wooten, Chief, Policy Development, Office of Federal Contract Compliance, DOL

Arnold L. Zempel, Deputy Director, Office of Labor Affairs, Agency for International Development

Lawrence T. Zimmerman, Attorney, Private Practice

Seth D. Zinman, Attorney, Solicitor's Office, DOL

Notable Invitees Who Sent Letters Expressing
Regrets and Fond Remembrances

Hale Boggs, Congressman and Majority Leader

John R. Brown, Chief Judge, U.S. Court of Appeals for the Fifth Circuit

Warren E. Burger, Chief Justice, U.S. Supreme Court

Tom C. Clark, Associate Justice, U.S. Supreme Court

Marvin E. Frankel, U.S. District Judge for the Southern District of New York

Warner W. Gardner, Attorney, Shea & Gardner; former Solicitor of Labor

Rufus C. Harris, President, Mercer University; former President of Tulane University

Clement F. Haynsworth Jr., Chief Judge, U.S. Court of Appeals for the Fourth Circuit

Joseph C. Hutcheson, Jr., Senior Judge, U.S. Court of Appeals for the Fifth Circuit

Louis Loss, Professor, Harvard Law School

Thomas F. McAllister, Judge, U.S. Court of Appeals for the Sixth Circuit

George P. Palo, former Chief Engineer, Tennessee Valley Authority

Simon Sobeloff, Judge, U.S. Court of Appeals for the Fourth Circuit

Robert L. Stern, former First Assistant to the Solicitor General

Joseph C. Swidler, Chair, State of New York Public Service Commission; former
    General Counsel, Tennessee Valley Authority

Elbert P. Tuttle, Judge, U.S. Court of Appeals for the Fifth Circuit

Harrison L. Winter, Judge, U.S. Court of Appeals for the Fourth Circuit

Sources: Guest book, photographs, and correspondence in Bessie Margolin Papers.

NOTES

ABBREVIATIONS

AJ	*Atlanta Journal*
BM	Bessie Margolin
BMP	Bessie Margolin Papers
INS	Isidore Newman School Archives
JCH	Jewish Children's Home Collection, Tulane University Special Collections, New Orleans
JCRS	Jewish Children's Regional Service, New Orleans
KNS	*Knoxville News Sentinel*
NCCRW	Newcomb College Center for Research on Women, New Orleans
NOI	*New Orleans Item*
NOS	*New Orleans States*
NYT	*New York Times*
SDT	*Seattle Daily Times*
TP	*Times Picayune,* New Orleans
TU	Tulane University, New Orleans
TULS	Tulane University Law School, New Orleans
WP	*Washington Post*
WSJ	*Wall Street Journal*
YUL	Yale University Library, New Haven, Conn.

1. CHILDHOOD

1. Birth Certificate for Becy Margolyn, New York City Health Department, Oct. 23, 1935, BMP; Harry Margolin, Affidavit, Nov. 12, 1935, BMP; Thirteenth Census of the United States, 1910, Brooklyn Ward 29, Kings, New York, roll T624983, p. 18B, enumeration district 964, FHL microfilm no. 1374996.

2. M. Trifon, R. Margolin, and C. Margolin interviews; Charlotte Margolin, email to author, Aug. 12, 2012.

3. Between 1901 and 1918 the Industrial Removal Office resettled approximately eighty thousand Jewish immigrants away from New York to more than a thousand towns and cities throughout the United States and Canada to find jobs, with the goal of assimilating them into American society. Glazier, *Dispersing the Ghetto,* 16.

4. Lewis, *Biblical People in the Bible Belt,* 67–68, 70–73; and Haas, "Jewish Settlement in Tennessee."

5. M. Trifon interview; Burial Permit for Mrs. Revika Goldsmith Margahan [*sic*], May 23, 1912, Memphis, Tennessee, Board of Health, http://register.shelby.tn.us/imgView.php?img-type=pdf&id=2664119120523 (accessed Dec. 30, 2013).

6. Magner, *Story of the Jewish Orphans Home,* 34–35; Jewish Children's Home, *Diamond Jubilee,* 5–6; Rubin, *Century of Progress,* 5.

7. Admission Registry of the Jewish Orphans' Home, vol. 2, entries 1248 and 1249, JCRS (hereafter "Home Admission Registry").

8. Rabbi Samfield recommended the admission of at least twelve Memphis children, in addition to the Margolins. Box 48, JCH.

9. "Jewish Orphans—The Opening of the New Home on St. Charles Avenue," *TP,* Sept. 5, 1887.

10. "Jewish Orphans." Detailed descriptions and images of the Home are also found in Child Welfare League of America, *Report on the Jewish Children's Home, New Orleans, Louisiana, Submitted to the Committee on Child Care of the Council of Social Agencies* (1925), box 51, JCH (hereafter "Child Welfare Report"); Anna Berenson, "A Study of the Jewish Children's Home," MSW thesis, TU School of Social Work (1932) (hereafter "Berenson thesis"); Magner, *Story of the Jewish Orphans Home;* and Jewish Orphans' Home, *Annual Reports* (1913–20), JCRS.

11. "36 times": Rabbi Uri Topolosky, eulogy for Lillian G. Rodos, Jan. 9, 2012, New Orleans. See, e.g., Exodus 22:22–23 ("Do not afflict any widow or orphan. If you do in any way, and if they cry unto me, I will surely hear their cry"); Preamble, Constitution, Association for the Relief of Jewish Widows and Orphans, Mar. 14, 1855, box 35, JCH ("For as long as the Faith in the 'Holy One' shall be our guide, teaching us that we are the children of one Heavenly Father, as long as Charity 'The Attribute of Heaven' shall animate our being, so long will the orphan be foremost among those who enlist the unwavering solicitude of every good Israelite").

12. Magner, *Story of the Jewish Orphans Home,* 9. Before 1880 the association housed indigent Jewish widows in the Home; thereafter, widows over age sixty resided in Touro Infirmary or received stipends (41–43, 62).

13. Although the orphanage and organization changed name and scope several times, the building was known throughout almost all of Margolin's time as the Jewish Orphans' Home; in 1924 it was renamed the Jewish Children's Home to reflect the fact that most residents were not orphans. Moise W. Dennery to W. P. O'Neil, Apr. 25, 1962, JCRS.

14. "Jewish Orphans." See Light, *That Pride of Race and Character,* for a critical analysis of the Home and other southern Jewish orphanages as vehicles for imbuing children of largely Eastern European Jewish immigrants with cultural citizenship and social legitimacy in America.

15. Beerman, Sizeler, and Smith interviews.

16. Home Admission Registry, vol. 2, entries 1248 and 1249, JCRS.

17. "New Superintendent for New Orleans Orphans' Home," *Jewish Herald,* Houston, Aug. 31, 1911, 1.

18. Remarks of Superintendent Leon Volmer, Proceedings of the Eighth Biennial Session, National Conference of Jewish Charities, Memphis, May 1914, reprinted in Lee Frankel, ed., *Jewish Charities—Bulletin of the National Conference of Jewish Charities,* Jewish Communal Service Association of North America, 4, no. 12 (1914): 7, www.bjpa.org/Publications/download Publication.cfm?PublicationID=14 (accessed Dec. 30, 2013).

19. Jewish Orphans' Home, *Sixty-First Annual Report* (New Orleans, 1916), JCH and JCRS (hereafter Home Annual Report).

20. The Home's annual reports provide enrollment data, including name and hometown of children admitted and discharged.

21. "770, 500": Friedman, *These Are Our Children,* 53. "Genteel" courtesy and "respect": Besmann, "Typical Home Kid Overachievers," 126–27, citing Scott Langston, "Interaction and Identity Jews and Christians in Nineteenth Century New Orleans," *Southern Jewish History* 3 (2000): 104 n. 3.

22. Home Annual Reports; Berenson thesis, 61–62.

23. Berenson thesis, 56; Sample admission applications from 1913, box 48, JCH; Lowenthal interview, quoted in Simons, *Jewish Times,* 172; Helen Gold Haymon, "Memories of Days in Jewish Children's Home—1920–1935," 3, JCRS; Pulitzer, *Dreams Can Come True,* 4.

24. "Confirmands at Jewish Altars," *TP,* June 12, 1913; Home Annual Report (1914).

25. Child Welfare Report, 7.

26. Karp interview (Karp, who entered the Home as a toddler in 1923, was "lovingly bathed and fed" by nursery helper Edna, whose last name Karp never knew). Haymon, "Memories," 1 ("One of the nurses was Henrietta, whom everyone called 'Mammy,' a dear, elderly mulatto"). See also Child Welfare Report, 7–8.

27. Berenson thesis, 95–96; Child Welfare Report, 8–9.

28. Home Admission Registry, entry no. 1271 for Jacob Margolin, July 2, 1914, JCRS.

29. "The Children's Fountain at the Jewish Home," *Daily Picayune,* Oct. 19, 1897.

30. Home Annual Report (1914), 114–17. The Home's annual reports and newsletters listed "Donations in Kind." Examples of press coverage of philanthropy for the Home: "Jewish Orphans Given Glorious Day by Junior Sunshiners," *TP,* Sept. 4 1913; "200 Orphans Are Guests of Kraemer at Strand," *NOS,* Mar. 19, 1918; "Jewish Orphans' Home Receives $1,000 Legacy," *NOS,* June 26, 1919; "Shuberts to Entertain Jewish Orphans Sunday," *TP,* Oct. 21, 1921.

31. Trestman, "Fair Labor," 43–45; Light, *That Pride of Race and Character,* 82 86, 94–97, 118.

32. Haymon, "Memories," 11; Pulitzer, *Dreams Can Come True,* 7.

33. Konigsmark, *Isidore Newman School,* 20–21.

34. Rubin, *Century of Progress,* quoting Jewish Orphans' Home Board Resolution, Apr. 27, 1902. The school's inclusiveness, in early-twentieth-century New Orleans, did not extend to race; Newman did not admit its first black student until 1968. Konigsmark, *Isidore Newman School,* 5.

35. Jewish Orphans' Home, *Golden City Messenger,* July 1923 (hereafter "*Golden City Messenger*").

36. Berenson thesis, 134–35, quoting Isidore Newman Manual Training School Prospectus.

37. "Children Act in Study," *TP,* Mar. 24, 1918, 45.

38. Simons, *Jewish Times,* 174.

39. Simons, *Jewish Times,* 174; Sizeler and Hornikel interviews.

40. See, e.g., "Pupils Give School Treat in Operetta," *TP,* June 4, 1922; Hornikel interview.

41. Bogen, *Jewish Philanthropy,* 164–65.

42. *Golden City Messenger,* Oct.–Nov. 1923, 3.

43. *Golden City Messenger,* Apr. 1, 1923, 2.

44. *Golden City Messenger,* Apr. 1, 1923, 2

45. Home *Annual Reports* (1915), 43; (1916), 45; and (1919), 14.

46. Home *Annual Report* (1915), 42.

47. Home *Annual Report* (1915), 42. Volmer gave a similar description eight years later. *Golden City Messenger,* Oct.–Nov. 1923, 3.

48. Berenson thesis, 96–97.

49. Pulitzer, *Dreams Can Come True,* 5; Besmann, "Typical Home Kid Overachievers," 138.

50. Haymon, "Memories," 11.

51. Haymon, "Memories," 3.

52. Besmann, "Typical Home Kid Overachievers"; Pulitzer, *Dreams Can Come True,* 9; Haymon, "Memories," 11; Smith interview.

53. Home Annual Reports (1914), 55 and (1915), 42.

54. *Golden City Messenger,* July 1923, 4

55. Englander, "History of Reform Judaism"; Meyer, *Response to Modernity;* Kaplan, *American Reform Judaism.*

56. Light, *That Pride of Race and Character,* 97–98. See also Friedman, *These Are Our Children,* 144–50.

57. "Many Confirmed at Synagogues," *NOS,* June 3, 1922.

58. See, e.g., "Jewish New Year Services Are Ended," *NOS,* Sept. 28, 1916.

59. Home Annual Report (1916), 45.

60. Simons, *Jewish Times,* 173, 175.

61. Karp interview.

62. Simons, *Jewish Times,* 174; Haymon, "Memories," 9–10.

63. Haymon, "Memories," 9; Simons, *Jewish Times,* 174.

64. M. Trifon and T. Trifon interviews.

65. BM to Robert W. Ginnane, Sept. 14, 1962, BMP; BM to William O. Douglas, Dec. 17, 1961, Douglas Papers.

66. Child Welfare Report, 18. Separating children from their families was common among Jewish orphanages of the time, leading to estrangement and feelings of abandonment, and making it more difficult for parents to resume their roles. Friedman, *These Are Our Children,* 169–72.

67. Nathan Cohn, Address, Jan. 23, 1916, in Home Annual Report (1916), 35–36.

68. J. W. Newman, "Annual Report of the President," *Golden City Messenger,* Jan. 1925, 2–3.

69. R. Margolin and C. Margolin interviews.

70. M. Trifon and T. Trifon interviews.

71. M. Trifon, email to author, Mar. 7, 2013.

72. Haymon, "Memories," 8.

73. *Golden City Messenger,* Apr. 1923, 1.

74. "Jewish Orphan Home Fifty-Ninth Jubilee," *Daily Picayune,* Jan. 14, 1914.

75. *Golden City Messenger,* Apr. 1923, 1, 5; "Jewish Orphans' Home Celebrates Its Anniversary," *TP,* Jan. 8, 1923, 9.

76. Rabbi Emil W. Leipziger, "The New Philanthropy," address at the Fifty-Ninth Anniversary of the Association for the Relief of Jewish Widows and Orphans, reprinted in Home Annual Report (1914), 40; "Jewish Orphan Home Fifty-Ninth Jubilee," *Daily Picayune,* Jan. 14, 1914.

77. Leipziger, "New Philanthropy"; "Jewish Orphan Home Fifty-Ninth Jubilee."

78. "Jewish Orphans to Be Given Start by Big Brothers," *TP*, Mar. 29, 1915; Home Annual Report (1915), 28.

79. Goodkind, *Eminent Jews of America*, 294–95.

80. Klein, *Passion for Sharing*, 47–48.

81. Klein, *Passion for Sharing*, 47–48; "Thieves Make Rich Haul at Maurice Stern's Home," *TP*, Feb. 23, 1904; "Maurice Stern's Funeral," *TP*, Apr. 16, 1919; Hannah B. Stern to Anna E. Many, Jan. 12, 1925, BM File, NCCRW.

82. Hanna B. Stern, Statement of Reference, Apr. 21, 1926, NCCRW; Hanna B. Stern to Anna E. Many, Jan. 12, 1925, BM file, NCCRW.

83. *Golden City Messenger,* May, July, and Dec. 1923.

84. English Collateral Reading for Bessie Margolin, INS.

85. BM Report Cards, INS.

86. Drowne and Huber, *1920s,* 182–83.

87. BM, "Gypsy Matchmakers," *Pioneer,* June 1924, 66–70; BM, "In Someone Else's Shoes," *Pioneer,* May 1924, 30–34.

88. Margolin, "Gypsy Matchmakers," 66–70.

89. Barbara Brin et al., "Alumni Feature: Newman's Representative in Washington," *Pioneer,* Isidore Newman School, May 1966, 8, BMP.

90. *Pioneer,* June 1925, 20.

91. Polack interview.

92. "Children's Page," *Golden City Messenger,* May 1925.

93. *Pioneer,* June 1925, 39.

94. Flonacher to BM, May 1939, BMP.

95. "Speakers Tell Story of Growth of Jewish Home," *TP*, Jan. 12, 1930, 7.

96. The Home's post 1946 history as a regional, nonresidential service agency for needy Jewish youth is available at www.jcrs.org/about/history/ (accessed Mar. 23, 2015).

97. Harold Rubin, "Orphanage to Court Career," *TP States and Roto Magazine,* Jan. 2, 1955.

98. Child Welfare Report, 35–40. Volmer departed one year after Bessie left, and his successors took increasingly larger steps to make the Home less institutional and better integrate the children with the community. They replaced the large, stark dormitories with bedrooms shared by a few children, closed the Home's synagogue to send the children to nearby Reform congregations, issued allowances instead of using money to reward or punish behavior, or to compensate for chores, and soon abolished the entire Golden City system. Berenson thesis, 96–98.

99. Booton Herndon, "Brain Investment Pays Dividends," *NOI,* Apr. 6, 1939.

100. Rubin, "Orphanage to Court Career," *TP States and Roto Magazine,* Jan. 2, 1955.

101. C. Margolin interview.

2. COLLEGE AND LAW SCHOOL

1. According to the Home's registry, Margolin first boarded on Soniat Street with "Mrs. Block," who had provided lodging for other newly discharged Home alumni.

2. L. A. Wogan to BM, July 24, 1925, BM file, NCCRW; Newcomb College Bulletin, 1926, 120–21, NCCRW; Newcomb College Bulletin for 1927, 118–19, NCCRW; Booton Herndon, "Local Girl Makes Good in Big Way," *TP,* Apr. 6, 1939, 1.

3. "Newcomb College, Prospectus of the New Department of the Tulane University," *TP,* July 3, 1887, 9.

4. Tucker and Willinger, *Newcomb College, 1886–2006,* 124.

5. Tucker and Willinger, *Newcomb College, 1886–2006,* 125.

6. Kessler-Harris, *Difficult Woman,* 37, 38 n. 5.

7. Banner, *Women in Modern America,* 153.

8. Banner, *Women in Modern America;* Kessler-Harris, *Difficult Woman,* 38.

9. "Scraps," *TP,* Dec. 12, 1926.

10. "Newcomb Notes, News of Campus," *TP,* Nov. 28, 1926, 6.

11. A comparison of the graduates in Manual's 1925 Commencement Program with Newcomb's freshman class in the *Tulane Jambalaya* for 1925–26 reveals that nine of the seventeen girls from Margolin's Manual class went to Newcomb. Sorority information obtained from *Tulane Jambalaya* for 1925–26.

12. "Newcomb Campus News Happenings," *TP,* Apr. 30, 1927, 7; "Newcomb Notes," *TP,* Dec. 12, 1926, 17; "Newcomb Sophs Defeat Juniors in Cage Finals," *TP,* Mar. 26, 1927, 14; "Newcomb Prom Next Saturday," *TP,* May 8, 1927, 4.

13. "Society," *TP,* Oct. 3, 1926, 5; "Society," *TP,* May 3, 1926; "Society," *TP,* Nov. 29, 1926, 15; "Society," *TP,* Oct. 4, 1926, 15; "Society," *TP,* Dec. 21, 1926, 19.

14. A. E. Many to Hanna Stern, Apr. 21, 1926, BM file, NCCRW.

15. Hanna Stern, Statement of Reference, n.d., BM file, NCCRW.

16. Counselor of women to BM, May 5, 1926, BM file, NCCRW.

17. BM application for admission to the bar, U.S. District Court for the District of Columbia, Dec. 12, 1952, BMP.

18. M. Trifon interview.

19. BM transcript, H. Sophie Newcomb Memorial College, Sept. 1925–June 1927, BM file, NCCRW.

20. Oct. 7, 1927, report, BM file, NCCRW. In 1931 a reporter described twenty-two-year-old Margolin as "modest," "extremely reticent," "earnest," and "a charming, unusually interesting but unspoiled young girl." Mazie Adkins, "New Orleans Girl Aid to Yale Savant," *TP,* Aug. 21, 1931. A TVA coworker described Margolin in 1934 as a "Washington prima donna." Undated, unsigned letter to Tommy Corcoran, apparently written by Howard Corcoran soon after Larry Fly's arrival at TVA, box 197, Fly folder, Corcoran Papers (located by Daniel Ernst). A young lawyer in the Labor Solicitor's office in the mid-1950s described forty-something-year-old Margolin as a "single, totally work driven . . . perfectionist" and "elitist." Jones, *Hattie's Boy,* 271. In 1967 Tulane's alumni magazine described 58-year-old Margolin's initial "hesitant smiles" and "shy nervousness." Llamas, "Labor and the Lady Lawyer," 2.

21. BM report card, 1924–25, INS.

22. Booton Herndon, "'Local Girl' Makes Good in Big Way," *NOI,* Apr. 6, 1939, 1.

23. Tucker and Willinger, *Newcomb College,* 126.

24. Friedman, "A Look Back at the Tulane Law School of John Minor Wisdom's Era," 2091; Friedman, *Champion of Civil Rights,* 19.

25. Clara Dinkelspiel, Newman, 1923, graduated from Tulane Law School in June 1927. Tulane University, *Jambalaya*, 1926–27. Dinkelspiel spent one year at Newcomb before transferring to Tulane Law School, where she earned a bachelor of laws degree; Margolin would attain bachelor degrees in both laws and liberal arts and sciences.

26. Drachman, *Sisters in Law*, 118–19.

27. Drachman, *Sisters in Law*, 118–19, 256 (table 7).

28. MacCrate, "What Women Are Teaching a Male-Dominated Profession," 991.

29. Tulane University, Jambalaya, 1929–30; Brierre interview.

30. Epstein, *Women in Law*, 62–65.

31. Recollections of Leon Stahl, "Tulane University, 50 Year Reunion Brochure, Class of 1930," May 10, 1980, BMP.

32. Recollections of Leon Stahl, "Tulane University."

33. Friedman, "A Look Back at the Tulane Law School of John Minor Wisdom's Era," 2093 and n. 3.

34. Tulane University Class of 1930 Fifty Year Reunion Booklet (May 10, 1980), BMP.

35. Margolin, "Immovables by Destination," "Usufruct of a Promissory Note—Perfect or Imperfect," and "Vendor's Privilege."

36. BM's "Vendor's Privilege" was cited in: *In re Trahan*, 283 F. Supp. 620 (1968); *W.T. Grant Co. v. Mitchell*, 269 So. 2d 186 (1972); and L. David Cromwell, Secured Interests in Louisiana Crops: The 2010 Legislative Revision, 71 *La. L. Rev.* 1175, 1179 n. 19 (2011). BM's "Immovables by Destination" was cited in Edgar H. Lancaster Jr., Civil Law Property—Immovables by Destination, 7 *La. L. Rev.* 429 n. 2 (1947), and was praised by U.S. Circuit Judge Joseph Hutcheson in his opinion in *Warren v. White*, 76 F. 2d 764, n.2 (5th Cir. 1935).

37. "Monte M. Lemann Named by President to National Law Enforcement Commission," *Jewish Telegraphic Agency*, May 22, 1929, www.jta.org/1929/05/22/archive/monte-m-lemann-named-by-president-to-national-law-enforcement-commission (accessed Mar. 23, 2015).

38. Thomas B. Lemann to Leon Rittenberg Jr., email forwarded to author, July 9, 2010.

39. Friedman, *Champion of Civil Rights*; "Miss Bessie": Shire and Nagle interviews.

40. BM Transcript, BM student file, TULS; BM to TU Registrar, Oct. 7, 1942, BMP.

41. "Tulane Students Cast Heavy Vote in Campus Poll," *TP*, Apr. 28, 1928, 5.

42. "Society," *TP*, Jan. 16, 1928, 19.

43. "Speakers Tell Story of Growth of Jewish Home," *TP*, Jan. 12, 1930, 7; BM Application for Attorney Position, U.S. Civil Service Commission, Board of Legal Examiners, Nov. 12, 1942, BMP.

44. Haymon, "Memories," JCRS.

45. "Speakers Tell Story of Growth of Jewish Home," *TP*, Jan. 30, 1930; "Newman School Founders' Day Exercises Held," *TP*, Mar. 1, 1929; Newman *Pioneer*, 1929, 26.

46. Newcomb Assistant Registrar to L. E. Lashman, May 9, 1927, BM file, NCCRW.

47. "Many Nurses Are Passed Upon by Examining Board," *States Times Advocate* (Baton Rouge, La.), June 10, 1927, 12; Home Admission Registry, Entry for Jacob Margolin, no. 1271, JCRS; "Tulane to Confer Degrees on 391 Graduates Today," *TP*, June 9, 1931. When Jack began working at the Home as a boys' supervisor in Dec. 1930, he was discharged permanently from the Home to his father in New Orleans. From Tulane, Jack went to Dartmouth, where he received his MBA degree in May 1933.

48. Fifteenth Census of the United States: 1930, New Orleans, Ward 14, Block 411, Enumeration District 36–241, Supervisor's District 11, Sheet 22A (Apr. 11, 1930).

49. "Society," *TP,* May 21, 1930, 26; "Society," *TP,* May 15, 1930, 27 (Kate Polack's wedding and pre-nuptial events); "Society," *TP,* May, 31, 1928, 15 (Flonacher's wedding); "Society," *TP,* Mar. 8, 1929, 23 (Flonacher's engagement party for Newman classmate Bertha Jacobson).

50. M. Trifon interview.

51. "Terrebonne Man Succeeds Wallis," *TP,* Mar. 1, 1924, 3; "Judge Butler's Rites Set Wednesday," *Advocate* (Baton Rouge, La.), Feb. 9, 1965, 1.

52. Hope, *Last Poems,* 4.

53. Melnick, *Life and Work of Ludwig Lewisohn,* 346. BM titled her Apr. 1931 poetry notebook "La Poésie" and on the dedication page, she typed only "To. . . ."

54. Ernest Lorenzen to BM, Dec. 17, 1933, BMP.

55. Butler interview; "Butler Funeral Services Today," *TP,* June 28, 1973, S1, 17.

56. Photographs, Tulane Law School Class of 1930 25th Reunion Dinner at Antoine's, June 1955, BMP.

57. "Four Seniors, Nine Alumni Initiated—Tulane Law Group Given Membership in Order of Coif," *TP,* May 13, 1933, 3.

58. Unidentified TU alumni publication, 1967, BM folder, Central Files, TU.

59. "Tulane College Students Honored by Yale," *TP,* May 28, 1930.

60. Milton Colvin to Charles E. Clark, Dec. 31, 1929, Student Records (RU 263), box 61, folder 5892—Bessie Margolin, YU (hereafter "BMYSR").

61. Clark to Colvin, Jan. 6, 1930, BMYSR.

62. Colvin to Clark, Jan. 13, 1930, BMYSR.

63. Arlene Hadley (for Clark) to Colvin, Jan. 18, 1930, BMYSR.

64. BM to Clark, Jan. 22, 1930, BMYSR.

65. Oren, *Joining the Club,* 67–68. See also, Karabel, *Chosen,* 114–19; Kalman, *Abe Fortas,* 14–15.

66. Hadley to Harris, Jan. 31, 1930, BMYSR.

67. Harris to Hadley, Feb. 6, 1930, BMYSR.

68. Hadley to Harris, Feb. 10, 1930, BMYSR.

69. Clark to Harris, Feb. 14, 1930, BMYSR.

70. Kay, "Future of Women Law Professors," 18.

71. Clark to Harris, Feb. 14, 1930, BMYSR.

72. Harris to Clark, Feb. 25, 1930, BMYSR.

73. William D. Hays Jr., "Women Termed Good Law Pupils, yet Poor Lawyers," *TP,* Dec. 26, 1937, 19. A photo of four female law students, half of the enrolled women, bore the patronizing caption "Law Lassies among Tulane's Honor Students."

74. BM application for admission to the bar of the U.S. District Court for the District of Columbia, Dec. 12, 1952, BMP. Beutel authored several treatises on negotiable instruments and banking law and, in 1946, became dean of University of Nebraska Law School.

75. "Oath of Office Given to 52 Young Lawyers," *TP,* July 19, 1930, S2, 11. According to the article, one other woman, Mrs. Nedra P. Bywater from Loyola Law School, was admitted to the Louisiana Bar that year.

76. "$1,500": Clark to BM, May 15, 1930, BMP. "Self-supporting" and "discharge": Home Admission Registry, entry 1248, JCRS.

77. Mazie Adkins, "N.O. Girl Aid to Yale Savant," *NOI,* Aug. 21, 1931.

78. Adkins, "N.O. Girl Aid."

79. Cornell Alumni News, Oct. 14, 1903, 21; Corbin, "Ernest Gustav Lorenzen," 579.

80. Corbin, "Ernest Gustav Lorenzen," 579.

81. Yale Law School, *General Catalogue Number for the Academic Year, 1933–1934,* Aug. 1, 1933, 443.

82. Kalman, *Abe Fortas,* 14.

83. See, e.g., Zaremby, *Legal Realism and American Law;* Dagan, *Reconstructing American Legal Realism;* Llewellyn, *Jurisprudence;* Kalman, *Legal Realism at Yale.*

84. Kalman, *Legal Realism at Yale,* 23, 24.

85. Murphy, *Wild Bill,* 86–87.

86. Kalman, *Abe Fortas,* 16.

87. "Woman Lawyer Joins Legal Aid," *New Haven Register,* July 10, 1932.

88. BM to Stevens, n.d., box 33, folder 7, Stevens Papers. Although undated, Margolin likely wrote the letter shortly before Feb. 19, 1933, as it contains the notation "Answered by personal conference with BM, Feb. 19, '33."

89. In Jan. 1932, during Margolin's second year at Yale, Douglas published an article in which he explored benefits that American law could gain from British bankruptcy law. Douglas, "Some Functional Aspects of Bankruptcy."

90. BM, "Corporate Reorganization Provision in Senate Bill 3866."

91. Following custom for a lengthy student work in a law journal, Margolin's authorship was marked only by her initials, "BM." Although several prominent law firms were sufficiently impressed by the comment to inquire at the *Yale Law Journal* about its author with a view to employment, Margolin later recounted that upon learning the author was female, their interest withered, yielding only one offer—to work as a law firm librarian. Law firms' interest & inquiry: Reeves to Lilienthal, memo, June 29, 1933, Records of the U.S. House of Representatives, Record Group 233, Select Committee to Investigate the Federal Communications Commission, box 9, folder BM, Subject Files, National Archives, Washington, D.C. (hereafter "NA-FCC-BM"). Library job offer: BM conversation with author, late 1970s.

92. Lorenzen to Harris, Mar. 1, 1932, BMP.

93. Harris to BM, Mar. 7, 1932, BMP.

94. Lorenzen to BM, n.d., BMP. Lorenzen likely wrote the letter in Apr. 1932 given his references to Margolin's move "tomorrow," which coincides with her move from her apartment on Howe Street to Whitney Avenue, and to her doctor's degree "next year," which reflects her anticipated JSD award in June 1933.

95. Lorenzen to BM, n.d., BMP. That Margolin did not strongly identify herself with Judaism can be gleaned from Lorenzen's letter, in which he impressed upon her the need to seek spiritual fulfillment never once referring to her being Jewish, which Lorenzen must have known.

96. Lorenzen to BM, Dec. 17, 1933, BMP.

97. The 1920 U.S. Census for New Haven (Jan. 1920) reports that Lorenzen was married to Charlotte (9 years younger) and had two sons, Frederick (12) and Hans (10). The 1930 U.S. Census (Apr. 1930) reports that Lorenzen was a widower, living with one son, Frederick (23).

98. Lorenzen to Harris, Dec. 5, 1932, BM student file, TULS.

99. Lorenzen to Harris, June 12, 1933, NA-FCC-BM.

100. Brosman to Lorenzen, June 21, 1933, NA-FCC-BM.

101. BM Transcript, June 21, 1933, Office of the Registrar, Yale Law School; Nancy F. Lyon, YUL, email to author, July 15, 2013.

102. Application for a Further Extension of Time Within Which to File a Petition for a Writ of Certiorari, June 28, 1960, *Mitchell v. Whitaker House Cooperative, Inc.*, 366 U.S. 310 (1960).

103. Margolin, "Corporate Reorganization in France"; Douglas to BM, June 23 1933, BMP.

104. BM Transcript, June 21, 1933, Office of the Registrar, Yale Law School.

105. BM Transcript, June 21, 1933.

106. Margolin, "Corporate Reorganization in France," 62–63. While analyzing several French cases to demonstrate the uncertainties in French law governing repayment of unsecured debts in bankruptcy, Margolin described one French court's refusal to rule that a lawsuit to recover on such a debt, filed by a law professor, had been frivolous or vexatious. The court, she explained with amusement, found the professor's legal expertise made him more appreciative of judicial subtleties and less likely to knowingly misstate the law.

107. "Four Seniors, Nine Alumni Initiated," *TP*, May 13, 1933, 3; "Yale Graduation Is Full of Color," *NYT*, June 21, 1933, 15.

3. SUMMER WITH A SUFFRAGIST

1. "Air of great vitality, great movement": Henry Fowler in Louchheim, *Making of the New Deal*, 228–29.

2. "House Moves for Women's Suffrage," *NYT*, Sept. 25, 1917, 11.

3. Stevens, *Jailed for Freedom*, 169–73.

4. "Feminine Achievements Given Recognition during Past Year," *Richmond (Va.) Times-Dispatch*, Jan. 1, 1932, 3; McKenzie, "Power of International Positioning," 132, 134.

5. "Carrie Chapman Catt Ends Long Career," *Greensboro (N.C.) Daily News*, Jan. 31, 1932, 8.

6. Douglas to BM, June 23, 1933, BMP; BM to Douglas, June 26, 1933, box 9, folder 13, Douglas Papers. Frank, one of legal realism's leading proponents, left his New York law firm that year for an appointment at Yale to develop an interdisciplinary course dealing with the legal and sociological aspects of the judicial process. "Yale Law School Announces Its Appointments," *New Haven Journal-Courier*, June 24, 1932.

7. BM to Doris Stevens, n.d., box 33, folder 7, Stevens Papers. The letter contains a notation: "Answered by personal conference with BM Feb. 19, '33."

8. BM to Stevens, Feb. 6, 1933, box 33, folder 7, Stevens Papers.

9. Stevens to Matthews, Mar. 23, 1933, box 34, folder 3, Stevens Papers.

10. *Baltimore Evening Sun*, July 17, 1925, 2, http://darrow.law.umn.edu/photo.php?pid=702 (accessed Jan. 9, 2014).

11. Marjorie J. Spruill, ed., "Historical Introduction," in Stevens, *Jailed for Freedom*, l–li.

12. "She's Doris Stevens, Not Mrs. D. F. Malone," *Wilkes-Barre (Pa.) Times-Leader*, Jan. 24, 1922, 10. "Too modernistic": Lorenzen to BM, Dec. 17, 1933, BMP.

13. BM to Stevens, Mar. 5, 1933, box 33, folder 7, Stevens Papers.

14. Stevens to BM, Mar. 23, 1933, box 33, folder 7, Stevens Papers.

15. Stevens to BM, Apr. 14, 1933, box 76, folder 20, Stevens Papers.

16. BM to Stevens, Apr. 29, 1933, box 76, folder 20, Stevens Papers.

17. BM to Boord, telegram, June 12, 1933, box 76, folder 2, Stevens Papers.

18. Boord to BM, telegrams, June 12, 1933 (6:35 a.m. and 2:25 p.m.), box 76, folder 20, Stevens Papers.

19. Virtue, *Family Cases in Court.* Maxine Boord Virtue's other books and articles include *Survey of Metropolitan Courts; Basic Structure of Children's Services in Michigan;* and "The Two Faces of Janus: Delay in Metropolitan Trial Courts."

20. Frances Maxine Boord Transcript, June 19, 1935, Office of the Registrar, Yale Law School; Virtue vertical file; Virtue, "Laws Affecting Women in Kansas." The author thanks Veronica Virtue for her help in obtaining information about her mother's legal education and career.

21. BM to Douglas, June 26, 1933, box 9, folder 13, Douglas Papers.

22. BM to Douglas, June 26, 1933, box 9, folder 13.

23. BM to Douglas, June 26, 1933, box 9, folder 13.

24. Wade, "Burnita Shelton Matthews"; Cushman, *Supreme Court Decisions and Women's Rights,* 15.

25. IACW "Country Codes," boxes 113–23, Stevens Papers.

26. The commission's agreement to "quietly table" the equal rights treaty was the quid pro quo for the United States's decision to support the equal nationality treaty, in accordance with President Roosevelt's instructions to Secretary of State Cordell Hull. McKenzie, "Power of International Positioning," 140.

4. DEFENDING THE NEW DEAL'S TENNESSEE VALLEY AUTHORITY

1. Epstein, *Women in Law,* 4, table I.1.

2. Drachman, "New Woman Lawyer," 227, 235.

3. Margolin, "Women in Law," 137.

4. Myers, "Women Lawyers in Federal Positions," 19–20.

5. "Tennessee Valley Program," *WP,* Aug. 19, 1933, 8; "Valley Plans Hold Work for Million," *WP,* June 28, 1933, 2; "White House Gets Shoals Bill Today," *WP,* May 18, 1933, 2.

6. Hubbard, *Origins of the TVA,* 2–5; Owen, *Tennessee Valley Authority,* 4–11; Badger, *FDR: The First Hundred Days,* 110–14.

7. Hubbard, *Origins of the TVA;* Owen, *Tennessee Valley Authority,* 8.

8. Franklin D. Roosevelt, "Message to Congress Suggesting the Tennessee Valley Authority," Apr. 10, 1933, www.presidency.ucsb.edu/ws/?pid=14614 (accessed Apr. 7, 2015).

9. Tennessee Valley Authority Act of 1933, 48 Stat. 58–59, 16 U.S. Code sec. 831.

10. Walter Lippmann, "TVA Is Most Interesting of New Deal Undertakings," *Omaha World Herald,* Feb. 26, 1936, 6.

11. BM to Douglas, June 23, 1933, box 9, folder 13, Douglas Papers; Margolin, "Women in Law," 137.

12. Jerome Frank recruited Abe Fortas to work at the Agricultural Adjustment Administration. Kalman, *Abe Fortas,* 32. Tommy Corcoran persuaded Henry Fowler to join the Reconstruction Finance Corp., another New Deal agency. Louchheim, *Making of the New Deal,* 231–32; Fowler interview, 1:2, 10. Corcoran also recruited C. Girard Davidson, who was two years behind Margolin at Tulane and Yale, to work at TVA. Davidson interview, 25–26.

13. Clark to TVA, June 23, 1933, NA-FCC-BM; Douglas to TVA, June 23, 1933, BMP.

14. BM Application for Employment, June 27, 1933, BM Personnel File, Tennessee Valley Authority, Knoxville, obtained by author under Freedom of Information Act (hereafter "TVA-BM").

15. BM to Douglas, June 23, 1933, box 9, folder 13, Douglas Papers.

16. Niehoff, *Floyd W. Reeves,* 193.

17. Reeves to Lilienthal, June 29, 1933, NA-FCC-BM.

18. Harris to Reeves, July 13, 1933, NA-FCC-BM.

19. Sturges to A. E. Morgan, July 13, 1933, NA-FCC-BM.

20. Smith to Lilienthal, July 8, 1933, BMP.

21. Lorenzen to Reeves, July 22, 1933, NA-FCC-BM.

22. "William A. Sutherland," Obituary, *Atlanta Journal-Constitution,* Nov. 11, 1987, C12; Sutherland to file re: BM, memo, n.d., NA-FCC-BM (apparently written shortly after BM's Aug. 9, 1933 interview).

23. Sutherland to Corcoran, Aug. 29, 1933, NA-FCC-BM.

24. Sutherland interview, 2:1; Storrs, *Second Red Scare,* 29.

25. Reeves claimed he "had to convince a reluctant Lilienthal to hire" Margolin. Neuse, *David M. Lilienthal,* 115.

26. A two-thousand-dollar salary in 1933 "was ample" in Washington, D.C., said another New Deal lawyer who rented an apartment for $60 a month, bought a car for $450, and could still afford a maid. Louchheim, *Making of the New Deal,* 138.

27. C. L. Richey to BM, Sept. 12, 1933, TVA-BM.

28. Sutherland interview, Vol. 1, 22.

29. BM to Douglas, Sept. 14, 1933, box 9, folder 13, Douglas Papers.

30. See, e.g., various memoranda regarding BM's assignments, box 81, folder "095 Margolin," Lilienthal Correspondence, Records of the Tennessee Valley Authority, Record Group 142, National Archives, Morrow, Ga. (hereafter "NA-TVA-LC").

31. Sutherland to V.D.L. Robinson, memo, Jan. 27, 1934, NA-FCC-BM.

32. Owen to C. L. Richey, memo, June 26, 1934, NA-FCC-BM.

33. Sutherland to Lilienthal, Apr. 13, 1934 and June 20, 1934, box 101, folder "095 Sutherland," NA-TVA-LC.

34. Lilienthal to Sutherland, June 26, 1934, box 101, folder "095 Sutherland," NA-TVA-LC; Lilienthal to Jerome Frank, July 17, 1934, box 53, folder "095 Fly through 1934," NA-TVA-LC.

35. Henderson, *Power and the Public Interest,* 23–24.

36. Complaint, *Central Ice Co. v. TVA,* filed June 14, 1934, U.S. District Court, Northern District of Alabama, box 7, folder "10.4 Central Ice Company," NA-TVA-LC.

37. Lilienthal to Owen, memo, July 2, 1934, box 7, folder "10.4 Central Ice Company," NA-TVA-LC.

38. See, e.g., Fly to Lilienthal, July 19, 1934; Lilienthal to Fly, telegram, Aug. 3, 1934; and other correspondence in box 53, folder "095 Fly though 1934," NA-TVA-LC. Other candidates

suggested to Lilienthal included Calvert Magruder and Douglas Arant. Lilienthal to Sutherland, June 26, 1934, box 101, folder "095 Sutherland," NA-TVA-LC.

39. Henry Pringle, "The Controversial Mr. Fly," *Saturday Evening Post,* July 22, 1944, 9; Brinson, *Red Scare,* 27.

40. "James L. Fly Given TVA's Attorneyship," *TP,* Aug. 8, 1934, 11.

41. Brinson, *Red Scare,* 27; Fortas interview, 2; John T. Moutoux, "New TVA Solicitor Is New Deal Type," Aug. 1934, *KNS.*

42. "A Man in the News," *Christian Science Monitor,* Feb. 11, 1936.

43. Fly to Lilienthal, memo, Aug. 10, 1934, box 3, folder "TVA Appointment—Set Up of Legal Division," Fly Papers.

44. Fowler interview by Crawford, vol. 1, 3–4.

45. V.D.L. Robinson to C. L. Richey, memo, Aug. 8, 1934, NA-FCC-BM.

46. First page of letter to "Tom," n.d., box 197, folder "James Lawrence Fly," Corcoran Papers. Daniel Ernst, who located this document, notes that an opening reference to Fly's recent visit and expected, permanent return suggests a date soon after Fly's Aug. 6, 1934, trip to Knoxville. Howard Corcoran likely was the unidentified writer, who lists "me" as one of the legal division's seven lawyers. Ernst, email to author, June 12, 2012.

47. Fly to Reeves, memo, Aug. 23, 1934, NA-FCC-BM.

48. A. S. Jandrey to Fly, memo, Feb. 8, 1935, box 115, folder "211.92 Legal Personnel," NA-TVA-LC; "Salary Histories for Selected TVA Employees—June 1934 through Jan. 1939," memo, box 115, folder "221 Salaries, pay wages, allowances 1938," NA-TVA-LC. Howard Corcoran, who had been promoted to the higher rank of senior attorney, was already making forty-five hundred dollars per year, while C. Girard Davidson, a 1934 Yale law graduate, was earning twenty-six hundred dollars per year in the lower rank of assistant attorney.

49. C. L. Richey to Gordon R. Clapp, memo, Dec. 28, 1938, box 115, folder "221 Salaries, pay wages, allowances 1938," NA-TVA-LC. Fowler's starting salary of thirty-two hundred dollars per year was lower than Margolin's thirty-six hundred dollars, by 1936 it was raised to match hers, and by the end of 1936 exceeded it by four hundred dollars.

50. "Herbert Marks Comes Here in TVA Work," *Chattanooga News,* Jan. 13, 1939, box 7, folder "TVA Clippings: HSM Personal," Marks Papers. By Feb. 1935 Fly promoted Marks to senior attorney at forty-eight hundred dollars per year and by 1938 to assistant general counsel at seven thousand dollars per year. Feb. 8, 1935, memo from A. S. Jandrey to Fly, box 115, folder "211.92 Legal Personnel," NA-TVA-LC; Civil Service Commission, *Official Register of the United States* (Washington, D.C.: Government Printing Office, 1938), 189.

51. Henderson, *Power and the Public Interest,* 12–21. After serving as assistant general counsel until 1945, Swidler became TVA's general counsel, a position he held until 1957.

52. Fowler interview by Crawford, 2:8; "Melvin Hirsh Siegel," obituary, *San Francisco Chronicle,* Jan. 13, 1997.

53. Fowler interview by Crawford, 1:6.

54. Fowler interview by Crawford, 1:7.

55. Report of the Joint Committee on the Investigation of the Tennessee Valley Authority, S. Doc. No. 56, 76th Cong., 1st sess. (Apr. 3, 1939), 68, box 5, Fly Papers.

56. Fitts interview by Connell, 2.

57. Fitts interview by Connell, 46.

58. Fly to Reeves, memo, Aug. 23, 1934, NA-FCC-BM; TVA Employee Status Change for BM, Aug. 29, 1934, NA-FCC-BM.

59. J. Swidler interview, 9–10.

60. J. Swidler interview, 11.

61. Best interview, 10.

62. Corcoran to Ethel Diamond, July 27, 1934, box 293, folder "321 Division of Law," Washington Office Correspondence, Records of the Tennessee Valley Authority, Record Group 142, National Archives, Morrow Ga. (hereafter "NA-TVA-WC").

63. John T. Montoux, "TVA Headquarters Here Is Beehive of Varied Activities," *KNS,* Dec. 3, 1933, 1.

64. BM to Marks, Apr. 25, 1939, Marks Papers.

65. Henderson, *Power and the Public Interest,* 27.

66. Clauss interview.

67. Clauss interview.

68. *Ashwander v. TVA,* 297 U.S. 288 (1936); *TEP. v. TVA,* 306 U.S. 118 (1939).

69. Henderson, *Power and the Public Interest,* 23–24.

70. Swidler and Marquis, "TVA in Court," 304–5.

71. On Oct. 31, 1934, Judge Grubb, without a written decision, declared the National Industrial Recovery Act unconstitutional. "NRA Is Invalid, U.S. Judge Rules in Lumber Case," *Dallas Morning News,* Nov. 1, 1934, 1, 4.

72. *Ashwander v. TVA,* 8 F. Supp. 893, 896 (N.D. Ala. 1934); Fowler interview by Crawford, 1:16.

73. Fowler interview by Crawford, 1:22–23.

74. Fowler interview by Crawford, 1:11; Fitts interview by Connell, 5.

75. "TVA Lawyers Burn Midnight Oil Preparing for Varied Suits," *KNS,* July 5, 1936, G-2.

76. TVA Travel Request for BM, Jan. 18, 1935, box 141, folder "Personal," Exhibits, Evidence, Etc., Re: Committee Investigations/James L. Fly, FCC Chair, Special Committee on Un-American Activities (Dies), National Archives, Washington, D.C. (hereafter "NA-FCC-JLF").

77. Louchheim, *Making of the New Deal,* 234.

78. "Basis for Attack on TVA's Program Laid at Hearings," *Springfield (Mass.) Republican,* Jan. 29, 1935, 6.

79. "Basis for Attack on TVA's Program"; "Feels Innocent, Hauptmann Says," *Springfield (Mass.) Republican,* Jan. 29, 1935, 1; "Lawyers for TVA Plan Answer to Injunction Plea," *TP,* Feb. 11, 1935, 22.

80. "TVA Right to Sell Power Outlawed by Court Ruling," *Richmond Times-Dispatch,* Feb. 23, 1935, 1.

81. *Ashwander v. TVA,* 9 F. Supp. 965 (N.D. Ala. 1935).

82. See Schlesinger, *Politics of Upheaval,* 364.

83. *Ashwander v. TVA,* 9 F. Supp. 965, 966 (N.D. Ala. 1935).

84. *Railroad Retirement Board v. Alton R.R. Co.,* 295 U.S. 330 (1935) (no opinion issued by the D.C. Cir.); *United States v. Certain Lands in City of Louisville,* 78 F. 2d 684 (6th Cir. 1935), affirming 9 F. Supp. 137 (W.D. Ky. 1935)

85. "Judge Rules TVA Can Not Sell Power," *Baton Rouge Advocate,* Feb. 23, 1935; "New Deal Appeals Decision on TVA," *Augusta (Ga.) Chronicle,* Feb. 24, 1935.

86. "Successful Defender of TVA," *Literary Digest,* Feb. 29, 1936, box 13, Fly Papers.

87. Fowler interview by Crawford, 1:24.

88. "Legal 'Cream' of New Deal to Aid TVA Appeal," *KNS,* Mar. 4, 1935.

89. "Legal Division Activities from May 16–31, 1935," box 293, folder 321, "Legal Department, Progress Reports, 1935," NA-TVA-WC; TVA Travel Request for BM, May 29, 1935, box 141, folder "Personal," NA-FCC-JLF.

90. John T. Moutoux, "Fate of TVA's Program Rests with 3 Judges," *KNS,* June 18, 1935.

91. Fly to Lilienthal, telegram, July 17, 1935, box 5, folder "010.4 Ashwander," NA-TVA-LC.

92. "TVA Wins in U.S. Court," *KNS,* July 17, 1935, 1.

93. "A Man in the News," *Christian Science Monitor,* Feb. 10, 1936, 4.

94. Frank R. Kent, "The Great Game of Politics," *WSJ,* July 19, 1935.

95. BM to *New Republic,* July 29, 1935, BMP. Margolin was referring to the Nov. 1934 legal opinion Newton Baker wrote for the Electric Institute, the utility holding companies' association, which concluded, not surprisingly, that TVA was "palpably unconstitutional." Schlesinger, *Politics of Upheaval,* 364.

96. Justice Department Press Release, Sept. 17, 1935, box 5, folder "010.4 Ashwander," NA-TVA-LC.

97. Fly to John B. Blandford, memo, Dec. 4, 1935, box 293, folder "321 Legal Division," NA-TVA-WC.

98. Fly to Lilienthal, Dec. 1, 1935, box 63, folder "095 Fly, James L. 1935," NA-TVA-LC.

99. Fly to Thurber D. Wolfe, memo, Nov. 22, 1935, box 5, folder "010.4 Ashwander," NA-TVA.

100. The first one hundred women were admitted to the Supreme Court by 1920. Cushman, *Supreme Court Decisions,* 220. Even by 1938, of the sixty thousand lawyers admitted to practice at the Supreme Court, only about four hundred were women. Drew Pearson and Robert S. Allen, "The Washington Merry-Go-Round," *Sunday Morning Star* (Wilmington, Del.), June 26, 1938. By 1935 only seventeen women had argued at the Supreme Court. Trestman, "First 101 Women to Argue at the United States Supreme Court."

101. *U.S. Supreme Court Journal* 109–10 (Dec. 19–20, 1935). See also Caldeira, "FDR's Court Packing Plan in the Court of Public Opinion," 38–39 n. 43.

102. A list of Margolin's Supreme Court arguments appears in app. 1.

103. "Transcript of Oral Argument in *Ashwander* at the U.S. Supreme Court," 4, box 7, folder "010.4 Ashwander, Oral Argument," NA-TVA-LC (hereafter "*Ashwander* Transcript").

104. *Ashwander* Transcript, 149.

105. *Ashwander* Transcript, 83.

106. *Ashwander* Transcript, 92.

107. *Ashwander* Transcript, 93.

108. *Ashwander* Transcript, 94.

109. Fowler described O'Brian's argument as "masterful," notwithstanding "hostile questions from Justice McReynolds who had a great time baiting his old friend." Fowler interview by Crawford, 1:26–27.

110. *Ashwander* Transcript, 120–21.

111. *Ashwander* Transcript, 120–21; Loucheim, *Making of the New Deal,* 234.

112. Milton V. Smith to Gordon R. Clapp, Jan. 2, 1936, NA-FCC-BM; TVA Employee Status Change for BM, Jan. 1, 1936, TVA-BM.

113. Even with the TVA victory, FDR had scored two wins and six losses in New Deal cases at the Supreme Court. Of eight major suits the administration had won only *Ashwander* and the gold clause cases decided almost exactly one year earlier. Of cases involving New Deal agencies, the Supreme Court had already declared unconstitutional the Agricultural Adjustment Administration in *Butler v. United States*, 297 U.S. 1 (1936) and the mandatory codes enforced by the National Recovery Administration, *Schechter Poultry Corp. v. United States*, 295 U.S. 495 (1935). More than a New Deal victory, the *Ashwander* decision remains best known for Justice Brandeis's concurrence, in which he outlined the importance of the Court's avoidance of constitutional issues when at all possible in disposing of a case. *Ashwander*, 297 U.S. 288, 346–348.

114. See, e.g., "Tennessee Valley Shouts with Joy," *NYT*, Feb. 18, 1936, 13; "Alabama Towns Wear Broad Smiles," *Mobile Times*, n.d., and "Town Joyous over TVA Case," *Mobile Times*, n.d., box 5, folder "010.4 Ashwander," NA-TVA-LC.

115. "Refused to comment": "Residents of TVA Area Hold Celebrations," *Tampa Tribune*, Feb. 18, 1936, 2; "Increased taxes": "Tennessee Valley Shouts with Joy," *NYT*, Feb. 18, 1936, 13.

116. "All but wrote the opinion": Fly to Abe Fortas, n.d. (responding to Fortas's Feb. 18, 1935, letter), box 3, folder "Personal—TVA, Lilienthal, Fortas, Fowler," Fly Papers.

117. Herbert Little, "O'Brian and Fly Are Real Heroes in Victory of TVA," unidentified source, n.d., BMP.

118. David Lawrence, "TVA Is Expected to Stay in Limits," unidentified source, n.d., BMP.

119. BM to Fly, memo, Mar. 12, 1936, box 5, folder "010.4 Ashwander," NA-TVA-LC.

120. BM to Fly, memo, Mar. 12, 1936, box 5, folder "010.4 Ashwander," 6.

121. O'Brian interview by Connell, 13–14.

122. *TVA v. TEP*, 90 F. 2d 885, 893 (6th Cir. 1937).

123. Fitts interview by Connell, 10 (Sally Fly Connell quotes BM).

124. *TVA v. TEP*, 90 F.2d 885 (6th Cir. 1937).

125. TVA Travel Request for BM, May 18, 1937, box 141, folder 2, NA-FCC-JLF.

126. *TVA v. TEP*, 301 U.S. 710 (1937).

127. Fly to O'Brian, July 14, 1953, box 54, folder "Fly—Biography," Fly Papers.

128. Fly to McKellar, July 23, 1937, box 5, folder "010.4 Ashwander," NA-TVA-LC.

129. Fly to O'Brian, July 14, 1953, box 54, folder "Fly—Biography," Fly Papers.

130. John Blandford to TVA Board, memo, Sept. 8, 1937, box 81, "folder 095 Mara-Marn," NA-TVA-LC.

131. TVA Employee Status Change for BM, Aug. 16, 1937, TVA-BM.

132. "TVA Lawyers Start Plans for Defense," *Chattanooga Free Press*, Nov. 8, 1937, box 13, folder "Publicity: TEP v. TVA," Fly Papers.

133. "TVA Goes on Trial for Its Life," *Life*, Nov. 29, 1937, 25; *Life*, Jan. 24, 1938, 21.

134. O'Brian interview by Crawford, 12.

135. Transcript, opening statement of James Lawrence Fly, *TEP v. TVA*, Nov. 15, 1937, box 7, Fly Papers.

136. TVA Employee Status Change for BM, Aug. 16, 1937, TVA-BM.

137. "A Woman Presides over the Tribunal Hearing One of Most Important Constitutional Cases in American History," *NYT*, Nov. 28, 1937.

138. Drew Pearson and Robert S. Allen, "Washington Merry-Go-Round," *Washington Daily*, Feb. 8, 1938.

139. Cook, "First Woman Candidate for the Supreme Court," 19.

140. *Walling v. Sanders,* 136 F. 2d 78 (6th Cir. 1943).

141. "Justice Depends on Understanding, Bible Class Is Told by Judge Allen," unidentified source, n.d. (refers to pending case of "eighteen power companies" v. TVA), box 13, folder "Publicity: TEP v. TVA," Fly Papers.

142. Compare photos of Margolin, "Crowded Court Awaits Ruling of Three Judges," *Chattanooga Times,* Sat. Jan. 22, 1938 and "Staff of TVA Counsel Happy over Decision," *Chattanooga Daily Times,* Jan. 22, 1938, 1, and Allen, "Members of Three-Judge Court Pose Informally," unidentified source, n.d. All photos in box 13, folder "Publicity: TEP v. TVA," Fly Papers.

143. "Excerpt, but Don't Argue Ruling, Judge Allen Tells Utility Lawyer," unidentified source, n.d., box 13, folder "Publicity: TEP v. TVA," Fly Papers.

144. "Big Stakes at Chattanooga," *KNS,* Nov. 28, 1937.

145. "Judge Allen Calls Hand of Fly for Pronunciation," unidentified source, n.d., box 13, folder "Publicity: TEP v. TVA," Fly Papers.

146. Fitts interview by Connell, 13–14.

147. "Flabbergasted," "all he could do": Fitts interview by Connell, 14. See also Fowler interview by Crawford, 2:5–6; Seymour interview, 4.

148. Sally Fly Connell, "The Most Dangerous Man in America," MS, box 54, folder "TMDM Outline," Fly Papers; Henry Pringle, "The Controversial Mr. Fly," *Saturday Evening Post,* July 22, 1944, 40.

149. O'Brian interview by Crawford, 8; Fowler interview by Crawford, 1:25.

150. Fowler interview by Crawford, 2:8.

151. Jackson became lead counsel role for the companies when his law partner, Newton Baker, died during the Christmas recess.

152. "Crowded Court Awaits Ruling of Three Judges," photo and article, *Chattanooga Times,* Jan. 22, 1938, box 13, folder "Publicity: TEP v. TVA," Fly Papers.

153. "Power—TVA Clear," *Time,* Jan. 24, 1938; *Tennessee Electric Power Co. v. Tennessee Valley Authority,* 21 F. Supp. 947 (1938).

154. "Court Rules TVA Program Lawful Federal Activity," *Chattanooga Daily Times,* Jan. 22, 1938, 1.

155. "Staff of TVA Counsel Happy over Decision," photo, *Chattanooga Daily Times,* Jan. 22, 1938, 1.

156. Fly to J. B. Blandford, memo, May 5, 1938, box 293, folder "321 Legal Department, Progress Reports, 1938," NA-TVA-WC.

157. As an imprecise indication of her role, Margolin's name appeared below Solicitor General Robert H. Jackson, Fly, O'Brian, Paul Freund, William Fitts, Melvin Siegel, and Henry Fowler and above the names of Herb Marks and Richard Mosher.

158. "500 exhibits/6000 pages": *Tennessee Valley Authority v. Southern States Power Co.,* 33 F. Supp. 519 (W.D. N.C. 1940).

159. Itemized Schedule of Travel and Other Expenses for Oct. 24 to Nov. 20, 1938, for BM, and Statement of Travel by Motor Vehicle for Dec. 15, 1938, to Jan. 2, 1939, for BM, box 141, folder No. 2 (of 2), NA-FCC-JLF.

160. Clapp to BM, Jan. 9, 1939, TVA-BM.

161. Itemized Schedule of Travel and Other Expenses for Oct. 24 to Nov. 20, 1938, for BM, and Statement of Travel by Motor Vehicle for Dec. 15, 1938, to Jan. 2, 1939.

162. Walsh, "Gender and the Automobile in the United States."

163. See, e.g., Hudson ads at http://oldcarandtruckads.com/Hudson/ (accessed Jan. 30, 2013).

164. M. Trifon and Clauss interviews; author personal experience.

165. Washington, D.C., police record for BM, June 3, 1948, Margolin FBI File, No. 121-518, obtained by author pursuant to FOIA request (hereafter "FBI-BM").

166. Lynn Homeier Rauch, email to author, Dec. 12, 2012, quoting her mother.

167. Margolin, "Women in Law," 137–38.

168. Evans Dunn to Herbert Marks, memo, Aug. 5, 1938, box 7, folder "TVA: Chattanooga Office," Marks Papers.

169. O'Brian interview by Crawford, 8–9.

170. Swidler, memos titled "Fitts" and "Fly," n.d., box 82, folder 17, Swidler Papers. Swidler likely wrote these memos shortly before filing his Sept. 1951 response to Loyalty Board charges.

171. *TEP v. TVA,* 306 U.S. 118 (1939).

172. BM to Marks, n.d., box 4, folder "Bessie Margolin," Marks Papers.

173. Barr to Fly, Sept. 1, 1938, box 3, folder "James A. Barr," Fly Papers.

174. Lilienthal to Roosevelt, Feb. 1, 1938, and O'Brian to Roosevelt, Jan. 21, 1938, box 1, folder "Franklin D. Roosevelt," Fly Papers.

175. Fitts interview by Connell, 47.

5. BACHELOR GIRL

1. Evelyn Flonacher and Kate Polack had married by 1930, and within a few years Kate had two children. In 1936 Margolin's sister married Harry Trifon, a doctor she met while he attended Tulane Medical School, giving Margolin her first two nephews before 1939. After Kate and Dora wed, neither worked outside the home; Evelyn went to work in an advertising firm only after her divorce.

2. McGuire, "Most Unjust Piece of Legislation," 516–41.

3. Banner, *American Beauty,* 273. For a study of single women and how they have been perceived through modern history, see Israel, *Bachelor Girl.* A more scandalous depiction of a "bachelor girl" in its time was the 1923 English translation of a French novel (first adapted into film in 1936) that portrayed the life of a young woman who, after leaving her cheating fiancé, lived freely, including having a lesbian love affair. Victor Margueritte, *La Garçonne,* 1922, translated into *The Bachelor Girl,* by Hugh Barnaby (London: Knopf, 1923); movie: *La Garçonne,* Franco London Films, 1936.

4. *Biography of a Bachelor Girl,* directed by Edward H. Griffith (Metro-Goldwyn-Mayer, 1935), trailer available at www.tcm.com/tcmdb/title/47/Biography-of-a-Bachelor-Girl/ (accessed Apr. 6, 2015).

5. Banner, *American Beauty,* 414–15; Banner, *Women in Modern America,* 216, citing fictional female characters who gave up their independence or careers to marry, portrayed by actresses including Claudette Colbert in *It Happened One Night* (1934), Rosalind Russell in *Take a Letter, Darling* (1942), Ginger Rogers in *Lady in the Dark* (1944), and most of eight films Katharine Hepburn made with Spencer Tracy; Haskell, *From Reverence to Rape,* 4–5.

6. Booton Herndon, "Local Girl Makes Good in Big Way," *NOI,* Apr. 6, 1939, 1.

7. Evelyn Flonacher to BM, May 1939, BMP.

8. Fitts interview by Connell, 41–42; Taylor interview by Connell, 45–46. While interviewing Taylor, Connell recounted: "I did interview her [Margolin], and I said that I would like to include this in the book simply because the story has to be complete in all its dimensions and she didn't cotton to that. [Margolin] said, 'No you can't and what's more if you do I'm going to sue you for libel.'" Taylor interview by Connell, 46. According to her husband and son, Connell could not find a publisher for Fly's biography. Karl Connell and Lawrence Fly Connell interviews.

9. Taylor interview by Connell, 45; Durr interview by Sargent, 163.

10. Durr interview by Connell, 7; James interview, 33.

11. R. J. Abbaticchio Jr. to J. Edgar Hoover, Jan. 21, 1948, quoting TVA employee Holly Walker, FBI-BM.

12. Mildred Fly's handwritten responses on May 24, 1967, letter from Sally Fly Connell to "Dearest Mom," box 54, folder "Fly—Biography—'born' etc.," Fly Papers.

13. James Dunn report "In re: Fly," May 1, 1943, box 141, folder "Personal," NA-FCC-JLF.

14. Abbaticchio to Hoover, Jan. 21, 1948, FBI-BM.

15. BM to Marks, n.d., box 4, folder "Margolin, Bessie," Marks Papers. The letter is dated only "Tues." but was likely written on Tuesday, Jan. 31, as BM referred to recent Supreme Court *TEP* decision (issued Jan. 30, 1939) and wrote she could be reached at Miami's Hotel Pierre. According to BM's TVA leave records, she requested annual leave for Wed., Feb. 1 through Friday, Feb. 3, 1939. NA-FCC-BM.

16. BM to Marks, Feb. 14 and 24, 1939, box 4, folder "Margolin, Bessie," Marks Papers.

17. BM to Marks, Feb. 19, 1939, box 4, folder "Margolin, Bessie," Marks Papers.

18. O'Brian to Fly, Feb. 21 1939, box 3, folder "O'Brian, John Lord," Fly Papers.

19. BM to Herb Marks, Feb. 24, 1939 letter, and Marks to BM, Feb. 27, 1939, box 4, folder "Margolin, Bessie," Marks Papers.

20. Fitts interview by Connell, 2.

21. E.g., Alvin Ziegler to Marjorie Merritt, Dec. 29, 1952, BMP.

22. Fly to Carl L. Richey, Dec. 11, 1935, box 115, folder 211.92 Legal Personnel, NA-TVA-LC; Richey to Clapp, Dec. 28, 1938, box 116, folder 221 Salaries, Pay Wages, Allowances and Compensation 1938, NA-TVA-LC.

23. "Transcript of Conference, May 9, 1938," 8, box 141, unlabeled folder, NA-FCC-JLF. Thompson later filed a lawsuit against Barr for ten thousand dollars, which she voluntarily dismissed after an out of court settlement. Summons and Pauper Oath, *Billie B. Thompson v. James A. Barr,* filed May 23, 1938, Civil Action No. 6158, First Circuit Court of Knox County, Tenn., box 141, unlabeled folder, NA-FCC-JLF.

24. Fly to W. P. O'Neil, May 2, 1938, box 3, folder "James A. Barr," Fly Papers; and "Confidential Memorandum on James Lawrence Fly," n.d., box 141, unlabeled folder, NA-FCC-JLF (hereafter "HUAC Memo on Fly"), 3–4. The ninety-five-page memorandum on Fly, a copy of which is also found in Fly's FBI file, was written between 1951 and 1954 by the House Committee on Un-American Activities (HUAC), according to information in the memo and in related FBI correspondence. Fly FBI file, No. 62-73756, obtained by author pursuant to Freedom of Information Act request (hereafter "FBI-JLF").

25. Barr to Fly, May 26, 1938, box 3, folder "James A. Barr," Fly Papers.

26. Fly to Elmer Andrews, Aug. 1, 1938, box 3, folder "James A. Barr," Fly Papers. Marks to Gerard D. Reilly, June 20, 1938; Melvin Siegel to Leon Keyserling, June 18, 1938; Marks to Calvert Magruder, Oct. 21, 1938, box 1, folder "James A. Barr," Marks Papers.

27. Fitts interview by Connell, 42–44.

28. Mildred Fly's handwritten responses on May 24, 1967, letter from Sally Fly Connell to "Dearest Mom," box 54, folder "Fly—Biography—'born' etc.," Fly Papers.

29. Plotkin interview, 15; Taylor interview, 45.

30. "Reply of John F. Pierce to Specifications of Charges Promulgated against Him by John B. Blandford, Jr., General Manager of the Tennessee Valley Authority," unsigned and undated, box 10, folder 38, Bolt Papers. Although he did not identify Fly and Margolin by name, there is no doubt Pierce was referring to them, given that she was the only woman in the legal department making five thousand dollars per year and he was the legal department's sole member with authority to recommend her salary.

31. "Reply of John F. Pierce."

32. Pierce interview, 11–12.

33. In *Vinson v. Meritor Savings Bank,* 477 U.S. 57 (1986), the Supreme Court recognized that a hostile work environment and quid pro quo conduct constitute unlawful forms of sex discrimination under Title VII of the Civil Rights Act of 1964.

34. BM to HM, Oct. 8, 1939, box 4, folder "Bessie Margolin," Marks Papers.

35. HM to BM, telegram, Oct. 14, 1939, box 4, folder "Bessie Margolin," Marks Papers.

36. BM to HM, telegram, Oct. 15, 1939, box 4, folder "Bessie Margolin," Marks Papers.

37. BM to HM, Dec. 17, 1939, box 4, folder "Bessie Margolin," Marks Papers.

38. Taylor interview, 46.

39. Brinson, *Red Scare,* 25–87. See also Edwardson, "James Lawrence Fly, the FBI, and Wiretappings"; Marcus Cohn, "How Liberals Rediscovered Free Speech," *Baton Rouge Advocate,* Jan. 11, 1975, 21.

40. U.S. Congress, House, Remarks of Representative E. Eugene Cox, 77th Cong., 2d sess., Cong. Rec., vol. 88, pt. 1 (Jan. 28, 1942), 794; "Cox Urges Inquiry on Fly and the FCC," *NYT,* Jan. 29, 1942, 7; "Fly Violently Attacks Cox Committee," *Broadcasting,* July 12, 1943, 20.

41. "L" to "My Own Darling," BMP. This is one of ten letters apparently written to Margolin by Fly, based on comparison to numerous other documents he wrote. Because the letter refers to the writer's tough time "yesterday" defending in an "open letter to Dies" his hiring of a "full professor at Columbia," the letter was most likely written in Dec. 1941 about Fly's hiring of Goodwin Watson. See Brinson, *Red Scare,* 70–72.

42. "L" to "Sweetheart dearest," n.d., BMP. This letter was apparently written at the end of 1941, based on reference to the announced move of Wage and Hours offices to Pittsburgh.

43. "L" to "My own sweetheart," n.d., and enclosed news clipping, Louis Stark, "High Court Upholds Portal Pay for Iron Ore Miners of Alabama, *NYT,* Mar. 28 1944," BMP. The case discussed was *Tennessee Coal, Iron and Railroad Co. v. Muscoda Local 123,* 321 U.S. 590 (1944), which held that the FLSA entitled miners to wages for the time they spent traveling underground to reach their job stations.

44. "L" to "Sweetheart mine," n.d.; "L" to "Darling mine," n.d., BMP.

45. "Thine" to "Darling Mine," n.d. (Sat. night), BMP.

46. "L" to "Sweetheart mine," n.d. (Mon. p.m.), BMP.

47. "L" to "My Own Darling," BMP. Because the letter refers to the writer's tough time defending his hiring of a "full professor at Columbia" in an open letter to Dies, Fly was apparently referring to his hiring of Goodwin Watson and most likely wrote the letter to Margolin in Dec. 1941. See Brinson, *Red Scare*, 70–72.

48. House Res. 21, 78th Cong., 1st sess., 89 Cong. Rec. 234 (Jan. 19, 1943).

49. U.S. Congress, House, Remarks of Representative E. Eugene Cox, 77th Cong., 2d sess., Cong. Rec., vol. 88, pt. 1 (Jan. 28, 1942), 794; "Cox Urges Inquiry on Fly and the FCC," *NYT*, Jan. 29, 1942, 7; "FCC Investigation Sought by Georgian," *Augusta (Ga.) Chronicle*, Jan. 29, 1942, A-2; "Newspapers Called Deserving of Radio," *Cleveland Plain Dealer*, Jan. 29, 1942, 8.

50. I. F. Stone, "Mr. Biddle Is Afraid," *Nation*, May 22, 1943, 735–36; Edwardson, "James Lawrence Fly." Fly also claimed that for months before the Pearl Harbor attack the FCC had fed the FBI the Tokyo-Berlin messages but that Hoover was unable to break the code. James Lawrence Fly, "Halo for Mr. Hoover?" *Saturday Review*, Dec. 29, 1956, 11–12.

51. Brinson, *Red Scare*, 82–86; Caro, *Years of Lyndon Johnson: Means of Ascent*, 90–92.

52. Wendell Berge to attorney general, memo, Apr. 29, 1942, box 34, folder: "Cox Investigation: FCC," Fly Papers.

53. Salmond, *Conscience of a Lawyer*, 106.

54. Bugeye to Garey, n.d., box 141, folder "Fly, J. L.—Personal," NA-FCC-JLF.

55. "Jimmie" to "Gen," n.d., box 141, folder "Fly, J. L.—Personal," NA-FCC-JLF.

56. Stenographer's notepad, NA-FCC-BM.

57. Dunn, report, Apr. 29, 1943, box 141, folder, "Fly, J. L.—Personal," NA-FCC-JLF.

58. Dunn, report, Apr. 30, 1943, box 141, folder, "Fly, J. L.—Personal," NA-FCC-JLF.

59. Dunn, report, May 2, 1943, box 141, folder, "Fly, J. L.—Personal," NA-FCC-JLF.

60. Dunn, report, May 1, 1943, box 141, folder, "Fly, J. L.—Personal," NA-FCC-JLF.

61. Durr interview by Sargent, 163–64.

62. Durr interview by Connell, 9, 20–21.

63. Durr interview by Sargent, 163–64.

64. Neal, *Dark Horse: A Biography of Wendell Willkie*, 43–44, 144–45; Culver, *American Dreamer*, 234, 241–42; William J. Vanden Heuvel, "In Praise of Wendell Willkie, a 'Womanizer,'" *NYT*, Dec. 19, 1987.

65. James interview, 33; Caro, *Means of Ascent*, 91–92.

66. James interview, 33; Caro, *Means of Ascent*, 91–92.

67. Margolin FBI file, 1964 name check.

68. Edwardson, "James Lawrence Fly's Fight for a Free Marketplace of Ideas," 20; House Select Committee to Investigate the Federal Communications Commission, Final Report, 78th Cong., 2d sess., 1945, H. Rept. 2095, 50–53.

69. Edwardson, "James Lawrence Fly's Fight for a Free Marketplace of Ideas," 20; "Fly Resigns after Stormy Career in FCC," *Chicago Tribune*, Nov. 3, 1944, 27; "Fly Has Enough," *Miami Herald*, Nov. 3, 1944, 6.

70. "L" to "Darling mine," n.d., BMP. The same seltzer water fiasco was described in detail in Henry Pringle, "The Controversial Mr. Fly," *Saturday Evening Post*, July 22, 1944, 9.

71. "L" to "Precious One," n.d. ("Tues. p.m.), BMP; "L" to "My darling dear," n.d. ("Wed. p.m."), BMP.

72. "L" to "Darling mine," n.d. ("Thurs. p.m."), BMP.

73. T. Trifon interview; Toby Trifon email to author, Oct. 24, 2012; Tracey Trifon emails to author, Mar. 30 and June 16, 2012 (with current photos of the Naval Academy Class of 1921 ring). The ring Margolin gave to her nephew appears to be the same one Fly wore in numerous photographs taken during his time at the FCC. Photographs, box 16, Fly Papers.

74. "Right to Job Won by Social Worker," *NYT,* Aug. 11, 1947; "Social Worker Is Reinstated: Arbitrator's Award Hailed by Both Sides of Dispute," *New York Sun,* Aug. 11, 1947; American Arbitration Association, Administrator, Voluntary Labor Arbitration Tribunal, "In the Matter of the Arbitration between the National Council of Jewish Women and Social Service Employees Union, Local 19, United Office and Professional Workers of America, CIO, Opinion, James Lawrence Fly," Aug. 8, 1947.

75. *United States v. Bridges,* 86 F. Supp. 922 (1949); Edwardson, "James Lawrence Fly: The FBI and Wiretappings"; Lawrence E. Davies, "Court Room Fight for Bridges Opens," *NYT,* Oct. 5, 1949.

76. "McGrath Backs Wiretapping Acts by FBI," *WP,* Jan. 9, 1950; editorial, "Dirty Business," *WP,* Jan. 11, 1950; Fly, "Mr. Fly on Wiretapping—Former FCC Member Expounds His Views on 'Dirty Business' in Reply to State Editorial," *Washington Evening Star,* June 13, 1949; Fly, "Threat to Liberty, Defiance of Law Seen in FBI Wiretapping," *WP,* Jan. 7, 1950, 9; James Lawrence Fly, "The Wiretapping Outrage," *New Republic,* Feb. 6, 1950, 14–15; Fly "Fly Scores Legal Profession for Its Apathy toward FBI Wire Tapping," *Harvard Law School Record,* Apr. 26, 1950; and transcript of "Should Wire Tapping Be Legalized?" panel discussion on WOR-TV's "America Speaks," with J. Edward Lumbard, U.S. attorney for the Southern District of New York, Dec. 8, 1950, and other papers in box 41, folder "Fly on Wiretapping," Fly Papers.

77. Numerous memos in Fly's FBI file, written by FBI personnel, recount Fly's criticisms of the FBI and characterize his attitude toward the FBI as "hostile" and "vicious." See, e.g., V. P. Keay to H. B. Fletcher, memo, Nov. 16, 1949; Ladd to the Director, Jan. 11, 1950; FBI-JLF. As late as 1968, two years after Fly died, FBI director Hoover refused to be interviewed by Fly's daughter for Fly's biography; internal memos explained Hoover's refusal by noting Fly's "lack of cooperation and a critical attitude toward the Bureau" both during and "long after" he was FCC chair. M. A. Jones to Mr. Bishop, memo, Nov. 11, 1968, FBI-JLF.

78. D. M. Ladd to the Director, memo, Aug. 28, 1951, FBI-JLF.

79. HUAC Memo on Fly, 1; "James L. Fly to Be Married," *Seattle Daily Times,* Dec. 19, 1950, 10.

80. BM to Charlotta Gallup, Aug. 21, 1959, BMP.

81. O'Brian to BM, May 29, 1962, BMP.

82. "James L. Fly Dies at 67," *Daytona Beach Sunday News-Journal,* Jan. 7, 1966.

6. WAGES AND HOURS

1. Grossman, "Fair Labor Standards Act of 1938," 24.

2. Franklin D. Roosevelt, "Fireside Chat," June 24, 1938, www.presidency.ucsb.edu/ws/?pid=15662 (accessed Apr. 6, 2015).

3. Grossman, "Fair Labor Standards Act of 1938," 23.

4. Franklin D. Roosevelt, "Excerpts from the Press Conference," Dec. 29, 1936, www.presidency.ucsb.edu/ws/?pid=15246. In *Hammer v. Dagenhart,* 247 U.S. 251 (1918), the Supreme

Court struck down a child labor law reasoning that production of goods was not commerce. In *Schechter Poultry v. United States,* 295 U.S. 495 (1935), the Court invalidated regulations issued pursuant to the National Industrial Recovery Act, finding that any effect Schechter's slaughterhouses, which sold chickens only to intrastate buyers, had on interstate commerce was indirect and beyond federal reach.

5. Franklin D. Roosevelt: "Message to Congress on Establishing Minimum Wages and Maximum Hours," May 24, 1937, www.presidency.ucsb.edu/ws/?pid=15405 (accessed Apr. 10, 2015).

6. Labor Department Press Release, "Twenty-Eighth Annual Report of the Secretary of Labor," Jan. 5, 1941, box 111, Secretary Perkins—General Subject File, 1940–45, Administrative, General Records of the Labor Department, Record Group 174, National Archives, College Park, Md. (hereafter "NA-DOL"), 10–11.

7. Grossman, "The Fair Labor Standards Act of 1938," 22.

8. BM to Marks, Feb. 15, 1939, box 4, folder "Bessie Margolin," Marks Papers.

9. BM to Marks, Feb. 19, 1939, box 4, folder "Bessie Margolin," Marks Papers.

10. BM to Marks, Apr. 25, 1939, box 4, folder "Bessie Margolin," Marks Papers.

11. "New Orleans Girl Represents U.S. at Hearing," *TP,* Apr. 6, 1939, 3; "Orleans Girl with Federal Counsel," *NOS,* Apr. 5, 1939, 1; Booton Herndon, "Local Girl Makes Good in Big Way," *NOI,* Apr. 6, 1939, 1.

12. "I'm not a radical": Booton Herndon, "Local Girl Makes Good in Big Way," *NOS,* Apr. 6, 1939, 1. TVA Communists: see Purcell, *White Collar Radicals.*

13. BM to Marks, May 22, 1939, box 4, folder "Bessie Margolin," Marks Papers.

14. "Woman Attorney Thinks Federal Career Is Best," *TP,* Nov. 23, 1939, 20.

15. BM to Marks, May 22, 1939, box 4, folder "Bessie Margolin," Marks Papers.

16. According to available records, TVA employed Janet L. Mayfield, the second female lawyer in its legal division, from 1948 to 1951. Carol Moody, email to author, June 6, 2014.

17. *Opp Cotton Mills v. Administrator,* 312 U.S. 126 (1941). In *Opp* the mill challenged the Administrator's 32.5 cents an hour minimum wage for textile workers, arguing that Congress had unlawfully delegated legislative authority to the executive branch to set higher wage rates (up to 40 cents an hour) in certain industries.

18. *Opp Cotton Mills v. Administrator,* 111 F. 2d 23 (5th Cir. 1940).

19. *United States v. Darby,* 312 U.S. 100 (1941); *Opp Cotton Mills v. Administrator,* 312 U.S. 126 (1941). The Supreme Court also rejected the claim that the FLSA's minimum wage provisions violated employers' rights, citing *West Coast Hotel v. Parrish,* 300 U.S. 379 (1937).

20. Death certificate for Harry Margolin, July 22, 1940, Louisiana State Board of Health.

21. Harry Margolin, affidavit, Nov. 12, 1935, BMP.

22. "Firm Fails to Enjoin Wage and Hour Action," *Florence (Ala.) Times Daily,* July 10, 1939, 5; "Makers of Mops Enjoined from Wage Violation," *TP,* Dec. 21, 1939; "Labor Injunction Is Given against Alexandria Firm," *TP,* Dec. 30, 1939.

23. T. Trifon interview.

24. Dorothy Williams headed the San Francisco office. The three women in Margolin's Washington office were: Anna Faye Blackburn, attorney, thirty-eight hundred dollars per year (the same grade and pay as two men attorneys, George L. Clarke and Joseph I. Nachman); H. Michele Olsson, assistant attorney, twenty-six hundred dollars per year; and Flora Chudson, junior attorney, two thousand dollars per year.

25. *Walling v. Peavy Wilson,* 49 F. Supp. 846 (W.D. La. 1943). Margolin's work on the case dated back to Dec. 1939. *Jacobs v. Peavy Wilson,* 33 F.Supp. 206, 207 (W.D. La. 1940).

26. BM, "Answers to Personal Data Questionnaire," Mar. 23, 1964, 18–19, BMP.

27. *Jacobs v. Peavy-Wilson Lumber Co.,* 33 F.Supp. 206 (1940) (W.D. La. 1940), quoting *West Coast Hotel Co., v. Parrish,* 300 U.S. 379, 399 (1937).

28. *Fleming v. Alterman Brothers,* 38 F. Supp. 94 (N.D. Ga. 1941).

29. *Fleming v. Alterman Brothers,* 38 F. Supp. 94 (N.D. Ga. 1941) at 101–2. The Supreme Court later endorsed this analysis in *Walling v. Jacksonville Paper,* 317 U.S. 564 (1943).

30. *Cudahy Packing of Louisiana, Ltd. v. Fleming,* 119 F.2d 209 (5th Cir. 1941).

31. "Almost every conceivable objection": BM, "Answers to Personal Data Questionnaire," Mar. 23, 1964, 18, BMP; *Cudahy Packing Co. of Louisiana v. Holland,* 315 U.S. 785 (1942).

32. *Cudahy Packing Co. of Louisiana v. Holland,* 315 U.S. 785, 788 (1942).

33. Gardner, *Pebbles from the Paths Behind,* 123–24.

34. *Walling v. Sun Publishing Co.,* 47 F. Supp. 180 (W.D. Tenn. 1942), 140 F.2d 445 (6th Cir. 1944).

35. "Most prominent": Michael Stamm, *Newspapers, Radio and the Politics of New Media* (Philadelphia: University of Pennsylvania Press, 2011), 79.

36. "Wage Law Cannot Be Used in Newspaper Cases," *Cincinnati Enquirer,* Dec. 1, 1943, 24.

37. *Walling v. Sun Publishing Co.,* 140 F.2d 445 (6th Cir. 1944).

38. *Sun Publishing Co. v. Walling,* 322 U.S. 728 (1944).

39. *Holland v. Lowell Sun,* 315 U.S. 784 (1942).

40. BM to Perkins, letter and memo, Sept. 28, 1942, box 158, folder "Solicitor of Labor," Secretary Perkins, General Subject File, 1940–45, NA-DOL.

41. BM to Perkins, letter and memo, Sept. 28, 1942, box 158, folder "Solicitor of Labor."

42. BM to Perkins, letter and memo, Sept. 28, 1942, box 158, folder "Solicitor of Labor."

43. BM to Perkins, letter and memo, Sept. 28, 1942, box 158, folder "Solicitor of Labor."

44. Smith to Perkins, Oct. 14, 1942, box 157, NA-DOL.

45. Levy to Smith, Personnel Recommendation, Oct. 20, 1942, BM Federal Personnel File, National Personnel Records Center, St. Louis, Mo. (hereafter "NPRC-BM").

46. Levy to Smith, Personnel Recommendation, Oct. 20, 1942.

47. BM Application for Federal Employment, Feb. 4, 1959, NPRC-BM.

48. Chafe, *Paradox of Change,* 126.

49. Kessler-Harris, *Out to Work,* 273–299; Stewart Robertson, "Ladies—Take a Bow!" *Family Circle,* Sept. 1943.

50. Lundberg and Farnham, *Modern Woman,* 370; Kessler-Harris, *Out to Work,* 297.

51. Banner, *American Beauty,* 417–18.

52. Chafe, *Paradox of Change,* 178.

53. Berebitsky, *Sex and the Office,* 142–43.

54. Maggs to Perkins, memo, Dec. 31, 1943, box 157, folder "Solicitor General," Secretary Perkins, General Subject File, 1940–45, NA-DOL.

55. *Tennessee Coal, Iron & Railroad Co. v. Muscoda,* 135 F.2d 320 (5th Cir. 1943).

56. BM notes for Chief Justice Earl Warren's remarks at her 1972 retirement dinner, n.d., BMP; typescript version of BM notes, box 832, folder "Remarks, Dinner Marking Retirement of Bessie Margolin," Warren Papers (hereafter "BM Notes for Warren").

57. Fahy to R. W. Van de Velde, Aug. 19, 1960, BMP.

58. *U.S. v. Darby* and *Opp Cotton Mills*, e.g., were argued on behalf of the Wage and Hour Administrator at the Supreme Court in Dec. 1940 by solicitor general Francis Biddle; *Walling v. A. H. Belo* in 1942 by solicitor general Fahy; *H. T. Overstreet v. North Shore Corp.* in 1943 by assistant attorney general Francis Shea; *Williams v. Jacksonville Terminal Co.* in Jan 1942 and *Walton v. Southern Package Corp.* in Dec. 1943 by assistant solicitor general Robert L. Stern; and *Addison v. Holly Hill Fruit Products, Inc.* in Jan. 1944 by labor solicitor Douglas Maggs. See also Rebecca Mae Salokar, *The Solicitor General: The Politics of Law* (Philadelphia: Temple University Press, 1992), 58, 64–67.

59. The others were Helen Carloss, a special assistant attorney general in the Justice Department's Tax Division, and Ruth Weyand, attorney for the National Labor Relations Board. Trestman, "First 101 Women to Argue at the United States Supreme Court."

60. Anne Palo to BM, Jan. 16, 1972, folder "Letters Concerning Retirement Dinner," BMP.

61. "What Does the Well Dressed Woman Lawyer Wear before the United States Supreme Court?" *Women Lawyers Journal* 30 (Jan. 1944): 15. Women advocates' attire at the Supreme Court is also discussed in Cushman, *Supreme Court Decisions and Women's Rights*, 231–32.

62. Clauss interview.

63. *A. H. Phillips v. Walling*, 324 U.S. 490 (1945).

64. *A. H. Phillips v. Walling*, 144 F. 2d 102 (1st Cir. 1944).

65. Douglas, *Court Years 1939–1975*, 184–85.

66. Jackson to BM, Mar. 1945, BMP.

67. John Q. Barrett, email to author, Dec. 20, 2012.

68. Barrett, "Supreme Court Bar Admission."

69. BM to Jackson, Mar. 5, 1945, box 15, folder 10, Jackson Papers. The author thanks John Q. Barrett for sharing this and other Jackson documents.

70. *A. H. Phillips v. Walling*, 324 U.S. 490, 493 (1945).

71. Perkins to BM, Mar. 29, 1945, BMP.

72. BM Notes for Warren. According to Fahy's records, however, as late as Mar. 10, 1945, Lane was assigned to argue both *Borden* and *10 East 40th St.* These records suggest that Margolin, contrary to her later recollection, may have been asked at the last minute to substitute for Lane in *both* cases. "Estimate for March 26 Session," Mar. 10, 1945, box 45, folder "Supreme Court (Oct. 1944 Term)—Assignments for Argument," Fahy Papers.

73. BM Notes for Warren.

74. *Borden v. Borella*, 325 U.S. 679 (1945); *10 East 40th St. Bldg. v. Callus*, 325 U.S. 578 (1945). Both cases focused on whether building maintenance employees, elevator operators, and watchmen were covered by the FLSA because their work was "necessary" to the production of goods in interstate commerce. This question turned on whether the building owner or major tenants were engaged in manufacturing of goods for shipment in interstate commerce. The difference was that in *Borden*, where the Court extended coverage to the building's maintenance employees, a manufacturer of goods shipped across state lines owned and occupied seventeen of the building's twenty-four floors. *Callus* presented a more difficult factual scenario because the employees serviced a building occupied by a variety of renters with no manufacturing—a situation that Justice Frankfurter declared "spontaneously satisfies the common understanding" of a local business, placing the building's maintenance employees beyond federal regulation. 325 U.S. at 583.

75. *Roland Electrical Co. v. Walling*, 326 U.S. 657 (1946).

76. Maggs to BM, Feb. 1, 1946, BMP.

77. *Boutell v. Walling,* 327 U.S. 463 (1946).

78. *Martino v. Michigan Window Cleaning Co.,* 327 U.S. 173 (1946).

79. BM Notes for Warren.

80. *Boutell v. Walling,* 327 U.S. 463, 472 (1946).

81. *Lenroot v. Kemp,* 153 F.2d 153, 154 (5th Cir. 1946), quoting Judge Mize.

82. *Lenroot v. Interstate Bakeries Corp.,* 146 F. 2d 325, 328 (8th Cir. 1945). Judge Mize issued decisions in both *Kemp* and *Hazlehurst* on Jan. 6, 1946, possibly unaware of the Eighth Circuit's decision on Jan. 2, 1945.

83. In pencil Margolin drafted these sentences on the back of several pages of Robert H. Jackson's Apr. 1945 speech to the American Society of International Law, which immediately preceded his selection by President Truman to serve as chief prosecutor for the Nazi war crimes trials. Folder "War Crimes," BMP. Using the speech as scratch paper suggests that she kept it close at hand but that its message was not a focus of her work. She ultimately kept the scribbled-on speech in a folder with legal research about war crimes trials, an assignment she accepted in Apr. 1946. See chap. 7, infra.

84. *Lenroot v. Kemp,* 153 F.2d 153, 156 (5th Cir. 1946).

85. Hugh McCloskey to BM, Jan. 30, 1946, and BM to McCloskey, Feb. 6, 1946, BMP. McCloskey had unsuccessfully argued *Walling v. Florida Hardware Co.,* 142 F. 2d 444 (5th Cir. 1944), affirming injunction denial absent "danger of a repetition of unlawful conduct."

86. "Court Enjoins Firm," *National Labor Tribune* (Pittsburgh, Pa.), Mar. 2, 1946, 1.

87. Perkins to BM, June 8, 1945, BMP.

7. AN INTERESTING ADVENTURE IN NUREMBERG

1. Executive Order 9547, Providing for Representation of the United States in Preparing and Prosecuting Charges of Atrocities and War Crimes against the Leaders of the European Axis powers and Their Principal Agents and Accessories, 10 Fed. Reg. 4961 (May 2, 1945).

2. Robert H. Jackson, "Address before the American Society of International Law, Apr. 13, 1945," BMP.

3. BM to Jackson, May 3, 1945, box 105, folder "Nuremberg War Crimes Trial, Personnel, Applications & Recommendations, J–Z," Jackson Papers.

4. Jackson to BM, May 15, 1945, BMP. Form letters: box 105, folders "Nuremberg War Crimes Trial, Personnel, Applications and Recommendations, A–I and J–Z," Jackson Papers. Although Jackson did not explain why Margolin could not fill one of those spots, his decision is not easily attributed to her religion or gender. Despite his insistence that the war crimes proceedings not become a "Jewish trial" with "too many" Jewish lawyers, Jackson nevertheless relied on Jewish men for crucial work on his war crimes legal staff, including Murray Bernays, Benjamin Kaplan, and Harold Leventhal, among others. Jackson interview, 1204–7; Taylor, *Anatomy of the Nuremberg Trials,* 48–49, 56–57; Bloxham, *Genocide on Trial,* 67–69. Jackson's legal team also included women lawyers: Katherine B. Fite, a State Department lawyer; Harriet F. Zetterberg, borrowed from the Board of Economic Warfare; Catherine E. Falvey, an army major who had previously served in the Massachusetts House of Representatives; and reportedly, Irma

Von Nunes, a Georgia lawyer who became a captain in the U.S. Women's Army Corps. Barrett, "Katherine B. Fite," 14 n. 6; Amann, "Portraits of Women at Nuremberg," 36.

5. Jackson repeatedly expressed concern over diminishing public support, difficulties of the pending trial, and critical personnel shortages. Box 3, folder 34, ser. 20, subser. 1, Taylor Papers: Jackson to Taylor, memo, Feb. 5, 1946; Jackson to Office U.S. Chief of Counsel, memo, Feb. 7, 1946; and Jackson to Betts and Fahy, Feb. 9, 1946.

6. Jackson to the President, Feb. 5, 1946, box 1, folder 2 (84-1), Nuremberg Administrative Files, Record Group 153, National Archives, College Park, Md. (hereafter "NA-Nuremberg").

7. Jackson to Betts, Feb. 9, 1946, box 3, folder 34, ser. 20, subser. 1, Taylor Papers.

8. Taylor, *Final Report to the Secretary of the Army*, 13–21; Heller, *Nuremberg Military Tribunals*, 12–17.

9. Horsky to Jackson, Apr. 25, 1946, box 102, folder 11, Jackson Papers. (The author thanks John Q. Barrett for sharing this document.)

10. David Marcus to J. M. Boyd, May 7, 1946, and Kimball to War Department, May 7, 1946, box 2, folder 1, bk. 1 (85-2), NA-Nuremberg.

11. Office of Chief Counsel to War Department, May 7, 1946, box 3, folder 2, bk. 2 (85-2), NA-Nuremberg.

12. BM to Polack Rittenberg, May 25, 1946, BMP.

13. BM to O'Brian, June 2, 1946, BMP.

14. BM to Polack Rittenberg, May 25, 1946, BMP.

15. BM to Polack Rittenberg, May 25, 1946.

16. Gaskin, *Eyewitness to Nuremberg*, 6–7.

17. Sally Moore, email to author, Mar. 22, 2013. The author thanks Jonathan Bush for facilitating this correspondence.

18. BM to Polack Rittenberg, May 25, 1946, BMP.

19. Gaskin, *Eyewitness to Nuremberg*, 114.

20. Taylor, *Anatomy of the Nuremberg Trials*, 129, 217.

21. Sally Moore, email to author, Mar. 22, 2013.

22. BM to O'Brian, June 2, 1946, BMP.

23. BM to O'Brian, June 2, 1946, BMP; West, "Extraordinary Exile: Nuremberg," 35–36

24. BM to O'Brian, June 2, 1946, BMP.

25. BM to O'Brian, June 2, 1946, BMP.

26. Taylor, "Organizational Memo No. II," June 26, 1946, box 1, folder 1: NMT Correspondence, 1947–49, ser. 5, subser. 1, Taylor Papers.

27. Taylor, "Organizational Memo No. II."

28. Barbara Brin and Dan Caplan, "Alumni Feature: Newman's Representative in Washington," *Newman School Pioneer* (May 1966): 7; BM, "Responses to Newman School Interview Questions," 1966, folder "Newman School," BMP. Although Jackson voiced to U.S. officials his opposition to a second international tribunal as early as Feb. 1946, President Truman did not adopt that approach until late Oct. and did not officially inform the other allies of his decision until Jan. 1947. Heller, *Nuremberg Military Tribunals*, 20, 24.

29. Taylor to Alvin Rockwell, Aug. 15, 1946, box 2, folder 1 (84-1), NA-Nuremberg. Before coming to Berlin as deputy counsel to the Office of Military Government of the United States,

Alvin Rockwell was general counsel to the National Labor Relations Board and had earlier worked for Charles Fahy in the Solicitor General's Office.

30. Guests at these Berlin social gatherings also included Charles Horsky and Max Lowenthal, a successful lawyer and advisor to Presidents Roosevelt and Truman, who was drafting legislation for the return of property seized by Nazis. Alvin Rockwell Diary, entries for Aug. 19, Sept. 4, and Sept. 26, 1946. The author thanks Jonathan Bush for sharing this resource.

31. "Subject: Establishment of Tribunals for Trials of War Criminals Pursuant to Allied Control Council Law No. 10," draft, n.d., BMP. Another draft of Ordinance No. 7 is in box 1, folder 12: "NMT—Military Government Memo—Ordinance No. 7: Organization of Military Tribunals: Draft (July–Aug. 1946)," ser. 5, subser. 1, Taylor Papers.

32. For a discussion of the significance of revisions during the drafting of Ordinance № 7, see Bush, "Prehistory of Corporations and Conspiracy," 1166–67.

33. BM, "Responses to Newman Interview Questions," folder "Newman School," BMP.

34. BM, "Responses to Newman Interview Questions."

35. BM, "Responses to Newman Interview Questions."

36. Bush, "Prehistory of Corporations and Conspiracy," 1161.

37. The actual number of defendants who were tried in the Subsequent Proceedings was somewhat lower than those charged, due to pretrial dismissals, illness, and deaths, including suicides.

38. BM to O'Brian, June 2, 1946, BMP.

39. "Army Wives in Germany to Wear Arm Bands," WP, Apr. 27 1946, 1.

40. BM to O'Brian, June 2, 1946, BMP.

41. D. M. Ladd to Director, memo, Dec. 16, 1947, FBI-BM (121-518-1); Director, FBI, to Attorney General, memo, Dec. 16, 1947, FBI-BM (121-518-2); Director to SAC, WFO, memo, Dec. 16, 1947, FBI-BM (121-518-13). These memos refer to, but do not currently contain, FBI reports from May and July 1947 and "four pieces of correspondence from Military Intelligence" regarding the recommendation that Margolin be separated from military service. In response to the author's FOIA requests, the FBI and the army stated that no such records could be located. Brad S. Dorris to author, INSCOM FOIA Case No. 0862F-13, Mar. 26, 2013; David M. Hardy to author, FOIPA Request No. 1192413-001, Dec. 12, 2012.

42. Ladd to Director, Dec. 16, 1947, FBI-BM (121-518-1); Director to Attorney General, Dec. 16, 1947, FBI-BM (121-518-2).

43. See pages 126–30, herein.

44. Taylor, *Anatomy of the Nuremberg Trials,* 381, 398.

45. BM to Jackson, July 26, 1946, Jackson Papers.

46. Photographs, July 29, 1946 dinner, box 255, folder 9, Jackson Papers.

47. M. Trifon interview; Edith Simon to BM, Feb. 1947, BMP.

48. "Triumphal entry, fashion show": Monneray to BM, Oct. 20, 1947, BMP.

49. Amann, "Cecilia Goetz," 618–20; Amann, "Portraits of Women at Nuremberg."

50. Taylor, *Anatomy of the Nuremberg Trials,* 217.

51. Jonathan Bush provides the tally of 130 lawyers whom Taylor brought to Nuremberg for the Subsequent Proceedings in "Nuremberg Prosecutors, Their Origins and Outlooks: New Dealers, Lady Lawyers, Refugees and Radicals," an unpublished manuscript that he graciously

shared. By this author's count, with help from Bush, the 12 women who served as lawyers during the Subsequent Proceedings were: Bessie Margolin, Sadie B. Arbuthnot, Mary Bakshian, Cecelia Goetz, Dorothy Hunt, Esther Jane Johnson, Mary M. Kaufman, Virginia Miller, Dorothea G. Minskoff, Sally Zeck Moore, Helen Shea, and Belle Mayer Zeck. See also Heller, *Nuremberg Military Tribunals,* 34; and Amann, "Portraits of Women at Nuremberg."

52. Throughout the 1940s women constituted approximately 3 percent of the American legal profession. They constituted 5 percent of federal government lawyers in 1939 and 7 percent in 1954. U.S. Department of Labor, *Women in the Federal Service,* 1954, 12. The 4 women lawyers who worked on the IMT during Jackson's tenure, listed in n. 4, constituted 3.6 percent of the 110 lawyers identified by Jonathan Bush working in Nuremberg for the IMT. Bush, "Nuremberg Prosecutors," 4.

53. Marcus, memo, Nov. 25, 1946, box 3, folder 2 (Bk-4, 85-2), NA-Nuremberg.

54. BM to Marcus, Jan. 13, 1947, BMP; BM to Taylor, Jan. 20, 1947, BMP.

55. BM, memo "Conferences re Nurnberg Judges," Dec. 1946, BMP. Margolin's recruitment notes also identify Paul Hebert, dean of Louisiana State University Law School, but do not reveal whether she personally recruited him. Hebert served on the tribunal that heard the prosecution of the executives of I. G. Farben Co., which manufactured the poison gas Zyklon B used at the extermination camps; Hebert issued a stinging dissent from the majority's acceptance of "the defense of necessity" to acquit all but five Farben executives of slave labor.

56. Opening Statement of Telford Taylor in "The Justice Case," case 3, Mar. 5, 1947, *Trials of War Criminals before the Nuernberg Military Tribunals under Control Council Law,* vol. 3, no. 10, 32–33, 41.

57. Taylor, *Final Report,* 28 n. 73.

58. Taylor to Schwellenbach, Nov. 2, 1946, BMP.

59. See, e.g., Answer and Memorandum in Opposition to Defendants' Motion to Dismiss No. IV and Motion to Strike No. 1, Military Tribunal No. IV, Case No. V, *United States v. Flick,* crate 23, box 5 (1998.A.0298), William L. Christianson Papers, U.S. Holocaust Memorial Museum; Judgment of the Tribunal, *United States v. Flick* (Dec. 22, 1947), *Law Reports of Trials of War Criminals* 9.6, 16–17. The author thanks Jonathan Bush for these materials.

60. "Contemporary Reflections on the Importance of the Nuremberg Trials," *Dimensions Online: A Journal of Holocaust Studies* 19 (Fall 2006), www.archive.adl.org/education/dimensions_19/section3/reflections.html#.U48x ZRdWEw (accessed June 4, 2014). According to one of Taylor's prosecutors, Ordinance No. 7 "laid a foundation not merely for the twelve subsequent trials at Nuremberg but also as a precedent which served as a guide for all similar international trials of war criminals in the future." Ben Ferencz, email to author, Dec. 12, 2004.

61. *Terminiello v. City of Chicago,* 337 U.S. 1, 22, 32 (1949) (Jackson, J., dissenting).

62. BM to Jackson, May 17,1949, box 156, folder 1, Jackson Papers.

63. Jackson to BM, May 31, 1949, BMP.

64. Edith Simon Coliver to BM, various letters, BMP.

65. Abram to Byron White, Mar. 9, 1962, BMP; Abram to BM, Mar. 9, 1962, BMP.

66. William Honan, "Morris Abram is Dead at 81," *NYT,* Mar. 17, 2000.

67. Abram to Byron White, Mar. 9, 1962, BMP; Abram to BM, Mar. 9, 1962, BMP.

68. Monneray to BM, Feb. 1, 1947, BMP.

69. Laura Monneray to BM, Mar. 20, 1972, BMP; BM to Ginnane, June 2, 1962, BMP.

70. Monneray to BM, Feb. 1, 1948, BMP.

71. Monneray to BM, June 8, 1949, BMP.

72. Abram to Byron White, Mar. 9, 1962, BMP.

73. Monneray to BM, Oct. 27, 1947, and Feb. 1, 1948, BMP.

74. Monneray to BM, Dec. 25, 1946, and Feb. 1, 1948, BMP.

75. Monneray to BM, Jan. 6, 1948, Feb. 1, 1948, and Nov. 8, 1948, BMP.

76. Monneray to BM, Jan. 6, 1948, BMP.

8. RETURN TO THE LABOR DEPARTMENT

1. Condé Nast Heritage, www.condenast.com/about-us/heritage#/1939-glamour-launches (accessed Jan. 22, 2014).

2. Alice T. Friedman, "The Luxury of Lapidus: Glamour Class and Architecture in Miami Beach," *Harvard Design Magazine* (Summer 2000): 1–2; Virginia Postrel, "The Power of Glamour," lecture recorded Feb. 2004, Monterey, Calif., http://blog.ted.com/2008/10/16/the_power_of_gl/ (accessed Feb. 1, 2013).

3. Condé Nast Heritage, www.condenast.com/about-us/heritage#/1939-glamour-launches (accessed Jan. 22, 2014).

4. "In America Every Third Woman Works," *Glamour Magazine,* Jan. 1948, 84–89.

5. Foster, "Jurisdiction, Rights, and Remedies for Group Wrongs under the Fair Labor Standards Act," 305.

6. Dodd, "Supreme Court and Fair Labor Standards," 369.

7. *United States v. Darby,* 312 U.S. 100 (1941); *Opp Cotton Mills v. Administrator,* 312 U.S. 126 (1941).

8. The author is indebted to Donald S. Shire for preserving and making available his extensive, yet incomplete, collection of Margolin's Case Analyses, No. 4 (Jan. 15, 1944) through No. 181 (Apr. 15, 1960).

9. Clauss and Shire interviews.

10. Clauss and Shire interviews.

11. Clauss interview.

12. *Rutherford Food Corp. v. McComb,* 331 U.S. 722 (1947).

13. Respondent's brief, *Rutherford Food Corp. v. McComb,* 331 U.S. 722 (1947), BMP.

14. Jackson to BM, n.d., BMP.

15. *McComb v. Jacksonville Paper Co.*, 336 U.S. 187, (1949). See also "U.S. Courts Have Power to Order Back Pay," U.S. Department of Labor, Labor Information Bulletin, Apr. 1949, 7. Margolin reviewed the importance of the *Jacksonville Paper* decision and subsequent circuit court rulings in her Feb. 28, 1950 Case Analyses No. 103, "Proper Scope of Section 17 Injunctions and Their Enforcement through Civil Contempt Proceedings," courtesy of Donald Shire.

16. *Powell v. U.S. Cartridge,* 339 U.S. 497 (1950), holding, among other things, that the munitions produced were "goods" and that the Walsh-Healey Public Contracts Act, which set wage and hour standards for employees of government contractors, and the FLSA are mutually supplementary.

17. BM to Stern, n.d., BMP (referring to *Powell v. U.S. Cartridge*).

18. H. P. Zarky to BM, n.d., BMP (referring to *Powell v. U.S. Cartridge*). Zarky, a special assistant to the U.S. attorney general, was passing along praise from a private attorney who argued later the same day.

19. Justice Tom Clark to BM, Dec. 13, 1949, BMP.

20. *Powell v. U.S. Cartridge Co.*, 339 U.S. 497 (1950).

21. "High Court Rules War Workers Were under Wage-Hour Law," *Labor Information Bulletin* (May 1950): 4.

22. Jeter S. Ray to Margaret Happer, memo, July 23, 1953, BMP.

23. Ray to Happer, memo, July 23, 1953.

24. Stuart Rothman to Department of Labor Incentive Awards Committee, n.d., BMP (likely written shortly before Nov. 14, 1956 when the Awards Committee announced its approval).

25. Soboloff to Mitchell, July 29, 1955, BMP.

26. *Mitchell v. Budd*, 351 U.S. 934 (1956), upholding administrator's definition of "area of production," which considered population as well as geography, for purposes of qualifying for FLSA agricultural exemption, and his ruling that "tobacco bulking" workers are not engaged in agriculture; *Mitchell v. Covington*, 229 F. 2d 506 (D.C. Cir.1955), cert. denied, 76 S.Ct. 546 (1956), upholding labor secretary's determination, under Walsh-Healey Public Contracts Act of 1936, of a dollar-per-hour industry-wide minimum wage for the textile industry; Sylvia Ellison to BM, n.d., BMP, referring to Mar. 26, 1956, decision in *Mitchell v. Budd* and denial of certiorari in *Mitchell v. Covington*.

27. *Mitchell v. Oregon Frozen Foods*, 145 F. Supp. 157 (D. Or. 1956); *Mitchell v. Oregon Frozen Foods*, 254 F. 2d 118 (9th Cir. 1958); *Mitchell v. Oregon Frozen Foods*, 359 U.S. 958 (1959).

28. Supplemental Memorandum for the Petitioner, filed Dec. 9, 1959, *Mitchell v. Oregon Frozen Foods*, box 3097, folder 33, OT 1959, U.S. Supreme Court Appellate Case Files, Record Group 267, National Archives, Washington, D.C.; *Mitchell v. Oregon Frozen Foods*, 361 U.S. 231 (1960).

29. *Mitchell v. H. B. Zachry Co.*, 362 U.S. 310 (1960).

30. BM to Joseph F. Dolan, Mar. 24, 1964, and "Answers to Personal Data Questionnaire," BMP.

31. The figures cited in text rely primarily on Margolin's own compilation, "Supreme Court and Court of Appeals Cases Prepared by or under Direction of Bessie Margolin as Assistant or Associate Solicitor of Litigation (1943–Sept. 1967)," BMP, in which she noted cases she personally argued, supplemented by the author's research on Margolin's appellate cases from Sept. 1967 through her Jan. 1972 retirement. The author notes, however, that Margolin and other Labor Department personnel referred in career summaries to her having "personally prepared briefs and orally argued about 200 appeals" in the circuit courts, in addition to her Supreme Court cases.

32. *Rutherford Food Corp. v. McComb*, 331 U.S. 722 (1947); BM Notes for Warren.

33. Audio recording, *Steiner v. Mitchell*, No. 22, Nov. 16, 1959, National Archives, Record Group 267, College Park, Md.

34. Audio recording, *Mitchell v. King Packing Co.*, No. 39, Nov. 16–17, 1959, National Archives, Record Group 267, College Park, Md.

35. Audio recording, *Mitchell v. H. B. Zachry Co.*, No. 83, Feb. 25, 1960, National Archives, Record Group 267, College Park, Md.

36. *Mitchell v. H. B. Zachry Co.*, 362 U.S. 310 (1960).

37. The following number of women (unduplicated) argued during each regular Supreme Court term (Oct.–June) during the 1950s: 1950, 1; 1951, 4; 1952, 3; 1953, 5; 1954, 3; 1955, 7; 1956,

4; 1957, 2; 1958, 7; 1959, 2. In 1955, e.g., 211 men argued, accounting for a total of 243 arguments. The same year 7 women presented a total of 11 arguments, with Margolin and Beatrice Rosenberg arguing 4 and 2 times, respectively. Trestman, "First 101 Women to Argue at the United States Supreme Court."

38. Justice Frankfurter's note, written one and two days after Margolin argued *Mitchell v. Frozen Foods* and *Mitchell v. DeMario Jewelry*, respectively, appears to capture a conversation between two persons identified only as "F" and "X":

> After some dithyrambic praise:
>
> F: She is a very good girl and a good advocate but not a lawyer of unsettling brilliance apart from the deft use of her feminine charms.
>
> X: Don't you think that female charms are terribly important!!!

Felix Frankfurter to Philip Elman, Nov. 18, 1959, file 3-91, Elman Papers. Another rather cryptic note from Justice Frankfurter, and which Elman placed in a folder labeled "Bessie Margolin," posed the following query using what appears to be a comically exaggerated pronunciation of her name: "I'll give you one guess who is the most susceptible to MAHR's [Margolin's] exploitation of her female talents?" The answer, or possibly Elman's guess, at the bottom of the note is "Harlan." Frankfurter to Elman, "May 9," file 3-91, Elman Papers. Margolin did not argue before the Supreme Court on May 9, 1959, but she argued the case of *Mitchell v. Kentucky Finance* on Mar. 3, 1959, and Justice Harlan authored the Court's Apr. 20, 1959, opinion.

39. Trestman, "Addenda to 'Fair Labor,'" 257–58 n. 15.

40. Frankfurter to Philip Elman, n.d., file 3-80, Elman Papers.

41. Frankfurter to Philip Elman, n.d., file 3-80, Elman Papers.

42. Audio recording, *Mitchell v. Lublin, McGaughy*, No. 37, Oct. 28, 1958, National Archives, Record Group 267, College Park, Md.

43. Audio recording, *Mitchell v. Kentucky Finance Co., Inc.* No. 161, Oct. 28, 1958, National Archives, Record Group 267, College Park, Md.

44. Audio recording, *Mitchell v. Kentucky Finance Co., Inc.* No. 161, Oct. 28, 1958.

45. *Mitchell v. Robert DeMario Jewelry, Inc.*, 180 F. Supp. 800 (M.D.Ga. 1957), aff'd, 260 F.2d 929 (5th Cir. 1958).

46. Audio recording, *Mitchell v. Robert DeMario Jewelry, Inc.*, No. 39, Nov. 16, 1959, National Archives, Record Group 267, College Park, Md.

47. *Mitchell v. Robert DeMario Jewelry Inc.*, 361 U.S. 288, 293 (1959).

48. BM to Maggs, Sept. 26, 1949, BMP; *McComb v. Scerbo*, 177 F.2d 137 (2d Cir. 1949).

49. Brown to Richard F. Schubert, Jan. 18, 1972, folder "Letters Concerning the Retirement Dinner," BMP. The case Judge Brown described appears to have been *Mitchell v. Empire Gas Engineering Co.*, 256 F.2d 781 (5th Cir. 1958). Margolin's efforts were unsuccessful; the Fifth Circuit ruled that the trial court did not abuse its discretion in denying the injunction.

50. Brown to Richard F. Schubert, Jan. 18, 1972, folder "Letters Concerning the Retirement Dinner," BMP.

51. "Parking space": M. Trifon interview; "Ambulance": Bessie Margolin, "Reckless Ambulances," *WP*, Feb. 6, 1951, 10.

52. BM to James R. Durfee, May 12, 1959, BMP.

53. Tuttle to Richard F. Schubert, Jan. 17, 1972, folder "Letters Concerning the Retirement Dinner," BMP.

54. Brown to Richard F. Schubert, Jan. 18, 1972, folder "Letters Concerning the Retirement Dinner, BMP.

55. Cooper, Christian and Clauss interviews.

56. Jerry Kluttz, "The Federal Diary," *WP*, Apr. 8, 1953, 25.

57. BM to Kluttz, Apr. 8, 1953, BMP.

58. Audio recording, *Mitchell v. Bekins Van & Storage Co.*, No. 122, Feb. 26–27, 1957, National Archives, Record Group 267, College Park, Md.

59. *Walling v. A. H. Belo Corp.*, 316, U.S. 624 (1942). In marginalia on her notes about the Judge Fahy anecdote, apparently for her 1972 retirement dinner, Margolin identified one of her detractors as Wayne Barnett, assistant to the solicitor general, 1958–65.

60. Margolin, "Cases and Materials on Government Regulation of Wages," 528.

61. BM, handwritten notes for legal training course, n.d., BMP.

62. Jones, *Hattie's Boy*, 271–72. Jim Jones started working in the labor solicitor's Legislation Division in the late 1950s. See also Clauss, Shire, and Nagle interviews.

63. Jones, *Hattie's Boy*, 271–72.

64. Shire interview.

65. Storrs, *Second Red Scare*, 110.

66. Department of Labor to FBI, Request for Report on Loyalty Data, Sept. 10, 1947, NPRC-BM.

67. See note 41 on page 206.

68. FBI remarks, dated Dec. 16, 1947, on Labor Department's Sept 1947 Request for Loyalty Report, FBI-BM.

69. FBI-BM.

70. William Slevin, report, Feb. 27, 1948, FBI-BM.

71. William Slevin to Director, memo, Feb. 16, 1948, FBI-BM.

72. Walker, *In Defense of American Liberties*, 178. Case studies of federal employees subjected to Loyalty Board inquiries are detailed in Storrs, *Second Red Scare*, 268–85.

73. SAC, New York to Director, Mar. 21, 1950, FBI-BM (121-518-25); Guy Hottel to Director, May 11, 1950, FBI-BM (121-518-25); SAC, Washington Field Office to Director, Jan. 14, 1955, FBI-BM (121-518-26); SAC, WFO to Director, Jan. 27, 1955, FBI-BM (121-518-27).

74. Howard Menhinick to Swidler, Aug. 31, 1951, box 82, folder 3, Swidler Papers.

75. Swidler to Harry Case, Sept. 20, 1951, box 82, folder 3, Swidler Papers; Swidler, Exhibits and Affidavits, Sept. 20, 1951, box 81, folder 11, Swidler Papers.

76. Ed Lemke to Swidler, Sept. 7, 1951, box 81, folder 7, Swidler Papers.

77. Harry Case to Swidler, Nov. 26, 1951, box 82, folder 3, Swidler Papers.

78. Marshall Miller to BM, Dec. 15, 1951, BMP; BM to Miller, Dec. 21, 1951, BMP; and Miller to BM, Mar. 18, 1955, BMP.

79. R. J. Abbaticchio to Director, FBI, Jan. 21, 1948, FBI-BM.

80. *United States v. Bridges*, 86 F. Supp. 931 (N.D. Cal. 1949).

81. William P. Fitzpatrick, report, Mar. 27, 1951, FBI-JLF; D. M. Ladd to the Director, Aug. 28, 1951, FBI-JLF.

82. BM to Oswald S. Colclough, Aug. 22, 1950, BMP.

83. BM to Douglas Maggs, Jan. 16, 1946, BMP; BM to Colclough, Aug. 22, 1950, BMP.

84. BM to Carl Spaeth (Stanford), Dec. 7, 1948, BMP; Wesley Sturges (Yale) to BM, Aug. 8, 1947, BMP; Sturges to Clarence Dykstra (UCLA), May 8, 1948, BMP; Ray Forrester (Vanderbilt) to BM, July 6, 1950, BMP; Roger Howell (U of MD) to BM, 1949, BMP; Fritz Mann (American University) to BM, Feb. 1951, BMP.

85. Kay, "Future of Women Law Professors," 5. Accreditation for a law school consisted of membership in the Association of American Law Schools (AALS) and approval by the American Bar Association.

86. BM to George L. Clarke, Sept. 1949, BMP; BM to Colclough, Aug. 22, 1950, BMP.

87. BM to Jeter S. Ray, memo, June 25, 1953, BMP.

88. BM to Eldon Lazarus, Oct. 1, 1953, BMP.

89. Bruce P. Spoon to BM, Mar. 10, 1960, BMP.

90. BM, notes for legal training course, n.d., BMP.

91. BM, notes for legal training course, n.d.

92. M. Trifon, B. Margolin, and C. Margolin interviews.

93. M. Trifon interview.

94. Toby Trifon to Aunt Bess, July 10, 1956, BMP.

95. M. Trifon and T. Trifon interviews.

96. M. Trifon and T. Trifon interviews.

97. M. Trifon interview.

98. T. Trifon interview.

99. M. Trifon interview.

100. M. Trifon, email to author, Mar. 30, 2013.

101. M. Trifon, email to author, Mar. 30, 2013.

102. M. Trifon interview.

103. M. Trifon interview.

104. T. Trifon interview.

105. "Ted" to BM, Oct. 22, 1954, BMP. None of Margolin's correspondence from "Ted" or "T." bears his surname or return address; the dates, foreign postmarks, and content, however, strongly support the conclusion that they were written by Clifton. M. Trifon interview.

106. "Ted" to BM, Jan. 24, 1955, BMP.

107. "Ted" to BM, Oct. 27, 1955, BMP; "T." to BM, Sept. 1, 1955, BMP.

9. EQUAL OPPORTUNITIES, PERSONAL AND PUBLIC

1. "Lest I forget": BM to Ginnane, Apr. 10, 1962. Intimate involvement: Ginnane to BM, Aug. 20, 1958, BMP; Gambrell interview.

2. BM to Ginnane, June 2, 1962, BMP.

3. BM to Ginnane, June 28, 1962, BMP.

4. BM to Ginnane, July 9, 1962, BMP.

5. BM to Ginnane, June 4 and 14, 1962, BMP. The other late-in-life marriage Margolin related was that of prominent Washington lawyer Edward B. Burling, at age ninety-two.

6. BM to Ginnane, Apr. 6 and 20, 1962, BMP. Margolin's close colleague Oscar H. Davis was first assistant to the solicitor general when Kennedy appointed him to the court of claims in Jan. 1962.

7. Burnita Shelton Matthews (D.C.) and Sarah Tilghman Hughes (N.D. Tex.) had both been appointed to the trial court within the last three years.

8. In her April 20, 1962, letter to Ginnane, Margolin reported that she had written to Boggs and planned to write to Peterson. Although Margolin did not keep a copy of her first letters to Boggs and Peterson requesting their help with her judicial candidacy, their responses confirm receipt of her requests. Peterson to BM, May 31, 1962, BMP; Boggs to BM, May 1, 1962, BMP.

9. Peterson to BM, May 31, 1962, BMP; Boggs to BM, May 1, 1962, BMP.

10. Fowler to Katzenbach, July 6, 1962, BMP.

11. John Herling, *Labor Letter Newsletter,* June 6, 1959, BMP; BM to Beverly Worrell, June 15, 1959, BMP; M. Trifon interview.

12. BM to Ginnane, Aug. 17, 1962, BMP.

13. BM to Boggs, Jan. 30, 1963, BMP. Abram's case was *Gray v. Sanders,* 372 U.S. 368 (1963), striking down Georgia's county unit system of legislative districting.

14. "Six Women Honored for Federal Service," *NYT,* May 3, 1963, 13; Louchheim, *By the Political Sea,* 184–85 and photo insert, 7.

15. BM to James T. O'Connell, May 22, 1963, BMP.

16. Cecil Stoughton, Photograph, President Johnson Taking the Oath of Office on Air Force One, 11/22/1963, 1A-1-WH-63, LBJ Presidential Library, http://transition.lbjlibrary.org/items/show/67588 (accessed Apr. 1, 2015).

17. BM to Clifton, Feb. 20, 1964, BMP; Clifton to BM, Mar. 23, 1964, BMP.

18. "The Perils of Portia," *Time,* Mar. 6, 1964.

19. BM to Louchheim, Mar. 6, 1964, BMP.

20. Louchheim to Dungan, memo, Apr. 16, 1964, BM file, Macy Papers.

21. O'Brian to Katzenbach, Mar. 9, 1964, BMP; Kennedy to O'Brian, Mar. 27, 1964, BMP.

22. Joseph F. Dolan to BM, Mar. 10, 1964, BMP.

23. Unidentified author, memo, Mar. 11, 1964, BM file, Macy Papers.

24. Moyers to Dungan, memo, Mar. 17, 1964, BM file, Macy Papers.

25. Goldman, *Picking Federal Judges,* 9–10, 160–61.

26. Clinton, Interview Record, Mar. 20, 1964, BM file, Macy Papers.

27. Shreve and Johnson, *Presidential Recordings,* 393.

28. Shreve and Johnson, *Presidential Recordings,* 402–3.

29. Shreve and Johnson, *Presidential Recordings,* 557–58.

30. BM to Joseph Dolan, Mar. 24, 1964, enclosing BM, "Answers to Personal Data Questionnaire," BMP. Margolin also submitted her questionnaire to the American Bar Association's Standing Committee on the Judiciary, which rates federal judicial candidates for the Justice Department. No information about the committee's rating of Margolin is available. According to its chair, by longstanding practice, the committee does not divulge ratings of individuals it evaluates but who are not later nominated. Bettina Plevan, email to author, Dec. 12, 2013.

31. BM, "Answers to Personal Data Questionnaire," Mar. 23, 1964, BMP.

32. Douglas to Johnson, Apr. 1, 1964, BM file, Macy Papers.

33. Boggs to Carpenter, Mar. 31, 1964, BM file, Macy Papers; Carpenter to Dungan, memo, Apr. 10, 1964, BM file, Macy Papers.

34. Catherine Crowley, "Spotlight on Distinguished Women Attorneys," *Federal Bar News,* Apr. 1964, 111–12; BM to Peterson, memo, May 6, 1964, box 52, folder 1019, Peterson Papers.

35. Peterson to Dungan, memo, May 20, 1964, BM file, Macy Papers; Peterson to Clinton, memo, June 2, 1964, BM file, Macy Papers.

36. Jones to DeLoach, Mar. 30, 1964, FBI-BM; "Memo re. Bessie Margolin," Mar. 27, 1964, FBI-BM.

37. President Truman's appointment of Federal Communications Commissioner Frieda B. Hennock to New York's federal district court raised numerous ethics complaints, not least of which was her relationship with a married New York State judge. Brinson, *Personal and Public Interests,* 149–50; Goldman, *Picking Federal Judges,* 96; Drew Pearson, "Secret Hearings Held on Appointing Woman Judge," *Baton Rouge Advocate,* Oct. 4, 1951, 17.

38. LBJ appointed Arnold Wilson Cowen and Linton McGee Collins to the court of claims in June and Sept. 1964, respectively. *Biographical Directory of Federal Judges,* www.fjc.gov.

39. BM to Peterson, memo, Sept. 23, 1964, box 39, folder 775, Peterson Papers.

40. Peterson to Clinton, memo, Nov. 30, 1964, box 39, folder 775, Peterson Papers.

41. Between Mar. and July 1965 LBJ nominated district judge Edward A. Tamm and Harold Leventhal to the circuit court and Howard Corcoran, William B. Bryant, and Oliver Gasch to the district court.

42. Marie Smith, "Where Are the 'Can-Do' Women?" *WP,* May 30, 1965, F-1.

43. BM to Fowler, July 14, 1965, BMP.

44. Boggs to Macy, July 16, 1965, BM file, Macy Papers.

45. BM to Boggs, Aug. 6, 1965, BMP.

46. Circuit judge George T. Washington retired. BM to Boggs, Nov. 19, 1965, BMP.

47. Boggs to BM, Nov. 23, 1965, BMP; Peterson to Macy, Nov. 29, 1965, BM file, Macy Papers.

48. Macy to Boggs, Dec. 3, 1965, BMP.

49. BM to Fowler, Nov. 19, 1965, BMP; BM to Wirtz, memo, Nov. 26, 1965, BMP; BM to Boggs, Nov. 29, 1965, BMP.

50. O'Brian to James A. Crooks, Nov. 29, 1965, BMP; Peterson to Katzenbach, Dec. 22, 1965, BMP; Fowler to Katzenbach, Dec. 3, 1965, BMP; Joseph Stone to Crooks, Nov. 29, 1965, BMP; Tyson to Crooks, Dec. 3, 1965, BMP; Marx Leva to Crooks, Dec. 22, 1965, BMP.

51. "Pins and needles," "Expected, soon": M. Trifon interview.

52. Trestman, "First 101 Women to Argue at the United States Supreme Court."

53. Margolin's argument in *Wirtz v. Steepleton General Tire Co.* immediately followed argument by labor solicitor Charles Donohue, his first at the Supreme Court, in *Idaho Sheet Metal Works, Inc. v. Wirtz,* 383 U.S. 190 (1965). The Supreme Court decided the cases jointly.

54. Macy also reported another name being "bandied about" was Margaret Brass, chief of general litigation for the Justice Department's Antitrust Division and a 1962 Federal Woman's Award recipient. Macy to Clinton, Dec. 8, 1965, BM file, Macy Papers.

55. Macy to Clinton, Dec. 8, 1965, BM file.

56. Macy to James Falcon, memo, Jan. 3, 1966, BM file, Macy Papers.

57. Clark to the President, memo, Jan. 29, 1966, BM file, Macy Papers.

58. Davis, "Third National Conference," 108.

59. LBJ also nominated Aubrey Robinson and John Lewis Smith Jr. to fill district court vacancies and Philip Nichols Jr. and Byron G. Skelton to fill new positions on the court of claims.

60. LBJ appointed a total of four men to the D.C. Circuit Court, seven to its district court, and four to the court of claims.

61. LBJ appointed June L. Green to Washington's district court in 1968. Deputy attorney general Warren Christopher called her the most highly regarded woman lawyer practicing in the District of Columbia, with substantial trial experience held by few women, although he acknowledged that her practice was limited to torts and domestic relations and that her qualifications "did not compare with those of the very best men." McFeeley, *Appointment of Judges*, 76, quoting Christopher to Larry E. Temple, memo, Mar. 30, 1968.

62. LBJ appointed Constance Baker Motley, an African American, to New York's federal district court in 1966 and Shirley M. Hufstedler to the Ninth Circuit in 1968.

63. James C. Falcon to Macy (with handwritten note, "Agree. JCM"), memo, Jan. 9, 1967, BM file, Macy Papers.

64. Although Spottswood Robinson was forty-eight at the time of his nomination, several of the men Johnson nominated to federal judgeships were older than Margolin's fifty-eight years: Howard Corcoran, fifty-nine; Oliver Gasch, fifty-nine; Philip Nichols Jr., fifty-nine; and Byron Skelton, sixty-one. Motley and Hufstedler were forty-five and fifty-three, respectively, at the time of their nominations. *Biographical Directory of Federal Judges*, www.fjc.gov/public/home.nsf/hisj (accessed June 14, 2014).

65. Although there is no record of Margolin claiming that she *personally* had been denied a judgeship on account of sex discrimination, she gave a speech to women lawyers in August 1966 in which she decried the "pitifully small percentage" of women as federal hearing examiners (7 of 546) and described this situation, in her prepared remarks, as "particularly difficult to explain on any basis other than sex discrimination." Two pages later in the same text, she cited the "present dearth of women federal judges" (2 out of 445) yet made no reference to discrimination. BM, "Speech to National Association of Women Lawyers: Some Observations on Women Attorneys Serving in the Federal Government, and on the Sex Discrimination Provision of Title VII of the Civil Rights Act," Montreal, Canada, Aug. 6, 1966, BMP. If Margolin believed the lack of women judges was due to sex discrimination, perhaps she did not want to undermine her own ongoing candidacy with a direct public allegation.

66. "Cigars": Lois Decker O'Neill, ed., *The Women's Book of World Records and Achievements* (New York: Doubleday, 1979), 353, "Bourbon": Isaac Stern, *My First 79 Years* (New York: Knopf, 1999), 178; "not teetotalers": Laura Kalman, email to author, Dec. 11, 2013.

67. M. Triton interview.

68. By 1968 Fortas agreed with other LBJ advisors that it was important to appoint a woman to the federal bench in light of Judge Burnita Shelton Matthews's retirement, but he apparently made no mention of Margolin. McFeeley, *Appointment of Judges*, 76–77.

69. BM to Ginnane, Mar. 13, 1962, BMP. The European Economic Community's 1957 Treaty of Rome, article 119, required that each member state adhere to the principle that men and women should receive equal pay for equal work.

70. U.S. DOL Report and Record of Training Received for Bessie Margolin, Jan. 14, 1964, NPRC-BM.

71. Executive Order 10980, Dec. 14, 1961; Presidential Commission on the Status of Women, *American Women: Report of the President's Commission* (Washington, D.C: Government Printing Office, 1963).

72. John F. Kennedy: "Remarks upon Signing the Equal Pay Act," June 10, 1963, www. presidency.ucsb.edu/ws/?pid=9267, accessed Apr. 1, 2015.

73. BM, "Talk before Federal Bar Association, Labor Law Section," June 1968, BMP.

74. BM, "Equal Pay and Equal Employment Opportunities for Women," *Proceedings of New York University Annual Conference on Labor* 19 (1967): 297 (hereafter BM, *NYU 19th Labor Conference*).

75. BM, "Talk before Federal Bar Association, Labor Law Section," June 1968, BMP.

76. BM, *NYU 19th Labor Conference*, 300.

77. BM, *NYU 19th Labor Conference*, 298.

78. BM, "Talk before Federal Bar Association, Labor Law Section," June 1968, 3–4, BMP.

79. BM, "Equal Pay and Equal Employment Opportunities for Women," remarks delivered to *NYU 19th Labor Conference*, Apr. 19, 1966.

80. In 1972 Congress empowered EEOC to file civil actions in cases involving employment discrimination. 42 U.S.C. sec. 2000e-5(f).

81. Llamas, "Labor and the Lady Lawyer," 2.

82. Llamas, "Labor and the Lady Lawyer," 5.

83. Shire, Nagle, Clauss, Fitzgerald, and Jahn interviews.

84. Audio recording, "Bessie Margolin Farewell Dinner, Jan. 28, 1972," Silberman Papers (hereafter "BM Retirement Recording"); Silberman interview.

85. Jahn interview.

86. Bessie Margolin delivered the following speeches prior to her January 1972 retirement: "Equal Pay and Equal Employment Opportunities for Women," remarks delivered to *NYU 19th Labor Conference*, New York, Apr. 19, 1966; "Equal Pay and Equal Employment Opportunity Legislation with Respect to Women," North Jersey Wage and Salary Association Dinner Meeting, May 17, 1966; "Recent Interesting Supreme Court Litigation and Observations on Title VII and the Equal Pay Act," Atlanta Lawyer's Foundation Third Annual Seminar on Labor Law, Atlanta, June 23, 1966; "Some Observations on Women Attorneys Serving in the Federal Government, and on the Sex Discrimination Provision of Title VII of the Civil Rights Act," National Association of Women Lawyers Annual Meeting, Montreal, Canada, Aug. 1966; "Equal Pay Act," Federal Bar Association, Harrisburg, Pa., Dec. 1966; "Equal Pay Act," Federal Bar Association Briefing Conference on Wages and Hours, Washington, D.C., Feb. 7, 1967; "Equal Pay for Women and Discrimination Based on Sex," Emory Law School and Corporate Counsel Association of Greater Atlanta, Fourth Biennial Institute on Corporate Law, Atlanta, Apr. 14, 1967; "Equal Pay for Equal Work," Chicago Bar Association Seminar on the Federal Wage and Hour Law—The Fair Labor Standards Act, Chicago, Jan. 31, 1968; Kentucky State Bar Annual Convention, Labor Law Section, "Equal Pay Act," Louisville, May 10, 1968; "Equal Pay Act and Title VII," Federal Bar Association, Labor Law Section, Washington, D.C., July 1968; "Discrimination in Employment on the Basis of Sex, Age and Veteran's Status," Southwestern Legal Foundation 15th Annual Institute on Labor Law, Dallas, Oct. 17, 1968; "Some Special Problems—Equal Pay for Women," Federal Bar Association First Annual Federal Public Law Conference, Labor

Law Session, Washington, D.C., Apr. 12, 1969; "Equal Rights vs. Free Bargaining," Boston Bar Association and Boston University School of Law Fifth Annual Labor Law Institute, Boston, Mar. 7, 1970; "What the Government Will Require," Urban Research Corp., Equal Opportunity for Women: Corporate Affirmative Action Programs, San Francisco, Oct. 21, 1971; "Management-Union Confrontation 1972 New Frontiers: Who Discriminates against Women?" NYU 25th Labor Conference, New York, May 25, 1972.

87. Margolin published the following papers in connection with her speeches: BM, *NYU 19th Labor Conference;* BM, "Discrimination in Employment on the Basis of Sex, Age, and Veteran's Status," Labor Law Developments 1969, *Proceedings of 15th Annual Institute on Labor Law,* Southwestern Legal Foundation (New York: Bender, 1969); BM, "Management-Union Confrontation 1972 New Frontiers: Who Discriminates against Women?" Proceedings of the *New York University* Annual *Conference on Labor 25* (1973): 205–24.

88. Sherman Carmell to Charles Donohue, Sept. 28, 1967, BMP; Susan Davis (Urban Research Corp.) to Morag Simchak, Aug. 18, 1971, BMP.

89. Program, Kentucky State Annual Convention, Louisville, May 8–10, 1968; Dan M. Byrd to Charles Donahue, Dec. 15, 1966, BMP; Byrd to BM, Jan. 9, 1967, BMP.

90. James W. Callison to BM, Jan. 26, 1967, BMP.

91. BM remarks, "Talk for Atlanta Meeting," Fourth Biennial Institute on Corporate Law, Atlanta, Apr. 14, 1967, BMP.

92. Bill Hunter, "Women's Job Rights Discussed Here," *Dallas Morning News,* Oct. 18, 1968, A-15.

93. Sarah Cash, "Very Few Women Bring Litigation," *AJ,* Apr. 14, 1967, 22.

94. BM marginalia on Harry Bernstein, "Debate Grows over Job Discrimination due to Sex," *Los Angeles Times,* Mar. 7, 1966, BMP.

95. BM marginalia on Carl N. Degler, "American Women in Social and Political Affairs—Change and Challenge," speech delivered at Southern Methodist University, Dallas, Jan. 27, 1966, BMP; BM marginalia on notes for Equal Pay Act remarks, Federal Bar Association, Harrisburg, Pa., Dec. 1966, BMP.

96. BM outline for Equal Pay Act remarks, Federal Bar Association, BNA Briefing Conference on Wages and Hours, Washington, D.C., Feb. 7, 1967, BMP.

97. The controversy over the genesis of Title VII's sex provision is discussed in Freeman, "How 'Sex' Got into Title VII"; Osterman, "Origins of a Myth"; and Brauer, "Women Activists, Southern Conservatives."

98. *Daily Labor Reporter* 77, Apr. 20, 1966, A-4; *BNA Labor Relations Reporter* (1966): 188–89.

99. Address of Herman Edelsberg, executive director, EEOC, to the American Society for Personnel Administration, May 20, 1966, reprinted in *Daily Labor Reporter* 99: F-1; undated BM notes for addenda to *NYU 19th Labor Conference* paper, BMP.

100. BM to Rawalt, May 26, 1966, BMP.

101. *NYU 19th Labor Conference,* 306 and n. 32, quoting Eleanor Roosevelt and Arthur Goldberg at 1962 Equal Pay Act hearings.

102. *NYU 19th Labor Conference,* 306–7.

103. 112 Cong. Rec. 13693–94.

104. Mattie Bell Davis to BM, June 29, 1966, BMP.

105. BM, "Speech to NAWL: Some Observations on Women Attorneys Serving in the Federal Government, and on the Sex Discrimination Provision of Title VII of the Civil Rights Act," Montreal, Canada, Aug. 6, 1966, BMP.

106. Freeman, "Origins of the Women's Liberation Movement," 797–99. See also National Organization for Women, "The Founding of NOW," www.now.org/history/the_founding.html (accessed June 19, 2014); Rosenberg, *Divided Lives,* 188–89; Paterson, *Be Somebody,* 168–69.

107. Mary Eastwood, email to author, Oct. 30, 2013; Oct. 29–30, 1966, Roster for NOW Organizational Meeting, box 4, folder 37, Eastwood Papers.

108. Audiotape, NOW Founding Conference, Oct. 29–30, 1966, NOW Audiotape Collection.

109. Audiotape, NOW Founding Conference, Oct. 29–30, 1966; Oct. 29–30, 1966, Minutes, NOW Organizing Conference, and Statement of Purpose, ser. 2, box 2, folder 1, NOW Papers.

110. Audiotape, NOW Founding Conference, Oct. 29–30, 1966.

111. Audiotape, NOW Founding Conference, Oct. 29–30, 1966; Oct. 29–30, 1966, Minutes, NOW Organizing Conference, and Statement of Purpose.

112. Joy Miller, "NOW Is the Time for Women to Demand Their Equal Rights," *Augusta (Ga.) Chronicle,* Nov. 24, 1966, B12; Karen Klinefelter, "NOW Starts Women's Rights Campaign," *Dallas Morning News,* Nov. 25, 1966, C1; "Betty Friedan," Photo Caption, *TP,* Nov. 22, 1966.

113. Sarah Cash, "Very Few Women Bring Litigation," *AJ,* Apr. 14, 1967, 22.

114. Llamas, "Labor and the Lady Lawyer," 4.

115. BM marginalia on her notes for Feb. 1967 Federal Bar Association speech, BMP.

116. Joan Geiger, "Labor Department Solicitor Helps Women Get Equal Pay," *SDT,* Apr. 1, 1968, 38.

117. Geiger, "Labor Department Solicitor Helps Women Get Equal Pay."

118. BM to Peter Seitz, Aug. 2, 1966, BMP. See also BM to Maurice E. Nichols, Mar. 7, 1969, BMP.

119. BM to Alfred Friendly, July 22,1968, BMP.

120. *Wirtz v. Basic Inc.,* 256 F. Supp. 786, 787 (D. Nev. 1966).

121. *Wirtz v. Basic Inc.,* 256 F. Supp. 786, 791 (D. Nev. 1966).

122. Wheeler interview; Mildred Lau Wheeler, email to author, Nov. 8, 2013.

123. BM speech to the Federal Bar Association, Labor Law Section, July 1968.

124. *Shultz v. Wheaton Glass Co.,* 421 F. 2d 259 (3rd Cir. 1970); *Shultz v. American Can Co.,* 424 F. 2d 356 (8th Cir. 1970); *Shultz v. First Victoria National Bank,* 420 F. 2d 648 (5th Cir. 1969); and *Hodgson v. Square D Co.,* 459 F. 2d 805 (6th Cir. 1972).

125. Ross and McDermott, "Equal Pay Act of 1963," 10 n. 53; Murphy, "Female Wage Discrimination," 649.

126. *Wirtz v. Wheaton Glass Co.,* 284 F. Supp. 23 (D. N.J. 1968).

127. *Wirtz v. Wheaton Glass Co.,* 253 F. Supp. 93 (D. N.J. 1966).

128. 284 F. Supp. at 28–30 and nn. 9, 11.

129. 284 F. Supp. at 33.

130. Nagle, Clauss, and Shire interviews.

131. Brief for Plaintiff-Appellant, Reply Brief for the Secretary of Labor as Appellant, and Plaintiff-Appellant's Supplemental Brief, *Shultz v. Wheaton Glass,* 421 F. 2d 259 (3rd Cir. 1970), cert. denied, 398 U.S. 905 (1970).

132. Jahn interview.

133. *Shultz v. Wheaton Glass Co.,* 421 F. 2d 259, 267 (3rd Cir. 1970).

134. Knoop interview; John Knoop, email to author, Mar. 24, 2013.

135. *Shultz v. Wheaton Glass Co.,* cert. den. 398 U.S. 905 (1970).

136. *Shultz v. Wheaton Glass Co.,* 319 F.Supp. 229 (D. N.J. 1970).

137. *Hodgson v. Wheaton Glass Co.,* 446 F.2d 527 (3rd Cir. 1971).

138. Francis LaRuffa to BM, Jan. 18, 1972, BMP.

139. *Corning Glass Works v. Brennan,* 417 U.S. 188 (1974).

140. BM research for speech, "What the Government Will Require," Urban Research Corp., San Francisco, Oct. 21, 1971, BMP.

141. Morag Simchak to Susan Davis, Aug. 23, 1971, BMP.

142. Ross and McDermott, "Equal Pay Act of 1963," 2.

143. Bill Fauver to BM, n.d., BMP.

144. *Hodgson v. First Federal Savings & Loan Association.,* 455 F.2d 818 (5th Cir. 1972).

145. Ginnane to BM, Sept. 30, 1972, BMP.

146. Clauss interview.

147. Laurence Silberman b. 1935, Peter Nash b. 1937, and Richard Schubert b. 1936.

148. Clauss, Shire, and Fitzgerald interviews.

10. RETIREMENT AND LAST YEARS

1. Margolin was the last Labor Department lawyer to present argument for the agency at the Supreme Court. Robert A. Shapiro, email to author, Sept. 30, 2014; Allen Feldman, email to author, Apr. 4, 2015.

2. BM Retirement Recording.

3. Robert E. Nagle, who served on Margolin's staff for a decade before advising the Senate committees that drafted the OSHA and ERISA laws, credited her with teaching him how to write a brief. An equally grateful attendee was Don Shire, who joined Margolin's staff in 1965, moved up the ranks in the Labor Solicitor's office, and retired forty years later as associate solicitor. Nagle and Shire interviews.

4. BM Retirement Recording and Warren, notes, n.d., box 832, folder "Remarks, dinner marking retirement of Bessie Margolin," Warren Papers.

5. BM Retirement Recording. The event program and abbreviated guest list appear in app. 2.

6. Memorandum for the Respondent in Opposition, *Hodgson v. Square D Co.,* 459 F.2d 805 (1972), cert. denied, 409 U.S. 967 (1972).

7. BM, "Management Union Confrontation 1972 New Frontiers," 206.

8. BM, "Sex and the Equal Pay Act," Practice of Equal Employment Seminar, sponsored by George Washington University, Washington, D.C., Sept. 12, 1974.

9. See, e.g., Jean D. Muirhead to BM, Dec. 11, 1973, BMP; Virginia C. Howard to BM, June 29, 1975, BMP; BM, Case Analysis: *United Airlines Inc.,* Docket No. 76-333, *Preview of United States Supreme Court Cases* 48, Apr. 28, 1977, 1–3.

10. *Corning Glass Works v. Brennan,* 417 U.S. 188 (1974).

11. BM, "Impact of Corning," 1.

12. Allan Abbott Tuttle, assistant to the solicitor general, argued the government's case in *Corning Glass Works v. Brennan, Journal of the Supreme Court of the United States* (1973): 443.

13. BM, folder "GWU Lecturer Information," BMP.

14. M. Trifon interview.

15. Robert Coulson to BM, Oct. 29,1973, BMP; L. Schultz to BM, Aug. 23, 1974, BMP.

16. BM folder "FMCS Arbitration File 77K/20844," BMP.

17. BM folder "FMCS Arbitration File 76K/11061," BMP.

18. BM folder "FMCS Arbitration File No. 80K/08217," BMP.

19. BM folder, "FMCS Arbitration File 81K-14088," BMP. Responding to the author's FOIA request, FMCS was unable to locate any documents about the arbitration. M. J. Bartlett, email to author, Jan. 15, 2013.

20. Jimmy Carter, "Department of Labor Nomination of Carin Ann Clauss to Be Solicitor," Feb. 24, 1977, www.presidency.ucsb.edu/ws/?pid=6943 (accessed Apr. 5, 2015).

21. "Woman Nominated to Key Federal Post," *Virgin Islands Daily News,* Mar. 4, 1977, 6.

22. Stuart Auerbach, "Clauss Ends Bid for Judge," *WP,* Jan. 13, 1979.

23. Clauss interview. See also http://law.wisc.edu/profiles/caclauss@wisc.edu (accessed Apr. 5, 2015).

24. M. Trifon, T. Trifon, R. Margolin, and C. Margolin, interviews.

25. Tracey Trifon, email to author, June 15, 2012.

26. M. Trifon, email to author, with attached photos, Mar. 30, 2013.

27. A. Swidler interview.

28. J. Marks and N. Marks interview.

29. Ginnane to BM, Sept. 30, 1972, BMP.

30. M. Trifon and T. Trifon interviews.

31. Clauss interview.

32. M. Trifon and T. Trifon interviews.

33. M. Trifon interview.

34. T. Trifon interview.

35. C. Margolin interview.

36. M. Trifon interview.

BIBLIOGRAPHY

PRIMARY SOURCES

Archival and Manuscript Collections

L. B. Bolt Jr. University of Tennessee, Knoxville.

Thomas Corcoran. Library of Congress, Washington, D.C.

Archibald Cox. Harvard Law School, Manuscript Division, Cambridge, Mass.

William O. Douglas. Library of Congress, Washington, D.C.

Mary Eastwood. Schlesinger Library, Cambridge, Mass.

Philip Elman. Harvard Law School, Manuscript Division, Cambridge, Mass.

Morris Ernst. Harry Ransom Center, University of Texas at Austin

Charles Fahy. Franklin D. Roosevelt Library, Hyde Park, N.Y.

James Lawrence Fly. Columbia University, Manuscripts, New York.

Robert H. Jackson. Library of Congress, Washington, D.C.

Jewish Children's Home Collection. Tulane University Library, New Orleans.

Jewish Children's Regional Service, Metairie, La.

Louisiana Collection. New Orleans Public Library, New Orleans.

John Macy. Lyndon B. Johnson Library, Austin, Tex.

Bessie Margolin. Private Collection of Malcolm Trifon.

Herbert S. Marks. Franklin D. Roosevelt Library, Hyde Park, N.Y.

National Organization for Women. Schlesinger Library, Cambridge, Mass.

Isidore Newman School Archives, New Orleans.

Nuremberg Administrative Files. Record Group 153. National Archives, College Park, Md.

John Lord O'Brian. University of Buffalo Law School, Buffalo, N.Y.

Esther Peterson. Schlesinger Library, Cambridge, Mass.

Laurence H. Silberman. Hoover Institution Archives, Stanford University, Stanford, Calif.

Doris Stevens. Schlesinger Library, Cambridge, Mass.

Student Records. Newcomb College Center for Research on Women, New Orleans.

Student Records. Tulane University Law School, New Orleans.

Student Records. Yale University Library, Manuscripts and Archives, New Haven, Conn.

Joseph Swidler. Library of Congress, Washington, D.C.

Telford Taylor. Columbia University Law School, New York.

Tennessee Valley Authority. Record Group 142. National Archives, Morrow, Ga.

U.S. Department of Labor. Record Group 174. National Archives, College Park, Md.

U.S. House of Representatives. Record Group 233. National Archives, Washington, D.C.

U.S. Supreme Court. Record Group 267. National Archives, Washington, D.C.

U.S. Supreme Court Sound Recordings, Record Group 267, National Archives, College Park, Md.

Maxine Boord Virtue. Vertical Files. Bentley Historical Library, University of Michigan, Ann Arbor.

Earl Warren. Library of Congress, Washington, D.C.

White House Tapes. Lyndon B. Johnson Library, Austin, Tex.

Documents Obtained by Freedom of Information Act Requests

James Lawrence Fly. File No. 62-73756. Federal Bureau of Investigation, Washington, D.C.

Bessie Margolin. File No. 121-518. Federal Bureau of Investigation, Washington, D.C.

———. Federal Civilian Personnel File. National Personnel Records Center, St. Louis.

———. Personnel File. Tennessee Valley Authority, Knoxville.

Interviews

Beerman, Ralph. By Marc Beerman, New Orleans, Feb. 1, 1998.

Best, Edwin J., Sr. By Mary Jane Lowe, May 14, 1991. Transcript in Tennessee Valley Authority Oral History Records, National Archives, Morrow, Ga.

Brierre, Ellen. By author, telephone, Aug. 10, 2012.

Butler, Robert B., III. By author, telephone, Jan. 14, 2014.

Cahn, Adele Karp. By author, telephone, June 26, 2012.

Christian, Betty Jo. By author, telephone, June 22, 2011.

Clauss, Carin A. By author, Madison, Wis., June 7, 2010.

Connell, Karl. By author, telephone, Jan. 22, 2013.

Connell, Lawrence Fly. By author, telephone, Jan. 16, 2013.

Conrad, Nancy. By author, Washington, D.C., Aug. 19, 2013.

Cooper, Jean Saralee. By author, telephone, July 11, 2011.

Davidson, C. Girard. By Jerry N. Hess, July 17, 1972. Transcript in Harry S. Truman Library and Museum, Independence, Mo., www.trumanlibrary.org/oralhist/davidsn1.htm (accessed Mar. 20, 2015).

Durr, Clifford J. By Sally Fly Connell, Sept. 17, 1967. Transcript in James Lawrence Fly Project, Columbia Center for Oral History, Columbia University, New York.

———. By James Sargent, Apr. 17, 1974. Transcript in Columbia Center for Oral History, Columbia University, New York.

Fitts, William C. By Sally Fly Connell, Aug. 14, 1967. Transcript in James Lawrence Fly Project, Columbia Center for Oral History, Columbia University, New York.
———. By Charles W. Crawford, Aug. 1, 1969. Transcript in Tennessee Valley Authority Oral History Project, Memphis State University Oral History Office.
Fishman, Louis. By author, telephone, June 27, 2012.
Fitzgerald, Eva Bowers. By author, Washington, D.C., June 17, 2010.
Fortas, Abe. By Sally Fly Connell, Aug. 3, 1967. Transcript in James Lawrence Fly Project, Columbia Center for Oral History, Columbia University, New York.
Fowler, Henry H. By Charles Crawford, Apr. 22, 1971. Transcript in Tennessee Valley Authority Oral History Project, Memphis State University Oral History Office.
Gambrell, Ellen Ginnane. By author, telephone, Mar. 8, 2013.
Hoover, William. By author, Millville, N.J., Mar. 13, 2013.
Hornikel, Fannie Weil Cohn. By Dorothy Schlesinger, Aug. 27, 1989. Audiotape in Friends of the Cabildo Oral History Program, New Orleans Public Library, Louisiana Division.
Jackson, Robert H. By Harlan B. Phillips, 1952–53. Transcript in Columbia Center for Oral History, Columbia University, New York.
Jahn, LeRoy. By author, telephone, Aug. 11, 2010.
James, W. Ervin "Red." By Michael L. Gillette, Feb. 17, 1978. Transcript in Lyndon Baines Johnson Library Oral History Collection, Austin, Tex.
Kaufmann, Bruce. By author, telephone, June 25, 2012.
Knoop, John. By author, telephone, Mar. 15, 2013.
Margolin, Robert, and Charlotte Margolin. By author, telephone, July 30, 2012.
———. By author, New Orleans, Mar. 22, 2013.
Marks, Jonathan, and Nina Marks. By author, Bethesda, Md., Oct. 2, 2013.
Nagle, Robert. By author, McLean, Va., Oct. 25, 2011.
O'Brian, John Lord. By Sally Fly Connell, June 13, 1967. Transcript in James Lawrence Fly Project, Columbia Center for Oral History, Columbia University, New York.
———. By Charles Crawford, Jan. 10, 1970. Transcript in Tennessee Valley Authority Oral History Project, Memphis State University Oral History Office.
Parsons, Pauline. By author, Millville, N.J., Mar. 13, 2013.
Pierce, John F. By Charles W. Crawford, July 15, 1972. Transcript in Tennessee Valley Authority Oral History Project, Memphis State University Oral History Office.
Plotkin, Harry M. By Sally Fly Connell, Dec. 27, 1967. Transcript in James Lawrence Fly Project, Columbia Center for Oral History, Columbia University, New York.
Polack, Joseph. By author, telephone, July 7, 2010.
Seymour, Walton. By Charles W. Crawford, Feb. 7, 1970. Transcript in Tennessee Valley Authority Oral History Project, Memphis State University Oral History Office.
Shire, Donald S. By author, Potomac, Md., Aug. 10, 2010.
Silberman, Laurence H. By author, Washington, D.C., June 1, 2005.

Silverman, Eldon. By author, telephone, June 8, 2011.

Sizeler, Helen Lubow. By Dorothy Schlesinger, Aug. 18, 1982. Audiotape in Friends of the Cabildo Oral History Program, New Orleans Public Library, Louisiana Division.

Smith, Lillian Hofstetter. By Dorothy Schlesinger, July 30, 1982. Audiotape in Friends of the Cabildo Oral History Program, New Orleans Public Library, Louisiana Division.

Sutherland, William A. By Charles W. Crawford, June 9, 1973. Transcript in Tennessee Valley Authority Oral History Project, Memphis State University Oral History Office.

Swidler, Ann. By author, telephone, Nov. 1, 2012.

Swidler, Joseph C. By Mary Jane Lowe, June 18, 1991. Transcript in Tennessee Valley Authority Oral History Records, National Archives, Morrow, Ga.

Taylor, Telford. By Sally Fly Connell, Dec 5, 1967. Transcript in James Lawrence Fly Project, Columbia Center for Oral History, Columbia University, New York.

Trifon, Malcolm. By author, Berkeley, Calif., Aug. 21, 2010.

Trifon, Tobias. By author, Los Angeles, May 20, 2012.

Virtue, Veronica R. By author, telephone, Jan. 10, 2014.

Wheeler, Mildred Lau. By author, telephone, Nov. 7, 2013.

WORKS BY BESSIE MARGOLIN

Book Review. "Cases and Materials on Government Regulation of Wages, by Ernest N. Votaw." *Dickinson Law Review* 71 (1967): 527–29.

"Case Analysis: United Airlines, Inc., Docket No. 76-333." *Preview of United States Supreme Court Cases* 48 (Apr. 28, 1977): 1–3.

"Corporate Reorganization in France: A Comparative Study of French and American Practices." JSD thesis, Yale Law School, 1933.

"The Corporate Reorganization Provision in Senate Bill 3866: A Proposed Draft of a New Bankruptcy Act." *Yale Law Journal* 42 (1933): 387–401.

"Discrimination in Employment on the Basis of Sex, Age, and Veteran's Status." Southwestern Legal Foundation, Labor Law Developments, 1969. *Proceedings of 15th Annual Institute on Labor Law, Southwestern Legal Foundation.* New York: Bender, 1969.

"Equal Pay and Equal Employment Opportunities for Women." *New York University Conference on Labor Proceedings* 19 (1967): 297–315.

"Immovables by Destination." *Tulane Law Review* 5 (1930–31): 90–106.

"The Impact of Corning." *Women Law Reporter,* Sept. 15, 1974.

"Management-Union Confrontations 1972. New Frontiers: Who Discriminates against Women?" *New York University Conference on Labor Proceedings* 25 (1973): 205–24.

"Usufruct of a Promissory Note—Perfect or Imperfect." *Tulane Law Review* 4 (1929–30): 104–16.

"Vendor's Privilege." *Tulane Law Review* 4 (1929–30): 239–52.

"Women in Law." *Columns of Alpha Epsilon Phi* 22 (May 1938): 137–38.

BOOKS, PERIODICAL LITERATURE, AND OTHER SCHOLARLY SOURCES

Amann, Dianne Marie. "Cecilia Goetz, Woman at Nuremberg." *International Criminal Law Review* 11 (2011): 607–20.

———. "Portraits of Women at Nuremberg." In *Proceedings of the Third International Humanitarian Law Dialogs* 31, edited by Elizabeth Andersen and David M. Crane. Chautauqua, N.Y.: Chautauqua Institute, 2010.

Anti-Defamation League. "Contemporary Reflections on the Importance of the Nuremberg Trials." *Dimensions Online: A Journal of Holocaust Studies* 19 (Fall 2006). http://archive.adl.org/education/dimensions_19/section3/reflections.html#.U48x_ZRdWEw (accessed June 4, 2014).

Association for the Relief of Jewish Widows and Orphans of New Orleans. Annual Reports.

Badger, Anthony J. *FDR: The First Hundred Days*. New York: Hill & Wang, 2008

Banner, Lois. *American Beauty: A Social History . . . through Two Centuries of the American Idea, Ideal, and Image of the Beautiful Woman*. Los Angeles: Figueroa Press, 2005.

———. *Women in Modern America: A Brief History*. New York: Harcourt Brace Jovanovich, 1974.

Barrett, John Q. "Katherine B. Fite: The Leading Female Lawyer at London and Nuremberg, 1945." *Proceedings of the Third International Humanitarian Law Dialogs*. In *Studies in Transnational Legal Policy*, no. 42, edited by Elizabeth Anderson and David Crane. Washington, D.C.: American Society of International Law, 2010.

———. "Supreme Court Bar Admission (1931)." *Jackson List*, May 27, 2011. www.thejacksonlist.com (accessed Mar. 20, 2015).

Berebitsky, Julie. *Sex and the Office: A History of Gender, Power, and Desire*. New Haven: Yale University Press, 2012.

Besmann, Wendy. "The 'Typical Home Kid Overachievers': Instilling a Success Ethic in the Jewish Children's Home in New Orleans." *Southern Jewish History* 5 (2008): 121–59.

Biography of a Bachelor Girl. Directed by Edward H. Griffith. Metro-Goldwyn-Mayer, 1935. www.tcm.com/tcmdb/title/47/Biography-of-a-Bachelor-Girl/videos.html (trailer accessed Feb. 16, 2014).

Bloxham, Donald. *Genocide on Trial: War Crimes Trials and the Formation of Holocaust History and Memory*. New York: Oxford University Press, 2003.

Bogen, Boris D. *Jewish Philanthropy: An Exposition of Principles and Methods of Jewish Social Service in the United States.* New York: Macmillan, 1917.

Brauer, Carl M. "Women Activists, Southern Conservatives, and the Prohibition of Sex Discrimination in Title VII of the 1964 Civil Rights Act." *Journal of Southern History* 49 (1983): 37–56.

Brinson, Susan L. *Personal and Public Interests: Frieda B. Hennock and the Federal Communications Commission.* Westport, Conn.: Praeger, 2002.

———. *The Red Scare, Politics and the Federal Communications Commission, 1941–1960.* Westport, CT: Praeger, 2004.

Bush, Jonathan. "Nuremberg Prosecutors, Their Origins and Outlooks: New Dealers, Lady Lawyers, Refugees and Radicals." MS.

———. "The Prehistory of Corporations and Conspiracy in International Criminal Law: What Nuremberg Really Said." *Columbia Law Review* 109 (2009): 1094–1262.

Caldeira, Gregory A. "FDR's Court Packing Plan in the Court of Public Opinion." Paper presented at the annual meeting of the American Political Science Association, Aug. 2004. www.ibrarian.net/navon/page.jsp?paperid=1632126 (accessed May 13, 2014).

Caro, Robert A. *The Years of Lyndon Johnson: Means of Ascent.* New York: Vintage Books, 1991.

Chafe, William C. *The Paradox of Change: American Women in the 20th Century.* New York: Oxford University Press, 1991.

Chester, Ronald. *Unequal Access: Women Lawyers in a Changing America.* South Hadley, Mass.: Bergin & Garvey, 1985.

Cook, Beverly. "The First Woman Candidate for the Supreme Court: Florence E. Allen." *Journal of Supreme Court History* 6 (1981): 19–35.

Coontz, Stephanie. *A Strange Stirring: The Feminine Mystique and American Women at the Dawn of the 1960s.* New York: Basic Books, 2011.

Corbin, Arthur L. "Ernest Gustav Lorenzen." *Yale Law Journal* 60 (1951): 579–80.

Culver, John C., and John Hyde. *American Dreamer: The Life and Times of Henry A. Wallace.* New York: Norton, 2000.

Cushman, Clare, ed. *Supreme Court Decisions and Women's Rights.* Washington, D.C.: CQ Press, 2001.

Dagan, Hanoch. *Reconstructing American Legal Realism and Rethinking Private Law Theory.* New York: Oxford University Press, 2013.

Davis, Mattie Bell. "Third National Conference of Commissions on the Status of Women, June 28–30, 1966—Washington, D.C." *Women Lawyers Journal* 52 (1966): 107–8.

Dodd, E. Merrick. "The Supreme Court and Fair Labor Standards, 1941–1945." *Harvard Law Review* 59 (1945–46): 321–75.

Douglas, William O. *The Court Years, 1939–1975: The Autobiography of William O. Douglas.* New York: Random House, 1980.

———. "Some Functional Aspects of Bankruptcy." *Yale Law Journal* 41 (1932): 329–64.

Downey, Kirstin. *The Woman behind the New Deal: The Life of Frances Perkins, FDR's Secretary of Labor and His Moral Conscience.* New York: Doubleday, 2009.

Drachman, Virginia G. "The New Woman Lawyer and the Challenge of Sexual Equality in Early Twentieth Century America." *Indiana Law Review* 28 (1995): 227–57.

———. *Sisters in Law: Women Lawyers in Modern American History.* Cambridge: Harvard University Press, 1998.

Drowne, Kathleen, and Patrick Huber. *The 1920s—American Popular Culture through History.* Westport, Conn.: Greenwood Press, 2004.

Edwardson, Mickie Edwardson. "James Lawrence Fly, the FBI, and Wiretappings." *Historian,* Jan. 1, 1999. www.spybusters.com/History_1939–54.html (accessed May 10, 2010).

———. "James Lawrence Fly's Fight for a Free Marketplace of Ideas." *American Journalism* 14 (Winter 1997): 19–39.

Englander, Lawrence A. "History of Reform Judaism and a Look Ahead: In Search of Belonging." *Reform Judaism* (Summer 2011). http://reformjudaismmag.org/Articles/index.cfm?id=2802 (accessed Feb. 17, 2014).

Epstein, Cynthia Fuchs. *Women in Law.* New York: Basic Books, 1981.

Farley, Reynolds, and John Haaga, eds. *The American People: Census 2000.* New York: Russell Sage Foundation, 2005.

Foster, G. W. "Jurisdiction, Rights, and Remedies for Group Wrongs under the Fair Labor Standards Act: Special Federal Questions." *Wisconsin Law Review* 75 (1975): 295–342.

Freeman, Jo. "How Sex Got into Title VII: Persistent Opportunism as a Maker of Public Policy." *Law & Inequality* 9 (1990–91): 163–84.

———. "The Origins of the Women's Liberation Movement," *American Journal of Sociology* 78 (Jan. 1973): 792–811.

Friedan, Betty. *The Feminine Mystique.* New York. Dell, 1963.

Friedman, Joel W. *Champion of Civil Rights: Judge John Minor Wisdom.* Baton Rouge: Louisiana State University Press, 2009.

———. "A Look Back at the Tulane Law School of John Minor Wisdom's Era." *Tulane Law Review* 70 (1996): 2091–2102.

Friedman, Reena Sigman. *These Are Our Children: Jewish Orphanages in the United States, 1880–1925.* Hanover, N.H.: University Press of New England for Brandeis University Press, 1994.

Gardner, Warner W. *Pebbles from the Paths Behind: The Public Path, 1909–1947.* N.p.: Warner Gardner, 1989.

Gaskin, Hillary. *Eyewitness to Nuremberg.* London: Arms & Armour Press, 1990.

Glazier, Jack. *Dispersing the Ghetto: The Relocation of Jewish Immigrants across America.* Ithaca, N.Y.: Cornell University Press, 1998.

Goldman, Sheldon. *Picking Federal Judges: Lower Court Selection from Roosevelt through Reagan.* New Haven: Yale University Press, 1997.

Goodkind, S. B. *Eminent Jews of America.* Toledo, Ohio: American Hebrew Biographical Co., 1918.

Grossman, Jonathan. "Fair Labor Standards Act of 1938: Maximum Struggle for a Minimum Wage." *Monthly Labor Review* 101 (June 1978): 22–30.

Haas, Peter J. "Jewish Settlement in Tennessee." *Tennessee Encyclopedia of History and Culture,* Dec. 25, 2009. http://tennesseeencyclopedia.net (accessed Feb. 16, 2014).

Harrison, Cynthia. *On Account of Sex: The Politics of Women's Issues, 1945–1968.* Berkeley: University of California Press, 1989.

Haskell, Molly. *From Reverence to Rape: The Treatment of Women in Movies.* Chicago: University of Chicago Press, 1987.

Heller, Kevin Jon. *The Nuremberg Military Tribunals and the Origins of International Criminal Law.* Oxford: Oxford University Press, 2011.

Henderson, A. Scott, ed. *Power and the Public Interest: The Memoirs of Joseph C. Swidler.* Knoxville: University of Tennessee Press, 2002.

Hubbard, Preston J. *Origins of the TVA: The Muscle Shoals Controversy, 1920–1932.* New York: Norton, 1968.

Irons, Peter H. *The New Deal Lawyers.* Princeton: Princeton University Press, 1982.

Irving, David. *Nuremberg: The Last Battle.* London: Focal Point, 1996.

Israel, Betsy. *Bachelor Girl: 100 Years of Breaking the Rules—A Social History of Living Single.* New York: Perennial, 2003.

Jewish Children's Home. *The Diamond Jubilee: Jewish Children's Home, 1855–1930.* New Orleans: Jewish Children's Home, 1930.

Jones, James E., Jr. *Hattie's Boy: The Life and Times of a Transitional Negro.* Madison: University of Wisconsin Law School, 2006.

Kalman, Laura. *Abe Fortas: A Biography.* New Haven: Yale University Press, 1990.

———. *Legal Realism at Yale, 1927–1960.* Chapel Hill: University of North Carolina Press, 1986.

Kaplan, Dana Evan. *American Reform Judaism: An Introduction.* New Brunswick, N.J.: Rutgers University Press, 2003.

Karabel, Jerome. *The Chosen: The Hidden History of Admission and Exclusion at Harvard, Yale, and Princeton.* Boston: Houghton Mifflin, 2005.

Kay, Herma Hill. "The Future of Women Law Professors." *Iowa Law Review* 77 (1991–92): 5–18.

Kessler-Harris, Alice. *A Difficult Woman: The Challenging Life and Times of Lillian Hellman.* New York: Bloomsbury Press, 2012.

———. *Out to Work: A History of Wage-Earning Women in the United States.* New York: Oxford University Press, 2003.

Klein, Gerda Weissman. *A Passion for Sharing: The Life of Edith Rosenwald Stern.* Chappaqua, N.Y.: Rossel Books, 1984.

Konigsmark, Anne Rochell. *Isidore Newman School: One Hundred Years*. New Orleans: Isidore Newman School, 2004.

Kronman, Anthony, ed. *History of the Yale Law School*. New Haven: Yale University Press, 2004.

Lachoff, Irwin, and Catherine C. Kahn. *The Jewish Community of New Orleans*. Charleston, S.C.: Arcadia Publishing, 2005.

Law Reports of Trials of War Criminals. London: United Nations War Crimes Commission, 1949.

Levinger, Lee J. *A History of the Jews in the United States*. Cincinnati: Union of American Hebrew Congregations, 1935.

Lewis, Selma. *A Biblical People in the Bible Belt: The Jewish Community of Memphis, Tennessee, 1840s–1960s*. Macon, Ga.: Mercer University Press, 1998.

Light, Caroline. *That Pride of Race and Character: The Roots of Jewish Benevolence in the Jim Crow South*. New York: New York University Press, 2014.

Llamas, James E. "Labor and the Lady Lawyer: Interview with Bessie Margolin." *Tulanian* (Nov. 1967): 2–5.

Llewellyn, Karl. *Jurisprudence: Realism in Theory and Practice*. New Brunswick, N.J.: Transaction Publishers, 2008.

Louchheim, Katie. *By the Political Sea*. New York: Doubleday, 1970.

———, ed. *The Making of the New Deal: The Insiders Speak*. Cambridge: Harvard University Press, 1983.

Lundberg, Ferdinand, and Marynia F. Farnham. *Modern Woman: The Lost Sex*. New York: Harper & Brothers, 1947.

MacCrate, Robert. "What Women Are Teaching a Male-Dominated Profession." *Fordham Law Review* 57 (1989): 989–94.

Magner, Joseph. *The Story of the Jewish Orphans Home in New Orleans*. New Orleans: J. G. Hauser, 1905.

McFeeley, Neil D. *Appointment of Judges: The Johnson Presidency*. Austin: University of Texas Press, 1987.

McGuire, John Thomas. "The Most Unjust Piece of Legislation: Section 213 of the Economy Act of 1932 and Feminism during the New Deal." *Journal of Policy History* 20 (2008): 516–41.

McKenzie, Beatrice. "The Power of International Positioning: The National Women's Party, International Law and Diplomacy, 1928–1934." *Gender and History* 23 (Apr. 2011): 130–46.

Melnick, Ralph. *The Life and Work of Ludwig Lewisohn*, vol. 1: *A Touch of Wildness*. Detroit: Wayne State University Press, 1998.

Meyer, Michael A. *Response to Modernity: A History of the Reform Movement in Judaism*. Detroit: Wayne State University Press, 1995.

Murphy, Bruce Allen. *Wild Bill: The Legend and Life of William O. Douglas*. New York: Random House, 2003.

Murphy, Thomas E. "Female Wage Discrimination: A Study of the Equal Pay Act, 1963–1970." *University of Cincinnati Law Review* 39 (1970): 615–49.

Myers, Mary Connor. "Women Lawyers in Federal Positions." *Women Lawyers Journal* 19 (1932).

Neal, Steve. *Dark Horse: A Biography of Wendell Willkie.* New York: Doubleday, 1984.

Neuse, Steven. *David E. Lilienthal: The Journey of an American Liberal.* Knoxville: University of Tennessee Press, 1996.

Niehoff, Richard O. *Floyd W. Reeves: Innovative Educator and Distinguished Practitioner of the Art of Public Administration.* Lanham, Md.: University Press of America, 1991.

Oren, Dan. *Joining the Club: A History of Jews and Yale.* New Haven: Yale University Press, 2000.

Osterman, Rachel. "Origins of a Myth: Why Courts, Scholars, and the Public Think Title VII's Ban on Sex Discrimination Was an Accident." *Yale Journal of Law and Feminism* 20 (2009): 409–40.

Owen, Marguerite. *The Tennessee Valley Authority.* New York: Praeger, 1973.

Paterson, Judith. *Be Somebody: The Biography of Marguerite Rawalt.* Austin, Tex.: Eakin Press, 1986.

Pringle, Henry F. "The Controversial Mr. Fly." *Saturday Evening Post,* July 22, 1944.

Proceedings of the Eighth Biennial Session, National Conference of Jewish Charities, Memphis, May 1914, reprinted in Lee Frankel, ed., *Jewish Charities—Bulletin of the National Conference of Jewish Charities,* Jewish Communal Service Association of North America, vol. 4., no. 12 (1914). www.bjpa.org/Publications/downloadPublication.cfm?PublicationID=14 (accessed Dec. 30, 2013).

Pulitzer, Samuel. *Dreams Can Come True: The Inspiring Story of Samuel C. Pulitzer.* New York: Advisions, 1989.

Purcell, Aaron. *White Collar Radicals: TVA's Knoxville Fifteen, the New Deal, and the McCarthy Era.* Knoxville: University of Tennessee Press, 2009.

Rosenberg, Rosalind. *Divided Lives: American Women in the Twentieth Century.* New York: Hill & Wang, 2008.

Ross, Albert H., and Frank V. McDermott, Jr. "The Equal Pay Act of 1963: A Decade of Enforcement." *Boston College Law Review* 16 (1974): 1–73.

Rubin, Harold, ed. *Century of Progress in Child Care: Jewish Children's Home, 1855–1955.* New Orleans: David N. Dover, 1955.

Salmond, John A. *The Conscience of a Lawyer: Clifford J. Durr and American Civil Liberties, 1899–1975.* Tuscaloosa: University of Alabama Press, 1990.

Schlesinger, Arthur M., Jr. *The Politics of Upheaval, 1935–1936, vol. 3: The Age of Roosevelt.* New York: Mariner Books, 2003.

Shreve, David, and Robert David Johnson, eds. *The Presidential Recordings: Lyndon B. Johnson.* New York: Norton, 2007.

Silber, Norman I. *With All Deliberate Speed: The Life of Philip Elman: An Oral History Memoir*. Ann Arbor: University of Michigan Press, 2004.

Simons, Howard. *Jewish Times: Voices of the American Jewish Experience*. Boston: Houghton Mifflin, 1988.

Stern, Robert L. "Reminiscences of the Solicitor General's Office." *Journal of Supreme Court History* 20 (1995).

Stevens, Doris. *Jailed for Freedom: The Story of the Militant American Suffragist Movement*. Edited by Marjorie J. Spruill. Chicago: Donnelley & Sons, 2008.

Stone, I. F. "Mr. Biddle Is Afraid." *Nation,* May 22, 1943, 735–36.

Storrs, Landon R. Y. *The Second Red Scare and the Unmaking of the New Deal Left*. Princeton, N.J.: Princeton University Press, 2013.

Swidler, Joseph C., and Robert H. Marquis. "TVA in Court: A Study of the TVA's Constitutional Litigation." *Iowa Law Review* 32 (1947): 296–326.

Taylor, Telford. *The Anatomy of the Nuremberg Trials: A Personal Memoir*. New York: Little, Brown, 1992.

———. *Final Report to the Secretary of the Army on the Nuernberg War Crimes Trials under Control Council Law No. 10*. Washington, D.C.: U.S. Government Printing Office, 1949.

Trestman, Marlene. "Addenda to 'Fair Labor: The Remarkable Life and Legal Career of Bessie Margolin': A Discussion of the Methodology in Tallying Margolin's Supreme Court Argument Record as Well as Those of Other Pioneer Female Advocates Mabel W. Willebrandt, Helen R. Carloss, and Beatrice Rosenberg." *Journal of Supreme Court History* 38 (2013): 252–60.

———. "Fair Labor: The Remarkable Life and Legal Career of Bessie Margolin, 1909–1996." *Journal of Supreme Court History* 37 (2012): 42–74.

———. "First 101 Women to Argue at the United States Supreme Court." Supreme Court Historical Society, July 2014, available at www.supremecourthistory.org (accessed Mar. 20, 2015)

Trials of War Criminals before the Nuernberg Military Tribunals under Control Council Law. No. 10. Washington, D.C.: Government Printing Office, 1951.

Tucker, Susan, and Beth Willinger. *Newcomb College, 1886–2006: Higher Education for Women in New Orleans*. Baton Rouge: Louisiana State University Press, 2012.

Tusa, Ann, and John Tusa. *The Nuremberg Trial*. New York: Atheneum, 1984.

U.S. Department of Labor. *Women in the Federal Service 1954, Women's Bureau Pamphlet Four*. Washington, D.C.: U.S. Government Printing Office, 1954.

Virtue, Maxine Boord. *Basic Structure of Children's Services in Michigan*. Ann Arbor: University of Michigan Press, 1952.

———. *Family Cases in Court*. Durham, N.C.: Duke University Press, 1956.

———. "Laws Affecting Women in Kansas." *University of Kansas Bulletin* 40, no. 10 (1939).

———. *Survey of Metropolitan Courts: Final Report.* Ann Arbor: University of Michigan Press, 1962.

———. "The Two Faces of Janus: Delay in Metropolitan Trial Courts." *Annals of the American Academy of Political and Social Science* 328 (March 1960): 125–33.

Wade, Christine L. *Burnita Shelton Matthews: The Biography of a Pioneering Woman, Lawyer and Feminist (1894–1988).* Women's Legal History Project, Stanford Law, 1996. http://wlh-static.law.stanford.edu/papers/MatthewsBS-Wade96.pdf (accessed Jan. 30, 2011).

Walker, Samuel. *In Defense of American Liberties: A History of the ACLU.* 2d ed. Carbondale: Southern Illinois University Press, 1999.

Walsh, Margaret. "Gender and the Automobile in the United States." *Automobile in American Life and Society.* Dearborn: University of Michigan–Dearborn and Benson Ford Research Center, 2004. www.autolife.umd.umich.edu/Gender/Walsh/G_Overview1.htm (accessed Jan. 30, 2013).

West, Rebecca. "Extraordinary Exile—Nuremberg, August 23, a Reporter at Large." *New Yorker,* Sept. 7, 1946.

Woolf, Virginia. *A Room of One's Own.* 1929. Reprint. New York: Harcourt Brace, 1991.

Zaremby, Justin. *Legal Realism and American Law.* New York: Bloomsbury, 2013.

INDEX

Abram, Morris, 111, 112, 137

Addison v. Holly Hill Fruit Products, Inc., 203n58

Age Discrimination in Employment Act (ADEA), 145, 161

Agger, Carolyn, 144–45, 174; photo, *following page 82*

Agricultural Adjustment Administration, 194n113

Allen, Florence Ellenwood, 39, 60, 61–62, 63, 136

Allred, James V., 110

Alpha Epsilon Phi (AEPhi), 17, 18, 22, 65

Arnold v. Ben Kanowsky, Inc., 172

Alstate Construction Co. v. Durkin, 172

Alterman Brothers, 88–89

American Arbitration Association, 167

American Civil Liberties Union, 81, 129

American Red Cross, 127

American University, 130

Anderson, Howard J., 173

anti-Semitism, 9, 26, 29, 110–11

arbitration, 167–68

Arbuthnot, Sadie B., 206n51

Ashwander, George, 51

Ashwander v. TVA: filing of, 47, 51; Margolin work on, 50, 52–53, 56; review in circuit court, 54–55; Supreme Court and, 50–51, 56–58, 194n113; trial of, 51–53

Association for the Relief of Jewish Widows and Orphans, 2

Atlanta Corporate Law Institute, 149–50

Avery, George T., 173

"bachelor girl," 67–68, 196n3

Baker, Newton, 60–61, 193n95

Bakshian, Mary, 206n51

Barker, Robert B. "Bugeye," 76

Barnes, B. Harper, 173

Barnett, Edith, 173

Barnett, Wayne, 211n59

Barr, James, 66, 71–72, 77, 197n23

Basic, Inc., 156–57

Baton Rouge, LA, 18

Beauvoir, Simone de, 150

Beck, James M., 56

Berger, Caruthers, 155, 173

Bernays, Murray, 204n4

Beutel, Fredrick, 28, 186n74

Biddle, Francis, 76, 203n58

Biography of a Bachelor Girl (film), 67, 196nn3–4

Black, Elizabeth, 169

Black, Hugo, 54, 87, 120, 169

Blackburn, Anna Faye, 201n24

Blair, Mallory B., 110

Block, Beate, 173

B'nai B'rith, 9

Boggs, Hale, 136, 137, 139, 142, 176

Boggs, Lindy, 140–41

Bonneville Power Administration, 73

Boord Virtue, Maxine, 38

Borden Company v. Borella, 96, 172, 203n74

Boutell v. Walling, 96–97, 100, 172

Boyle, Fannie M., 173

Brandeis, Louis, 87, 194n113

Brass, Margaret, 214n54

Bridges, Harry, 81, 129

Brosman, Paul, 27, 33

Brown, Helen Gurley, xiv

Brown, John R., 124, 176

Many, Anna, 18

Margolin, Bessie

—birth and death: 1, 170

—career: arbitrator, 167–68; awards, 117–18, 135, 137–38; circuit court record, 119, 209n31; Equal Pay Act advocate, 24, 40, 145, 146–47, 149–53, 156–62, 216–17nn86–87; and FBI investigation, 107, 127–28, 129, 141, 211n67; Inter-American Commission of Women, 33, 35–40; International Labor Office, 135; judgeship aspiration, 40, 136–45; Labor Department advocate, 83–99, 114–26; Louisiana Bar admittance, 28, 186n75; loyalty board inquiry, 126–27, 129; mentor to women lawyers, xv, 88, 148, 291n24; New Haven's Legal Aid Bureau, 30–31; and newspaper coverage, 30, 68, 69, 77, 78, 113, 124–25, 141; retirement, 162, 163–65, 173–77; salaries, 28, 38, 43, 45, 46, 48, 57, 64, 84, 88, 91–92, 137, 148; Supreme Court record, xiv, 96, 118–19, 125, 171–72; teaching law, 130–31, 166–68; TVA, 43–66, 74; Yale Law School research assistant, 25–34

—personal life, qualities, and skills: alcohol, 43–44, 124, 144–45; as aunt, 131–33, 168–69; dress and hairstyle, 17, 18, 19, 28, 90, 92, 94, 113, 139, 148–49, 163; elitism, xv, 19, 86, 126, 184n20; "feminine charm," 121, 147–48, 210n38; feminism, 39, 40, 150, 154–56, 163; foreign languages, 21, 37, 38; friendships and contacts, 21–22, 28–30, 111–12, 134, 169; housing, 18, 28, 38, 103; humor, 68, 119–20, 150; Jewish identity, 8, 9–10, 26, 29, 104, 140, 187n95; legal researcher, 33, 36, 37, 39, 43, 45, 46; love of cars, 64; marriage perspectives, 23, 24, 38, 67, 169–70; perfectionism, xv, 88, 126, 184n20; perfume, 112, 134; poker and gaming, xiv, 65, 129, 133, 134; political views, 13, 40, 85; reading, 13, 14, 23–24; romantic affairs, 23–25, 32, 36–37, 68–71, 72–73, 74, 135–36, 169–70; social life, 13, 17–19, 29, 107–8, 133–34; speaking

and argumentation, 13, 65, 120–24; travel, 9, 64, 102, 108; wordsmithery, 68, 156; work schedule, 148–49; writing, 12, 24, 34, 65, 115

—youth and schooling: doctorate received, 33–34; at Jewish Orphans' Home, 3–5, 8–12, 15; at Newcomb College, 16–19; at Newman School, 6–8, 12–13; at Tulane Law School, 19–25; writings, 12–13

Margolin, Charlotte (nephew's wife), 170

Margolin, Harry (father), 23, 87; Bessie's relationship with, 9–10, 87–88; giving up of children by, 1–2; photo, *following page 82*

Margolin, Jacob "Jack" (brother), 1, 15, 22, 87, 185n47; photo, *following page 82*

Margolin, Rebecca Goldschmidt (mother), 1

Margolin Trifon, Dora (sister), 10, 132; death of, 34, 133; at Jewish Orphans' Home, 1–2, 4, 15, 22–23; marriage of, 23, 87, 196n1; photo, *following page 82*

Markham, Edwin, 23

Marks, Herbert S., 54, 63, 72, 73–74, 128, 169, 191n50; background of, 48; and Margolin, 65, 66, 69, 70, 71, 76–77, 84, 85, 86; photo, *following page 82*

Marks, Jonathan, 169

Marks, Morton J., 175

marriage: film depiction of, 67, 196nn3–5; Margolin and, 23, 24, 38, 67, 68, 69, 136, 169–70

Marshall, Thurgood, 143

Martin, John D., 60

Martino v. Michigan Window Cleaning Company, 97

Mather, Katherine: photo, *following page 82*

Matthews, Burnita Shelton, 39–40, 144

Maxwell-Fyfe, David, 104

McAllister, Thomas F., 177

McComb v. Jacksonville Paper Co., 116–17, 166–67, 172, 208n15

McNarney, Joseph T., 105

McParland, Rita, 169, 175

McReynolds, James C., 56

Memphis, TN, 1, 2, 10, 29